Character
Styles

By the Same Author

The Symbiotic Character

"Here is a rich and original book, grounded on solid clinical knowledge. . . . it clearly formulates the process, blockages, and treatment traps related to the symbiotic character. In short, *The Symbiotic Character* is a stimulating, thought-provoking book."

— *The Psychiatric Times*

Humanizing the Narcissistic Style

"I found Stephen M. Johnson's new book . . . a surprisingly stimulating, sensitive and well-written treatment of the troublesome topic of pathological narcissism. . . . the author, by virtue of theoretical synthesis, generous case histories, insight, compassion and wisdom gleaned from extensive professional and personal experiences with narcissism, has created a helpful handbook for all clinicians."

— *The California Therapist*

Characterological Transformation: The Hard Work Miracle

"Stephen Johnson has written an extraordinarily useful book. . . . It was easy to recognize many of my patients, indeed myself, in his descriptions of characterological process. The book is very worthy of time and energy. . . . I am looking forward to the promised future volumes addressing additional character styles."

— *Psychotherapy in Private Practice*

A NORTON PROFESSIONAL BOOK

Character
Styles

STEPHEN M. JOHNSON, Ph.D.

W. W. NORTON & COMPANY • *New York* • *London*

Library of Congress Cataloging-in-Publication Data
Johnson, Stephen M.
    Character styles / Stephen M. Johnson.
        p.   cm.
    ISBN 0-393-70171-9
    1. Nature and nurture.   2. Personality development.   3. Individual differences.   4. Personality and culture.   5. Personality disorders.
    I. Title.
    BF342.J   1994   155.2′5—dc20   93-42540 CIP

W. W. Norton & Company, Inc., 500 Fifth Avenue, New York, NY 10110
W. W. Norton & Company, Ltd., 10 Coptic Street, London WC1A 1PU

For my wonderful daughters, Kate and Rebecca

The more original a thought, the richer its Unthought becomes. The Unthought is the highest gift that a thought can give.

—Jacques Derrida

ACKNOWLEDGMENTS

IT HAS BEEN A TEN-YEAR JOURNEY, writing the series of books that ends with the publication of this one. The guides, companions, and followers on this journey have honored me with their knowledge and their trust.

It was Dr. Edward Muller of Phoenix, Arizona, who had the knowledge I needed to make sense of all I had learned and to point me toward further discovery. With the generativity of a true teacher, he gave the knowledge away with no strings attached—no demands for orthodoxy, no limits on change, no expectations of franchise. Thanks, Ed, for free access to the Unthought of all those thoughts. It is in this spirit that I pass the knowledge along.

My family has provided me with the secure base I needed to do my profession my way, to go out on those limbs, to resign those tenured professorships. My mother and father and wife Ellen have allowed me to risk, knowing that somewhere I would always be loved and supported. My most loyal and long-standing friends, Peter Alevizos, Larry King, and Ron Wagner, have lent the same support, often coaching, reasurring or booting me as the situation demanded.

Many others have contributed to this work: the students of 22 years of academic life, the members of all ongoing training and consultation groups that I have either taken or led, some wonderful fellow faculty whom I will never forget, all the psychotherapy clients who have shared their pain and growth with me, my own psychotherapists. Instead of trying to list them all and leave someone out, I have decided to individually name just one. That is Robert Morgan, the only academic administrator who ever really succeeded in promoting the creativity-generating, secure environment that higher education aspires to but so often actively destroys. Thanks, Bob, for all you did and for all you had to take to even partially realize our dream.

Finally, I want to acknowledge my editor at Norton Professional Books, Susan Barrows Munro, who shepherded all four volumes through editing and production with a deep understanding of the work and a very human understanding of the workman. And thanks, Susan, for Margaret Farley who did much of the editing on this particular book so very well.

CONTENTS

APPENDICES

INTRODUCTION

THIS IS THE BOOK I WISH I'd had when I began the serious study of psychology over thirty years ago. Like many young people, I went into the field with broad, straightforward, significant questions— What makes people tick? Why are we so crazy? What can be done about it? Eight years later, with a Ph.D. in hand, I knew far more about experimental design, statistics, and the learning of nonsense syllables than I did about what had initiated my quest. It wasn't until six years after that, with tenure in a respectable psychology department and the freedom of a sabbatical, that I finally returned to these more fundamental questions. It required abandoning the restrictive narrowness then required by mainstream academic psychology concerning what forms of knowledge are valid. Empirically derived knowledge, acquired by sticking to the rules sanctioned at any particular time, just won't suffice for such questions. I found that the answers had to involve a number of ways of knowing and the integration of many, often independent, contributions. Completing this book has closed a circle, if it has not brought me full circle, in answering the questions that brought me to the field. Elements of the answers come from within the mainstream, but much comes from outside it. What you will find here is the product of intuition, theory, experience, deductions and, yes, a good deal of mainstream empirical research.

"What makes people tick?" is very similar to the equally broad, important question "What is human nature?" It seems to me that developmental research and theory, in their essence, attempt to answer that question. Sustained watching of infants, babies, and children leads one to speculate about the essential nature of this being who is so initially helpless and potentially accomplished. Careful and often contrived observation is sometimes necessary to discover how already accomplished this little one really is. Theories are particularly useful in this endeavor to suggest the right questions.

What developmental theory and research have given us is an increasingly broad yet increasingly precise description of human nature. This particularly includes the kinds of needs humans must have met and the kinds of environments that must be provided to achieve human potential. Similarly, observations of children in development tell us what happens when these needs are chronically frustrated or when the needed environments are not provided. Again, the theories suggest what to look for and posit the most central relationships between early environment and resulting development.

I've always found the most fascinating application of this basic knowledge to involve answering the second question: "Why are we so crazy?" It's obvious that were it not for our craziness, there would be so much less suffering and destruction in the world. Humans solve problems far better than any other life-form but our craziness interferes profoundly with that process at every level. It is in the family, the workplace, and the politics of humankind that we see the colossal waste and pain of our proclivity for destructive dysfunctionality.

In answering the second question, I have found it particularly useful to study the most common patterns or syndromes in which our craziness expresses itself. These patterns are best described by those clinicians who have attempted to treat pathology. Among these, those who have described character structures, styles, or disorders have often been the most astute. The resulting character syndromes have stood well the tests of time and clinical practice and have done relatively well under the scrutiny of more systematic research. In their more extreme forms, these disorders of character or personality are widely used for diagnostic purposes around the world.

Now, here is the integration of two ways of knowing that help us to answer these questions. The studies of human development or human nature fit very nicely with the descriptions of the patterns of human craziness. Furthermore, these patterns don't just occur in the most severe forms of mental illness. Such patterns are clearly documented in normal populations and in less severely pathological groups. I believe there are several useful continua of human dysfunction from the most to the least severe, which reflect quintessential building blocks of human nature. I believe I've found seven such building blocks around which personality and psychopathology are organized. There may be more.

Critical to any individual's adjustment on any of these continua is *interaction*. That interaction is between the individual, with his changing but basic needs, and the changing environment's ability to meet them. Such interaction makes personality and produces psychopathology. In an era when our most basic science, particle physics, asserts that matter itself is made of interaction, we are ripe to understand and experience our personality and our personal pathology as the product of interaction.

The interactional perspective in psychiatry is far from new. Fairbairn (1974, originally published 1952) and Guntrip (1968, 1971) are among its earliest, clearest, and most seminal contributors. These figures represent part of what has come to be known as the British School of Object Relations Theory, which emphasizes the role of the parent-child relationship in the development of personality and psychopathology. Theirs is a variation of psychoanalytic theory that emphasizes theoretically derived dimensions of child development and psychopathology based on early interactions.

Character is not usually a central focus for these theorists though they do address it. And, their theories are not typically informed or modified by child development research. What is necessary, then, for a more profound understanding of the essential questions is the integration of developmental process, interactional determinants, and characterological syndromes.

While all the building blocks for this have been available for some time, they are just now, here and there, being brought together. I've attempted to do this in my prior books written for therapists in practice and training (Johnson, 1985, 1987, 1991). Each of these books addresses one or two characterological patterns with an emphasis on treatment. I have tried to write each of these books in sufficiently nontechnical language so that any educated layperson could read them. Yet, the bulk of each book does not speak to nontherapists, and any serious student would have to pull together all of my books and those of others to complete the picture. This book brings all of this together, first to describe the overall theoretical-empirical model, which integrates development, character, and inter-action. Then, each of the character structures reflecting the seven basic existential life issues are thoroughly described.

My hope is that this work will be accessible to anyone on the mature side of college sophomore and that it will help you answer your own questions about human nature and craziness. I hope it will help set the stage for your discovering what you can do about the craziness not only in psychotherapy but in your life and relation-ships. I also hope that you, like me, will relate to this as a work in progress. These questions are too important and the problems too intricate to lend themselves to any last words or final solutions. Theoretical, empirical, intuitive, deductive, experiential, and other forms of knowing will continue to inform and correct our work.

Answers to the third question, what can we do about human craziness, is where I experience the least closure. These answers will certainly continue to evolve and will come from fields as varied as psychopharmacology to ecology and others we haven't even dreamt of. I have, however, held to the strategy of my earlier books in retaining the section on psychotherapeutic objectives for each char-acter type. Here, I tend to address the therapists, but the considera-tions encountered may be applied to one's own personal develop-ment or that of another.

The first four chapters of this book present the overall theoretical-empirical model. They were originally published in *The Symbiotic Character* (Johnson, 1991) and Chapters 2 through 4 review the model in reference to each of the seven basic existential issues and their characterological manifestations. The novice reader might con-sider skipping Chapters 2 through 4, at least initially, because they are more research-oriented than the chapters that follow.

Each of the subsequent chapters describes one existential life issue and the etiology, expression, and treatment objectives for the charac-ter formed by its mishandling. With minimal updating and editing I have then used the descriptive chapters from my earlier books. Chap-ters 5 and 6 come from *Characterological Transformation* (Johnson, 1985), Chapter 7 comes from *The Symbiotic Character* (Johnson, 1991), and Chapter 8 comes from *Humanizing the Narcissistic Style*

(Johnson, 1987). Chapters 9 through 11 were written explicitly for this book to complete the description of all seven character types.

For the most part, each chapter stands on its own, and one could read this book in any order. The first chapter presents the overall theory, however, and would be generally useful for more fully understanding the others. For those readers familiar with personality disorders, this chapter also will show how my treatment relates to the currently employed categories of personality disorder.

Sophisticated readers have, on occasion, asked me what is new or different about my approach. The answer is there's not much here that's new. What's different is this: It is not psychoanalytic, not object relations, not self-psychology or ego psychology. It is not behavioral or cognitive or affective. It is not characterological, developmental, interactive, phenomenological. It is not theoretical, empirical, experiential, intuitive, or deductive. It is all of this and more in a mix. It attempts to answer important questions with the information available. For each of us who are curious about such questions, this is what we must do. Here's my answer. I hope it helps.

PART I

A THEORY OF CHARACTER FORMATION

CHAPTER 1

A Characterological-Developmental Theory

IN THESE INITIAL CHAPTERS I WILL ATTEMPT to integrate what we now know about human development with what we know about the common constellations of character. Though our knowledge of both character and development is evolving and determined by our cultural perspective, I believe this integrated view gives us the most useful map of the territory of personality and psychopathology. An approach to understanding and helping people, which is grounded in the significant issues of their development, provides a generalized map which calibrates the most essential territory—it is a map that is sufficiently general yet appropriately targeted so that it fits the task at hand. Particularly, when a characterological-developmental perspective can remain open to the evolution of knowledge and culture, it provides a view that integrates the effects of the developing human potential with the effects of environmental conditions, and it documents how potentials affect learning and how either can be derailed from an optimal course.

Psychoanalytic developmental psychology, which is an umbrella label for object relations, ego, and self psychology, has been of great clinical use to many of us because it has consistently asked some of the most useful questions: What are the child's most basic needs and drives? What does the child need to achieve optimal human development? How does the person formulate a cohesive, robust sense of self? How does cognitive development unfold, and how does it relate to character and psychopathology? How does indulgence, trauma, or chronic frustration affect the development of the human being? Are there critical periods for the development of certain human qualities? If so, what are they? Does the human being internalize aspects of the environment; if so, how?

A cognitive map, which is to serve as the underpinning for this endeavor, also does well to include the most prevalent constellations of personality and psychopathology. The current *Diagnostic and Statistical Manual* of the American Psychiatric Association (1994) certainly provides a running start for this, albeit atheoretical and democratically derived. In my earlier work (Johnson, 1985, 1987), I have argued that a contemporary character-analytic point of view provides a very similar yet more theoretically derived view of the constellations of personality and psychopathology. Further, when this approach is informed by more developmental and interpersonal perspectives, one can derive a clinically useful model which can hold a wide variety of therapeutic techniques and suggests their appropriate application.

In this characterological-developmental view, each character structure is the outgrowth of one basic existential human issue. Each issue is fundamental to the human experience and requires a constant resolution over the life span. Yet, there are predictable periods in life during which each issue is of particular importance. And the first time the issue is dealt with can be particularly important, especially when the individual's experience is severely traumatic. In that case, early forms of resolving the issue tend to become fixed. In other words, the current model is not one of lockstep development asserting that crucial life issues are resolved in one life phase so that the child may move on to resolve others in subsequent phases. These issues are too important for that. Rather, what is proposed is that these extremely fundamental human issues are faced early on in life, and that some early attempts at resolving them are based both on limited equipment and limited experience of the world. Furthermore, when the issues are faced in trauma, their early resolutions tend to become rigid and resistant to change. In this view, these early solutions were often quite adaptive given the limitations of the environment and the limitations of the individual's capacities, but they often achieved an imperfect escape from trauma.

The work of Solomon and Wynne (1954) has documented the extreme resistance to extinction of a response learned in an analogous escape conditioning paradigm. In these experiments, dogs learned to avoid electric shock when signaled. Once established, the avoidance response never extinguished unless the dogs were confined in the original box and only then with a great deal of "resistance" and emotionality. The rigidity of similarly established solutions may explain the character and psychopathology of humans who come for psychotherapy. People often need to learn that the shock has been turned off—that their original escape solutions are no longer necessary.

The characterological-developmental model is further appealing as a cognitive map for all this because it suggests a resolution of one of the central conflicts of psychoanalytic theorizing. This conflict has been elucidated best by Greenberg and Mitchell (1983), who argue for the essential irreconcilability of the classical drive theory of psychoanalysis, which conceptualizes unconscious conflict resulting from instinctual impulses and societal inhibitions, and the interpersonal model, which conceptualizes the contents of the psyche as all interpersonally derived. In the interpersonal view, the dynamic conflict between two or more internalized aspects of the person derives from others in the interpersonal matrix.

The contemporary character-analytic model includes recognition of primary instinctual impulses such as sexuality and aggression but places equal importance on the environmental response to the individual's impulses and needs. Most importantly, the theory asserts that what is also definitional of character and resulting psychopathology comes from the person's pattern of dealing with the natural organismic response to the environment's frustration of the instinctual needs. Thus, much of what is character and much of what makes up psychopathology are understood in terms of the individual's complex reaction to environmental frustration. Conflict is interpersonally derived, but based on what is inherent in the human being.

More and more, contemporary theorists are willing to acknowledge the humanly inherent need for relationship (e.g., Fairbairn, 1974; Mitchell, 1988; Stern, 1985), as well as the sometimes competing need for individuation (e.g., Mahler, Pine, & Bergman, 1975; Masterson, 1976, 1981). With these latter "instincts" firmly in place, constellations of personality and psychopathology can productively be conceptualized as deriving from those existential lifelong issues: the extent to which they are allowed, frustrated, or resolved, and the individual's reactions to their continued frustration. Developmental knowledge, not only about babies but about people over the life span, informs us of the various expressions of each issue, as well as the developing nature of the human equipment at various ages and the nature of the kinds of cognitive and other errors and distortions made over the life span (e.g., see Kegan, 1982).

There are additional practical advantages to this characterological-developmental approach for psychotherapy. First among these is the beneficial effect that this essentially "therapeutic reframe" can have on both the client and the therapist. With respect to the client, this is a reframe which often finds easy acceptance because one's problematic behavior, attitudes, and feelings often seem so immature. Presented correctly, this reframe can have a beneficial effect on the self-labeling process, prompting compassion and understanding for oneself in place of self-denigration. As with any other hermeneutic intervention that "takes," one achieves the satisfaction of understanding and thereby achieving some control over the problem. But the developmental therapeutic reframe can do much more. For purposes of prescribing new learning and the intervention required to achieve it, the reframe can specify what has not been learned or resolved and can elucidate the required context and learning processes necessary for growth or resolution.

These same advantages of compassion, understanding, and control accrue to the therapist as well. Of particular importance here is the reframe's effect in helping the therapist distance from her own negative personal reactions. For example, the narcissistic client, who can relate only through idealization and ultimately devaluation or, alternatively, through using one as an audience for his grandiosity, will easily stimulate some not-very-therapeutic reactions in most people. But a therapist who can see the child in the adult and understand that this form of relationship is all that he is up to at that moment can attenuate her reactions and more easily respond with what is useful. It will often be important for the therapist to remember that this developmental model is merely that—a model or analogue of reality that can both generate and justify a plethora of therapeutic responses. Finally, the characterological-developmental model not only directs the therapist's attention to some of the more important issues, but also offers a model of how these issues may be resolved.

To the extent that we are correct about the basic processes of resolution in the infant or child or adolescent, we can assist the client in going through that very process. Developmental research on such things as perception-taking and object constancy, for example, has shown that the ability to take another's perception or to simultaneously hold conflicting feelings about an object develop through a number of iterations as one develops cognitively and emotionally. The young adult can take another's perception at a much higher level of sophistication than can a latency-aged child, who, in turn, can have empathy for another at a much more sophisticated level than can the 18-month-old who has demonstrated such abilities. Similarly, when an adult client needs to learn such an ability, that learning will not be the same as in an infant or a latency-aged child or an adolescent, but some of the essential processes will be the same. The therapeutic encounter, the learning procedures, and the level of conceptualization will be age- and situation-appropriate in good developmental psychotherapy, but knowledge of the process at each documented iteration cannot help but be useful.

Kohut's (1971) formulation of the archaic transferences of merger, twinship, mirroring, and idealization offer another useful example of this iterative maturing process. While, on the one hand, these transference behaviors are definitional of narcissistic personality disorder for Kohut, they are also the basic building blocks for his conceptualization of the development of self. Kohut asserts that a need for these selfobject relationships continues throughout the life span, but that, as the individual matures psychologically, the selfobject needs also mature, so that the individual needs others and ideals to respect, relations with others who are similar to him and who admire him, etc. Seen in these ways, the therapeutic derivatives from this developmental perspective are reparative but not regressive, in that they acknowledge the analogue nature of the model and recognize the contemporary strengths of the client.

According to the theory I will present here, personality and psychopathology develop in particular constellations as a consequence of the interaction of a broad but finite range of instinctual needs of the person and the environment's ability or inability to respond appropriately to them. These instinctual needs go well beyond those oral, anal, and phallic internal pressures posited by Freud and include the infant's well-documented need to attach or bond to a primary caregiver (e.g., Bowlby, 1969); the child's need to individuate through exploration, self-determined activity, and the building of psychic boundaries (e.g., Mahler, 1968); the need for self-determined expression (e.g., Kohut, 1971, 1977; Lowen, 1958, 1983); and the need for an attuned self-other relationship (e.g., Kohut, 1971; Stern, 1985). In this theoretical construction, the nature of personality and psychopathology is, then, largely determined by the kinds of interpersonal frustrations that are encountered by the developing person as she attempts to meet these many needs. Personality and psychopathology are further defined by both her natural instinctive response to the frustration in question and the methods she chooses to use in dealing with, adjusting to, or suppressing those natural responses. Her choice of adjustment maneuvers is further determined by the structural capacities at her level of development at the time of frustration as well as by the possible maneuvers that are modeled or accepted by the interpersonal environment. It is this interplay of instinctual needs with the impact of the interpersonal environment that makes this a truly integrative theory.

Character-analytic theorists (e.g., Levy & Bleecker, 1975) have delineated the development of character in five stages: (1) *Self-affirmation* is the initial expression of the instinctual need. (2) The *negative environmental response* is the social environment's blocking or frustration of that need. (3) The *organismic reaction* is the natural, "wired in" response to frustration by the environment—usually the experience and expression of intense negative affect, particularly rage, terror, and grief at loss.

These first three stages are relatively straightforward. It is in the final stages that character is formed. (4) The fourth stage is labeled *self-negation*. This more comprehensive form of turning against the self involves the individual's imitating the social environment in blocking the expression of the original instinctual impulse *and* blocking the instinctual response to that block as well. It is this identification with the environment that sets the person against himself, makes the block to self-expression internal, and creates psychopathology. This is the beginning of an internal conflict, which can persist throughout a lifetime, between the irrepressible instinctual need and reaction, on the one hand, and the internalized blocking of those needs and reactions, on the other.

Wilhelm Reich, Alexander Lowen, and other energetically oriented therapists have emphasized how the blocks to self-expression are literally present in the body, represented by chronic muscular tension which can result in postural distortion. This blocking or self-negation originally served the purpose of avoiding the pain and frustration of experiencing the environment's block. It continues to serve that purpose, and thus it is very resistant to change. The blocking on a body level is simply the organism's way of not experiencing the original need and the uncomfortable reaction to its frustration. Furthermore, the body blocks avoid the inevitable anxieties of being vulnerable again and risking the anticipated reinjury.

Fairbairn's (1974) position appears completely consistent with this and adds to it. Fairbairn's view was that these original organismic self-expressions (i.e., instincts, libidinal impulses, etc.) were object-seeking. When the objects (others) were frustrating or blocking, the individual internalized them and then rendered them unconscious. The original impulses, as well as what Fairbairn characterized as the individual's "aggressive" responses to frustration, became unconscious. What Fairbairn's view adds, which will be reviewed in more detail in Chapter 9, is the emphasis on the resulting unconscious and fixed internal object relations, which account for the resulting static psychopathology and the resistance to new relationships, learning, and change. Change is resisted not only because it may cause the resurrection of internalized "bad objects" and repressed impulses toward them—an intolerable psychic state that motivated repression in the first place—but also because of the individual's attachment to these objects as internalized. "It is above all the need of the child for the parents, however bad they may appear to him, that compels him to internalize bad objects; and it is because this need remains attached to them in the unconscious that he cannot bring himself to part with them" (Fairbairn, 1974, p. 68).

In other words, the self-negation process is relational and uniquely personified in each case. The constructs emphasizing splits in the self and explaining pathology and resistance in terms, for example, of an internalized object suppressing "libidinal" expression, are very useful clinically. Much of gestalt therapy is based on processes that bring to consciousness and actualize these splits of the self and play out their interrelationships.

(5) The fifth and final step in the sequence, labeled the *adjustment process*, essentially consists of making the best of it. This involves the construction of any number of compromises in an attempt to resolve the unresolvable conflict. This is analogous to Sullivan's concept of the "security operation" or Winnicott's "false self." In this conceptualization, the budding narcissist, for example, who cannot get well-attuned prizing from caretaking figures by his natural self-expression, will identify with the image of himself that these caretakers require for their own purposes, and he will do everything in his power to live up to it. By so doing, he can achieve some semblance of the mirrored attunement that he requires. Simultaneously, he can avoid the recurrence of painful narcissistic injuries, which come as a result of his true self-expression. To the extent that he can live up or down to the environment's expectations, the compromise appears to work, and this, in part, explains why the successful narcissist is notoriously difficult to change.

The self-negation process defines what the individual must deny or suppress. The adjustment process defines what he must exaggerate. What parts of the real self the individual suppresses and what parts he exaggerates succinctly define his character as discussed here. Psychopathology is seen in the suppression, in the exaggeration, or most often, in the individual's natural reaction to this kind of habitual, unnatural accommodation to avoid pain while maintaining contact.

The infusion of psychoanalytic development theory and developmental research (both observational, à la Mahler, and experimental, à la Stern) enriches and continually updates this model of character development. These sources provide data on the exact nature of the original organismic self-expressions (instincts) and document when they first seem to appear as naturalistically observed or as experimentally demanded. Further, these sources directly catalog environmental-social frustrations and the infant's or child's responses to them. Finally, these sources suggest the kinds of structural abilities and inabilities that occur throughout the life span and provide the basic equipment for the self-negation and adjustment processes. Though these sources all contain a mixture of empirically derived fact and inductive and deductive theory, there is a remarkable degree of convergence concerning the essential processes, despite all the apparent disagreement concerning their timing or the debates concerning what is inherent vs. what is learned. Further, there are empirically derived facts from the data that, without much interpretation, provide solid building blocks for a characterological-developmental theory.

The perspective of ego psychology can be useful here, if only at the level of description, by helping us make sense of a continuum of psychopathology. Along with others in this field (e.g., Masterson, 1976, 1981; Meissner, 1988), I have suggested that we see various basic forms of psychopathology along a spectrum. I believe the most central underlying dimension of such a spectrum involves the structural (often termed ego) functioning of the individual. This model posits that the same basic underlying characterological issue may be expressed all along this spectrum.

Just as other authors have discussed high-, medium-, or low-functioning borderlines or narcissists, I have been suggesting a similar demarcation along other characterological dimensions. Since I see these characterological dimensions as reflecting existential issues, the categorization will reflect the extent of psychic and behavioral disruption in relation to the issue in question. I am asserting that people are best understood *in relation to* these existential issues, recognizing that people can operate at different levels of structural integration depending on which issue they are dealing with. For example, an individual who typically operates with a high level of integration may more or less disintegrate or regress when faced with perceived threats to safety, threats to self-esteem, threats of another's abandonment, etc. This model is similar to that of Gedo and Goldberg (1973), who asserted that differing psychoanalytic *Models of the Mind* were appropriate to understand the differing types of psychopathological functioning.

Table 1 provides as comprehensive a map of all this as I could get into one table. Each characterological issue is subsumed under one of three developmental periods suggested by the developmental research and theories — attachment/bonding, self and other development, and self in system development. The six basic characterological issues and their respective expressions in behavior and attitudes are briefly presented. On the right side of the table the continuum of structural development is presented with three marker points along that continuum: personality disorder, character neurosis, and char-

Table 1
CHARACTEROLOGICAL ISSUES AND STRUCTURAL DEVELOPMENT

Developmental Period	Character	Issue	Characterological Expression	Structural Development Continuum and *DSM-IV* Diagnosis		
				Personality Disorder	Character Neurosis	Character Style
Attachment/ Bonding	Schizoid (safety)	Others the source of pain not comfort	Dissociation, withdrawal. Polarity: Presence-absence	Schizoid —————————— Avoidant ————→ Schizotypal Functional Psychoses		
	Oral (need)	Needs are denied or too great to be met	Dependency on or gratification of others at the expense of the self. Polarity: Seeking dependency gratification—providing dependency gratification	Dependent ————— Compensated Dependent* ————→		
Self and Other Development	Symbiotic (self boundaries)	Identity found in others, not in the self	Fusion defines an alien self-expression. True self elicits guilt. Polarity: Autonomy-enmeshment	Borderline ——————————————————————→ Dependent ——————————————————————→		

Self in System Development			
Narcissistic (self-esteem)	Identity found in the "false self," not in the impoverished real self	Attempts to maintain the grandiose self. Polarity: Worthlessness-grandiosity	Narcissistic ———
Masochistic (freedom)	Control of self-initiative surrendered to overpowering other	Subservient, guilt inducing, passive-aggressive, spiteful. Polarity: Controlled-controlling	Self-defeating*
Oedipal (love-sex)	Disruption and often splitting of the sexual and love impulses	Denial or exaggeration of sexuality, competition, and love. Polarity: Sexual-asexual	Obsessive-Compulsive ——— Histrionic ——— mixed ———

Note: Psychoanalytic developmental psychology = ego psychology (Hartmann, A. Freud), object relations (Mahler, Masterson, Kernberg, Stern, Winnicott, Fairbairn), self psychology (Kohut, Gedo, Goldberg), and character analysis (Reich, Lowen, Horowitz, Shapiro).

*Diagnoses not recognized by *DSM-IV*.

acter style. The continuum reflects a descending disruption in structural or ego functioning, particularly as it relates to that particular characterological issue.

Considering the schizoid (safety) issue, for example, full-blown schizoid personality disorder would be characterized by a very low level of structural development and high disruption in functioning, particularly around issues of social involvement, safety, and smooth affective regulation, with a tendency toward extreme use of dissociation and withdrawal in defense of threatening involvement. Schizotypal personality disorder and functional psychoses would also be listed under the character disorder column, evidencing high disruption in ego functioning, particularly around these kinds of issues.

All personality disorders are characterized by a very low tolerance for and difficulty in containing any increase in a number of affective states: anxiety, frustration, aggression, grief or loss, love or intimacy, etc. In response to these difficult to contain emotions, people with personality disorders tend to defend by the basic defense of splitting. In the schizoid case such splitting may be at the most global and primitive level with the individual dissociatively splitting off from current experience to an entirely different state. Or, like the narcissist or symbiotic personality disorder, there may be more specific, higher order splitting of the other or the self. Such splitting involves holding only one and usually extreme view of another, one's self, or of life itself. This experience of things dissociated or in dissociated extremes protects from the stress of working out a more adult, mixed view or integrated understanding and experience of things as they are. Thus, someone with a personality disorder may idealize or devalue another or see himself as either omnipotent or worthless. Furthermore, these extreme views can shift back and forth.

Projection is another common defense associated with personality disorder. Here the hard to contain emotion is thrown out onto others so that it need not be experienced internally. Another common defense is fusion or merger with others such that comfort is taken in the illusion of such oneness as long as the illusion can be maintained and as long as fusion and projection do not coexist. In the latter case, the projected feelings become even more threatening and require additional defense in that one still identifies with them, even to the point of experiencing the legitimacy of them being aimed at the self. This is called projective identification. When this occurs, the individual will engage in behaviors to defend against this perceived threat, often becoming very controlling and provoking just the reaction he has projected.

While all personality disorders share this basic primitive or immature structure, which Kernberg (1967) has labelled borderline personality organization, the different character styles predict the particular issues that are most likely to be the subject of splitting, projection, merger, projective identification, etc., as well as the manner in which they will be expressed.

Together with this defensive structure, personality disorder is often associated with damage to the internalization of values or the development of conscience. Among such difficulties may be an absence or at least impairment of guilt on the one hand, or the presence of an exaggerated and sadistic self punishment for imagined or real offences on the other.

Finally, personality disorder is often associated with the most troubled interpersonal histories from childhood to old age. Relationships, particularly intimate ones, may be absent, severely limited, or chronically dysfunctional. From an object relations viewpoint, all relationships become reruns of the original ones that created the trouble in the first place. Until the internalized representations of others and the self are repaired and maturation of defenses and coping are achieved, the future will always be a replay of the past.

Thus, the goal of therapy or any program of growth for one with a personality disorder must be maturation and integration. Understanding, catharsis, abreaction, cognitive or behavioral restructuring—anything we can name—will be inadequate unless this basic internal structure is matured and the polarities that determine the character style are integrated.

At middle levels of structural development with the schizoid issue, one is more likely to find the behavior more characteristic of the avoidant personality disorder in *DSM-IV* terms. Here there is an overuse of social withdrawal as a defense, with some cognitive and affective dissociation, especially under social stress, but serious structural disruption is absent, particularly outside this area of concern. What defines this midpoint character neurosis is a long-standing and life-disrupting internal conflict, which yields behavior that is "neurotic." In Shapiro's words, "The neurotic personality or character . . . is one that reacts against itself; it reacts, reflexively, against certain of its own tendencies. It is a personality in conflict" (Shapiro, 1989, p. x). Thus, in *DSM-IV*, what distinguishes a schizoid from an avoidant personality disorder is that the avoidant wants to be with others but is anxious about doing so. The tendency to approach reflexively brings on anxiety, but the tendency to avoid yields dissatisfaction. This "house divided against itself" personality can then produce elaborate compromise solutions to simultaneously accommodate the competing tendencies that carry that unmistakable neurotic quality.

Wherever the characterological adjustment is neurotic, one sees the predominance of defenses based on the repression of whatever creates conflict. Therapy with a neurotic character revolves more around the uncovering and resolution of such unconscious conflicts and the relinquishing of these compromise solutions. Such "solutions" are often obviously neurotic or self-defeating, but on closer examination they serve to appease both sides of the conflict while damaging the individual who has chosen them. With the neurotic character, there is often a greater role for guilt, especially unconscious guilt, in that his value structure is more solidly internalized and consistently determines his behavior over time.

Where those suffering personality disorder have difficulty tolerating or containing affect, the neurotic character can employ more mature defenses to hold even conflicting feelings for very extended periods. But such a person is often over-contained and out of touch with the raging forces that determine her behavior. Such held emotions can poison the individual, leading to the classic neurotic symptoms, which produce suffering in the somatic, behavioral, cognitive, or affective realms. Psychosomatic illness, compulsions, obsessions, or depression are all examples.

What I am proposing here is that the conflicts that can be florid and obvious in the personality disorder are also present in the neurotic character, but they have been rendered unconscious and are maintained as such by more mature, well-oiled defenses. Rather than maturation and integration, the goal of growth is the uncovering and resolution of such unconscious conflict. A natural result of such resolution is the relinquishing of neurotic compromise solutions.

In character style, there is greater consciousness concerning what gives the individual discomfort or conflict, a relative absence of symptoms, and a healthier reliance on coping and adaptation. It is unreasonable to expect human life to be conflict- or discomfort-free, but it is possible to defend nondestructively, to be aware, and to strive for greater levels of wisdom. Theoretically, the extreme right endpoint of the structural functioning continuum may be unattainable, but consistent movement in that direction is.

In the schizoid personality style, for example, even a trained clinician might have trouble classifying the person because coping, adaptation, and defenses work so well. But on close examination of all levels of functioning, one would detect some residual issues around safety, social exposure, and optimal contact with others. But the individual's intimate relationships, job, social life, defenses, etc., will operate relatively effectively both to limit pathology and enhance growth.

It is critical to remember here that this is a *dimensional* model rather than one based on fixed categories. Just as any given person may best be understood by a mixture of these characterological issues, so too may he be best comprehended by a mixed model of his structural functioning. He may, for example, function at the level of personality disorder when dealing with his key issues, when under extreme stress, or when given minimal support. Under more benign circumstances, however, he may be best understood as one who needs to resolve unconscious conflict or achieve higher levels of coping or adaptation.

In the structural-development continuum of the table, I have attempted to do a loose, generalized translation of *DSM-IV* personality-disorder terminology. With the exception of the avoidant personality classified under the schizoid issue, there are really no middle and high-end positions, because, in general, the manual is devoted to a description of severe personality disorders. The arrows within the structural development section are meant to communicate that the basic issues represented in these personality disorders may be extended to understand the character neuroses and the character styles that could just as well carry the same names. The table, which plots a characterological issue by level of structural development, can also be used in a general way to evaluate a client on more than one dimension, much like an MMPI profile. Thus, any given individual may show structural development in the low to middle range on the issue of narcissism, with a higher, yet disrupted, level of functioning on the schizoid and oedipal issues, etc. I have found that an orientation to all of this, which emphasizes the existential life issue as opposed to character typology, deepens and broadens understanding of ourselves and others and humanizes our approach to psychological problems.

It is critical in considering similarities between this characterological system and the DSM-IV diagnostic system to recognize their essential difference. DSM-IV begins with behavior; this system begins with etiology. I am outlining common developmental stories which, operating according to certain psychological principles, result in common characterological adaptations. DSM-IV is outlining commonly seen constellations of personality disorders. So, while there is overlap there will never be a one-to-one correspondence between the two systems.

I am not saying that every case of narcissistic or histrionic personality disorder derives from the archetypal story I will be telling here, though in these two cases this story appears to be by far the most common etiological pathway. The overlap of the two systems is probably lowest in the case of borderline and dependent personality disorder. Borderline is a clinically useful but very heterogeneous diagnosis which reflects many etiologies, including organic involvement. In my experience, individuals who are diagnosed borderline by DSM-IV guidelines usually have difficulty with at least two or often more of the life issues around which the present system is organized. Similarly, individuals with a diagnosis of dependent personality disorder could have an oral etiology as shown in Table 1 or a symbiotic etiology or a more idiosyncratic story that brought them to display such highly dependent behavior.

This system aims at explicating the primary life issues with which all humans must contend and understanding any given personality on the basis of those issues. Similar behaviors or attitudes can derive from different issues or stories as they play themselves out in the unique varieties that make for a kind of uncertainty principle in human affairs. Yet, the basic issues remain constant.

The model of character and psychopathology presented here is a "functional" one, meaning that it covers that which can be attributed to environmental as opposed to organic or genetic causes. Thus, those severe disorders that are documented to be organically or genetically related are not listed. Here I would include psychoses, bipolar disorders, antisocial (sociopathic or psychopathic) disorders, and autism. Some object-relations theorists would argue that sociopathic functioning is arrested development in the earliest (i.e., schizoid) period, but I have come to feel that much of it may be organically related.

Table 2, a companion to Table 1, further elucidates the structural development continuum. Here I've simply listed the characteristics of higher vs. lower structural development, which can be evaluated for an individual overall or, even more interestingly, for each characterological issue. An individual may have very good reality perception in general, but, because of his narcissistic issue, may misperceive social cues which are seen to affect his self-esteem in any way. Or, one's modulation of affect might be quite good except when one's fear of abandonment is triggered, etc. It is my experience that understanding this intersection of characterological issues and structural development for an individual provides the most useful diagnostic information and accurately predicts the themes of psychotherapy, its likely pace, and, to some extent, the interventions that will be useful, ineffective, or harmful.

This approach, which emphasizes looking at all personality issues in a pattern, is also consistent with the available data on personality disorders. For example, reviews of research on narcissistic personality disorder (Gunderson, Ronningstam, & Smith, 1991), histrionic personality disorder (Pfohl, 1991), and self-defeating personality disorder (Fiester, 1991) all show significant levels of overlap among these diagnoses and other personality disorder diagnoses. In other words, individuals who receive these diagnoses are likely to receive other diagnoses of some form of personality disorder.

Those who judge the validity of a diagnosis by its discriminant function have trouble with these results, but they are completely consistent with the theory presented here and with my experience. The lower the level of structural functioning, the more likely it is that a person will be dealing with disturbance in a number of these essential areas. In these cases, the clinician's understanding of the etiology, dynamics, and structural functioning associated with each characterological expression is necessary to understand and help the patient.

Now, I will turn to an exposition of the six basic characterological issues and the developmental factors that influence their course.

Table 2
THE STRUCTURAL DEVELOPMENT CONTINUUM

HIGH	LOW
Affective	*Affective*
Affective stability	Affects highly labile
High anxiety tolerance	Low anxiety tolerance
Anxiety serves as signal	Anxiety traumatic and disorganizing
Good self-soothing abilities	Poor self-soothing abilities
Good differentiation of feelings	Poor differentiation of feelings
Smooth modulation of feelings	Feelings undermodulated
High frustration tolerance	Low frustration tolerance
Experience of self-cohesion	Self-fragmentation
Insusceptible to regressive states	Susceptible to regressive states
Cognitive	*Cognitive*
Objective self-perception (good "observing ego")	Self-perception not reality based
Constancy of self-perception	Self-splitting
Predominance of mature defenses	Predominance of immature defenses
Mature development of moral sense	Morality founded on immature bases
High-quality reality perception	Poor reality perception
High quality of judgment	Impaired judgment
High quality of synthetic abilities	Impaired synthetic abilities
Formulation and execution of clear intentions	Intentions and planning impaired
Regressions creative and ego mediated	Regressions not ego mediated
Projections or regressions "owned"	Projections and regressions not "owned"
Interpersonal	*Interpersonal*
Object constancy	Object splitting
Good self-other differentiation	Blurring of boundaries
Distance and closeness well modulated	Relationships characterized by clinging, detachment, or ambivalence
Intimate others usually assumed to show object constancy	Relationships characterized by fears of other's abandonment, rejection, or destructiveness
Perception of others is reality based	Relationships characterized by merger, twinship, mirroring, or idealization transference behavior

CHAPTER 2

Characterological Issues of Attachment and Bonding

HAVING NOW REVIEWED the basic theory, in the remaining chapters of this section I will follow the central dimensions of Table 1 in presenting a summary of characterological issues. In this chapter, I will present the characterological issues that derive from the earliest period—attachment and bonding. These *schizoid* and *oral* issues will be discussed with illustrations of their expressions along the structural continuum—personality disorder, character neurosis, and character style. Similarly, in Chapter 3, I will present those issues of self development—symbiotic, narcissistic, and masochistic—along the same continuum. Finally, Chapter 4 will be devoted to the issues of the "oedipal" period, where the negotiation of self beyond the dyad becomes more crucial.

THE SCHIZOID ISSUE

The bulk of recent developmental research indicates that the human infant is seemingly "hardwired" at birth for social interaction. The data indicate, for example, that the neonate can discriminate its own mother's voice from another woman's voice reading the same material (DeCasper & Fifer, 1980). These same authors have shown that at one week, infants can recognize the difference between a passage read aloud to them in utero and a control passage which had never been read before. This shows a kind of social interaction even across the birth gap. Stern (1977, p. 36) notes that, even in the first few weeks of life, infants' eyes converge at approximately eight inches from the face, which is the typical distance between the mother's and the infant's face during nursing. Indeed, by the end of the first week, the behavioral evidence strongly suggests that the infant is sufficiently familiar with the mother's face to become visibly disturbed if it is obscured by a mask or matched with a voice other than the mother's (Tronick & Adamson, 1980, p. 141).

By one month, infants begin to show appreciation of more global (nonfeatured) aspects of the human face, such as animation, complexity, and even configuration (Sherrod, 1981). Even in the first two days of life, infants can discriminate between and even imitate happy, sad, and surprised expressions (Field et al., 1982). By three weeks of age, babies are able to perform the fairly complex activity of audiovisual crossmodal matching the absolute level of stimulus intensity (Lewcowicz & Turkewitz, 1980), indicating that they are, even at this point, up to the kind of mutual attunement with another that Stern (1985) characterizes as the essence of early human relations. Young infants are so predetermined to be social that they react emotionally to signals of distress from another individual (Sagi & Hoffman, 1976; Simner, 1971). Other studies have shown that infants will work to receive human contact or the opportunity to watch others. Lichtenberg (1983, p. 6) concludes that, "study after study documents the neonate's preadapted potential for direct interaction."

All this indicates that the infant is preprogrammed and attuned to the kinds of social responses he receives. So, very early on, a baby will track not only whether he is being handled roughly or subjected to painful stimulation, but he will be able to track the affective tone with which he is handled and the attunements, or lack of it, to his needs, emotional states, etc. Tronick et al. (1978) have documented that three-month-old infants will react with mild upset and social withdrawal if parents simply go "still-faced" in the middle of an interaction with them. Stern's (1985) work also shows that, from birth, the child can do things to tune out overstimulation. While challenging Mahler's earlier view of a "stimulus barrier," these findings further demonstrate the child's ability to discern and respond to aversive stimulation of a more social nature.

The schizoid issue (see Table 3) is one of safety in the social world. It is clear that the infant has more than the necessary equipment to discriminate the nurturing or depriving nature of the social environment. Babies can very quickly discriminate if caretakers are cold, distant, unattuned, even indirectly hostile. Essentially, the schizoid and oral issues come first developmentally because they involve the frustration of instinctual needs that are present at birth and that can be discriminated at birth or very shortly thereafter.

Yet, while the infant's ability in the discriminative realm is impressive, there are obvious limitations to its repertoire of adaptations to serious frustration. Turning away from and tuning out aversive stimulation are essential aspects of the infant's limited repertoire of responses to aversive stimulation. While these mechanisms may certainly be used extensively to deal with later traumas, they can be used as early as the beginning of life. The characterological-developmental theory merely states that to the extent that these mechanisms are used in the earliest period of life to avoid and escape nonoptimal frustrations in that period, they will tend to persist throughout life in response to situations that are perceived as similar (i.e., harsh, threatening, cold, etc.). Furthermore, to the extent that the early environment is indeed harsh, the theory simply asserts that the individual will be inclined to generalize his early experience and anticipate harshness in subsequent social situations. That harshness, both early and contemporary, may involve anything from abuse to inattention to poor attunement. The theory predicts that individuals with the schizoid issue will be particularly vigilant to harsh social environments, especially to harshness that resembles the early forms in which it was experienced. Further, the theory predicts a tendency toward social isolation, withdrawal, and forms of mental migration that will help avoid or escape any stress, particularly of a social nature.

Up to now, this process is all very simple and straightforward. However, what many clinicians have noted about schizoid individuals is that (a) they tend to be harsh with themselves, and (b) they often tend to gravitate towards relationships and environments that are themselves harsh. These phenomena are explained by the self-negation hypothesis of the characterological theory, which is consistent with the hypotheses of a number of relational-interpersonal theorists (e.g., Fairbairn, 1974; Mitchell, 1988; Weiss & Sampson, 1986; Winnicott, 1958, 1965). The individual is thought to imitate the caretakers and eventually internalize their attitudes toward the self. Fairbairn (1974) suggests that this internalization is particularly important when the child's objects are traumatically frustrating or "bad," because the child will render the internalized object and his own identification with it unconscious in order to escape pain. Thus, an internalized self and self-other relational model are rendered unconscious and thereby permeate his experience of self and his relationships with others. Also, the individual's relational needs are met in the context of this kind of negative self-other relationship, and the modes of self-negation and compromise solutions arrived at earlier are designed for just that kind of interpersonal entanglement. So, the patterns persist, both intrapersonally and interpersonally.

Because a common experience of character expressions is very valuable in communicating about them, I use illustrations from films in teaching about them whenever possible. In the schizoid's case, Timothy Hutton's portrayal of Conrad in *Ordinary People* is illustrative of one in the character neurosis range. William Hurt's portrayal of Macon Leary in *The Accidental Tourist* illustrates the extreme social withdrawal of a well-adapted schizoid personality disorder, if one discounts his quick recovery in falling in love with Muriel, portrayed by Geena Davis. The multiple personality portrayed by Sally Field in *Sybil* illustrates the dissociation that can be used to escape pain.

Psychotherapy of a person with a schizoid issue revolves around the projection as well as the reality of harshness in the social environment and harshness toward the self. People with this issue tend to see harshness where it's not, to be persistently harsh with themselves, and also to gravitate unnecessarily to harsh environments where their relational needs have been met, albeit very imperfectly, and their coping defenses are appropriate. At lower levels of structural development, there is typically a history of more severe and prolonged trauma. One finds the extreme inability to bond with another and the capacity for dissociation and withdrawal developed to a high degree. At higher levels of development, there tend to be more social skill and involvement, with concomitant tendencies toward intellectualization and spiritualization of life. Anxiety in social situations, while better compensated, is nevertheless present.

In this clinically derived correlation among personality, symptom constellation, and reconstructed history, therapists have frequently emphasized the role of terror in explaining and maintaining the often extreme levels of dissociation and withdrawal of these individuals. This is exemplified most dramatically with those who have experienced the kind of physical violence, sexual abuse, and sadistic torture that leads to the extreme dissociative cases of multiple personality. But we often find such intense terror present where we are able to uncover far more benign, if troubled, histories. It is unclear in many of these cases what exactly has happened to the individual, though it is quite conceivable that one very traumatic incident which has been repressed, and/or a chronically cold and barren social environment could be the cause.

In any case, schizoid individuals at all levels of structural development will show an almost automatic tendency to dissociate—to be unaware of their feelings and out of touch with thoughts or even visual memories that might disturb them. To some significant degree, these individuals are really out of touch with themselves and significant aspects of their experience. They tend, in particular, to isolate their feelings from thoughts. It is believed that this tendency to separate themselves from their own experience keeps them safe from the intense levels of terror that may emerge as this defensive strategy is relinquished. As this occurs, these individuals also typically access a good deal of retaliatory rage, which has also been kept in check by this ability to separate oneself from one's own experience. Typically, the treatment of the schizoid individual will involve not only the uncovering and expression of these difficult feelings but also some learning of better ways to control them. As all this occurs, the individual becomes more and more able to be vulnerable with respect to others and to access and connect to truly affectionate and nurturing feelings about others.

Successful therapy with a schizoid person really involves a desensitization to people, to intimacy, even to the experience of dependency on another for understanding, attunement, compassion, and love. It also involves attenuating the hostile "evoked companion" (Stern, 1985) or internalization of the harsh other and the hostile, retaliatory self. Finally, a good therapeutic outcome with a schizoid person involves the development of relational needs met in a more highly relational context, not in the context of a harsh, unwelcoming other.

Therapeutic errors with these individuals typically revolve around the timing of the process of desensitization to dissociated feelings

Table 3
SCHIZOID CHARACTER

---

1. *Etiological constellation*: Parenting is abusive to harsh to unattuned, cold, distant, and unconnected. The child experiences itself as hated, unwanted, or insignificant. With the limited resources of an infant the individual can only withdraw, dissociate, or internally migrate. The blocking of the most basic expressions of existence and the withdrawal of energy from external reality, others, and life itself produce deadness and disconnectedness.

2. *Symptom constellation*: Chronic anxiety, avoidant behaviors, conflict over social contact, trust, and commitment are definitional. There is usually evidence of self-destructive or self-damaging behavior, self-hatred or disapproval of self, poor self-care and self-soothing. The individual often shows an inability to know her own feelings and to make sustained social or intimate contact. To a great extent, this individual can be defined as one who is out of contact with self and others.

3. *Cognitive style*: Isolation of thinking from feelings with abstract thinking often well developed. Concrete operations in relation to the physical world often poorly developed. "Social" intelligence is often impaired.

4. *Defenses*: Projection, denial, intellectualization, "spiritualization," withdrawal, isolation of affect, dissociation, and fugue states. The individual may have poor memory, especially for interpersonal events, conflict, and childhood.

5. *Script decisions or pathogenic beliefs*: "I have no right to exist. The world is dangerous. There is something wrong with me. If I really let go, I could kill someone. I will figure it all out. The true answers in life are spiritual and other-worldly."

6. *Self-representation*: The self is experienced as damaged, perhaps defective or evil. The individual questions his own right to exist and invests in intellectual or spiritual pursuits identifying with his intellect and spirit.

7. *Object representations and relations*: Others are seen as nonaccepting, threatening, and more powerful than the self. The individual is particularly sensitive to harshness in the social environment. She often projects hostility onto others and elicits hostility through projective identification.

8. *Affective characteristics*: The person experiences chronic fearfulness and often terror. Affect is isolated and/or suppressed. The individual doesn't know how he feels and can appear cold, dead, and out of touch with himself. Primitive, suppressed rage underlies the fear and terror.

---

and thoughts as well as to other people. At one extreme, a very distant therapist might collude with the schizoid in very intellectualized reconstruction or mechanical, behavioral therapy for some aspect of this problem. At the other end of the spectrum, a very feeling-oriented therapist might rush such a client to premature affective and social experiences which would retraumatize him and thereby deepen the dissociative defense. Very often, these clients elicit impatience in therapists who fail to appreciate the profound level of terror that motivates their stubborn, out-of-touch demeanor. Retaliation for the very slow and uneven progress of these individuals, if not quickly repaired, can provide the death knell for their therapy. It is perhaps more with the schizoid issue than with any other that the therapist needs to provide at least a potentially holding environment while, at the same time, being careful not to push the client with more closeness, intimacy, or understanding than his shaky structure can handle. It is the "corrective emotional experience" offered in therapy and engineered outside it that is the essence of the required psychotherapy.

For each character issue or structure, I have composed a table summarizing some of the central features. In each summary, I have used the following categories: (1) etiological constellation, (2) symptom constellation, (3) cognitive style, (4) defenses, (5) script decisions or pathogenic beliefs, (6) self representation, (7) object representations and relations, and (8) affective characteristics. Though these summary statements are oversimplified and, in general, do not discriminate along the dimension of structural development, I have found them to be very useful heuristically. They are repetitive in places, but that repetitiveness is deliberate; in part, because I have found it often necessary for the real learning of this material, and also, because the slightly different slants or particular choice of words may be quite useful clinically in more accurately matching a specific client.

THE "ORAL" ISSUE

In clinical practice, problems that revolve around the themes of need, dependency, and dependency gratification are fairly common, giving rise to the labels of "oral" character, dependent personality disorder, and co-dependent (see Table 4). As with all other characterological patterns outlined here, this one derives from clinical experience with adults. The developmental theorizing has been derived from a combination of clinical experience with these individuals involving a reconstruction of their history and the developmental data (both naturalistic and experimental) that is available. In formulating this theory, it has always been obvious that infants ask to be fed almost immediately after birth and that their relationship to "feeding" may very well become isomorphic for their relationship to need gratification in general. In recent psychoanalytic theorizing, we emphasize more the interpersonal needs for relationship and mother-infant attunement. All the developmental research is consistent in emphasizing these themes, making the "oral" label a bit out-of-date as far as the regional specificity it implies, but it is still an appropriate label if it is understood metaphorically.

In any case, what clinicians have repeatedly found with those patients who present with problems in the "need constellation" is a history marked by either deprivation or unreliability in the need-fulfilling capacity of their parents. The severely "oral" patient gives one the impression that he has never really been thoroughly filled with those nutritional and emotional supplies that all human beings require. The body language as well as the presenting complaints and historical data all tend to confirm this impression of deprivation. In trying to reconstruct the etiological picture for these individuals, we notice that their defenses, from a psychodynamic point of view, are rather primitive in nature, and that their relationships have a distinctly one-up-one-down character revolving around need gratification.

In looking for developmental origins of these patterns, we have always known that young children need a great deal of attention and attunement quite early on; now, observational research documents these facts as never before (e.g., Mahler, Pine, & Bergman, 1975; Stern, 1985). Clinically, we also notice that people with these issues often have parents who, even in the first months of life, were unable to hold up their end of the relationship. We may see a history of depression, alcoholism, or extreme circumstances which made normal parenting difficult (e.g., single-parent families, stresses of war, or dire economic circumstances). This environmental block or frustration of natural dependency is, almost without exception, replicated by the individual, who harbors unresolved dependency issues.

Even in those individuals with this etiology who appear the most dependent, one typically sees self-disapproval of the neediness, as distinct from the more self-syntonic dependency of the symbiotic character.

In those individuals who have achieved a higher level of adjustment, the self-negation process is usually seen most clearly. The individual's needs are typically denied and/or expressed very minimally. Indeed, these individuals often experience their needs as alien or wrong and require themselves to be extraordinarily deprived before their own needs can be seen as legitimate. The adjustment process in these higher functioning individuals often involves a great deal of caretaking of others, as has often been observed in adult children of alcoholics. Often, these same individuals tend to take on much more caregiving than they can really sustain, ultimately breaking down and failing to deliver the level of gratification that they promised. It is at these times of breakdown that their needs become so great that they must be acknowledged and, at least to some extent, met. But, once this painfully won indulgence is allowed (and often guiltily), the individual will quickly return to the pattern of denying his own needs and attempting to gratify those of others. In this adjustment process, I believe there is the attempt: (1) to maintain contact with the environment which is essentially ungratifying, (2) to experience need gratification vicariously, and (3) to "fix" others so that they may at last gratify the self.

Developmental data, both observational and experimental, as well as psychoanalytic theory, can allow for this self-blocking of need and the attempts to nurture the insufficient caretaker from very early on. The developmental research shows that young infants respond empathically to others' distress (Sagi & Hoffman, 1976; Simner, 1971), that infants condition early and rapidly to frustrated feeding experiences (Gunther, 1961), and that by 10 weeks infants show differential responses to joy, anger, and sadness when these are displayed by the mother (Haviland & Lelwica, 1987). By three months of age children respond differentially to another's depression as expressed by facial expression and voice cues (Tronick et al., 1982), by nine months children can notice congruences between their own affective state and the affective expression observed on another's face (MacKain et al., 1985) and demonstrate attunement through crossmodal matching to the mood state of the mother (Stern, 1985), and by 10 months, they have the ability to match joyful and angry responses (Haviland & Lelwica, 1987). Further, Stern (1985) reports data that document that the quality of the attachment at one year is an "excellent predictor of relating in various other ways up through five years" (see pp. 77–78 for an extended review of this attachment research).

Psychoanalytic theory posits a number of instinctual vicissitudes and early developed defensive strategies that allow for the kind of self-denial and other-directed need gratification that orals exhibit. These strategies are: identification, displacement, reversal, and turning against the self. Blanck and Blanck (1974), in summarizing psychoanalytic ego psychology theory, indicate that all of these cognitive operations develop early and just after the most primitive defenses of denial and projection. Further, children begin to show primitive caretaking responses early.

The characterological-developmental position is that, once there is a blocking of the need "impulse" and the ensuing compromises and internalizations are in place, these solutions will be quite fixed and resistant to change, in spite of experiences that could potentially change them. This is due to the fact that, among other things, one's relational needs have been met with these blocks and adjustments and that these maneuvers were forged in the crucible of painful deprivation. The "pathogenic belief" (Weiss & Sampson, 1986) or "script decision" (Berne, 1964) underlying all this typically involves the idea that releasing the block and experiencing the need will lead to a repetition of the painful disappointment and deprivation. Further, it is often believed, albeit unconsciously, that failing to meet the needs of others will also lead to abandonment. Other common underlying beliefs are: "I don't need. I can do it all myself. I find myself in giving and loving. My need is too great and will overwhelm others."

As a result of living her life in this untenable, undernourished, and inhuman way, the oral character is prone to drop into very collapsed states. This often involves physical illness and depression. The physical illness is common because the individual is chronically undernourished in many respects and, therefore, more susceptible to all kinds of illness. Furthermore, getting sick is a culturally sanctioned way to procure nurturance, both from others and the self, and may well have been the only circumstance in which the compensated oral person was able to get caretaking from her parents. Serious illness, in particular, is a sort of honorable discharge from the often overwhelming and unconsciously resented responsibilities of adult life.

The "emotional illness" of depression can occur for the same reasons and be sustained by the same secondary gains or payoffs. Of course, depression also serves the function of defensively suppressing the oral's aggression, hostility, and much more intense but real grief at deprivation and the consequent loss of self that she feels. In any oral character with even marginally effective compensation, there is a compensatory state juxtaposed with this state of collapse, which is often more positive but can often veer off into elation, euphoria, and, in extreme cases, to manic episodes. In such states, the compensated oral character tends to exhibit the overnurturing of others, to take on more responsibility and independent action than she can sustain, and to make plans that are optimistic to grandiose.

The oral character is typically quite grandiose in her underlying omnipotent belief that she can meet the needs of others, and this oral grandiosity serves a defensive function. It is during these times of compensation that the individual takes especially poor care of herself, effectively setting up the collapse that inevitably follows. All character structures may show a juxtaposition of what I have alternatively termed the symptomatic or *collapsed self* and the compensated or *false self*. Both characterological expressions are defensive of the underlying real-self structure, which includes the archaic, real, and vulnerable demands of the child. This alternating pattern is perhaps just more obvious in many oral personalities, who tend to show this cyclothymic-like pattern.

The oral character is also typically out of touch with his natural aggression and his considerable hostility. Even where he can identify his needs, he is not able to mobilize aggression in such a way that he can get what he wants or organize his life so that it really works. As a function of his character development, his nature is passive, and he usually becomes more passive when anxious. In other words, anxiety does not serve as a signal to mobilize aggression, but is more traumatic in nature, increasing passivity. After all, the arrested dependent child believes that it is really someone else's job to take care of her. While she may defensively take care of others or collapse, she cannot take care of herself. The aggression and hostility often show up residually in a kind of chronic irritability, which is typically self-dystonic but which she is, nevertheless, unable to fully control. That irritability is the leaking through of the rage at chronic disappointment and the deep resentment at having to rise to self-sufficiency and the care of others prematurely.

The oral self-representation also follows this compensated-collapsed polarity. The person alternately sees himself as all-giving, all-nurturing, and even all-powerful in his abilities to heal the world in the compensated state, and as defective, powerless, damaged, and depleted in the collapsed state. This same polarity is useful in observing and understanding the relationships of the oral character, which tend to be characterized by dependency. The description of the compensated oral character and the co-dependent are virtually indistinguishable, although the co-dependent behavior can derive from other characterological solutions. Yet, in all but the most well-compensated oral personalities, others often get the message that this individual is really after his own dependency gratification. This message can come through in the longing look in the eyes, the manipulative feeling of the oral collapse, or in the transparency of the oral's nurturance, which demands even more nurturance in return.

One way or another, sooner or later, with the oral personality, we often feel that nothing will ever be enough, and that this person is truly a bottomless pit. And there is truth in that. The very real, legitimate needs of the infant, the child, and the adolescent were not really met. In a very real sense, he can never go back. What was missed then will be missed forever. To resolve this is as much a part of the oral's recovery as is his realization that human needs are legitimate and *can* be met within the real limits of adult relationships.

The characterological-developmental theory posits that releasing the block and relinquishing the adjustment will also remove the block to the natural organismic reaction of rage at the depriving other. It is true that one gripped by overwhelming need and rage may well alienate others and elicit abandonment and retaliation.

Successful therapy with the oral character addresses all of this and essentially repairs the individual's relationship to his own need; reclaiming the *right* to need; learning to discriminate one's own needs and express them; desensitizing the fear of disappointment, abandonment, or rejection at such expression; and legitimizing the very natural rage at being frustrated for being a normal human being who needs. Where the needs are, indeed, infantile and in some sense

Table 4
ORAL CHARACTER

---

1. *Etiological constellation*: Parents are unreliable or insufficient in response to the child's needs and are frequently excessively needy themselves. The child relinquishes the dependent position before being satisfied, thereby remaining chronically needy and dependent. He attempts to consistently deny the dependency that may be apparent or compensated but that is always disapproved of by the self.
2. *Symptom constellation*: The individual cannot get his needs met. Failures include the inability to identify needs, the inability to express them, disapproval of one's own neediness, inability to reach out to others, ask for help, or indulge the self. Self-soothing and self-nurturing abilities are impaired. The individual tends to meet the needs of others at the expense of the self, to overextend, and to identify with other dependent people while denying the similarity. Frequent illness, depression, or other forms of collapse, which coerce and justify support while permitting self-indulgence, are common. Compensations for dependency continue to be attempted irrespective of how well they work.
3. *Cognitive style*: Prone to swings of overactive, euphoric, and sometimes creative thought to underactivated, depressed, and uninspired cognition. May show poor judgment and reality testing in elated periods.
4. *Defenses*: Denial, projection, identification, reversal, displacement, and turning against the self. The compensation of caring for others and elation as well as the collapse of illness and depression are defensive and involve splitting of self and object representations. Grandiosity is shown in the oral's exaggerated responsibility for and attempts to meet other's needs.
5. *Script decisions and pathogenic beliefs*: "I don't need; I can do it all myself. I find myself in giving and loving. My need is too great and will overwhelm others. If I express my needs, I will be disappointed, abandoned, or rejected."
6. *Self-representation*: Split, emphasizing the giving, loving, healing, nurturing, and empowered self in the compensated state and the damaged, depleted, weak, defective, and powerless self in the collapsed state.
7. *Object representations and relations*: Split, with others seen as figures with more resources who may give the needed supplies or as weak and unable to take care of themselves and in need of gratification. These individuals tend to relate as dependent or co-dependent. When the individual's dependency is apparent, others feel they can never do enough — that the person is never really able to be satisfied.

Table 4
(*continued*)

---

8. *Affective characteristics*: These individuals are prone to a cyclothymic-like pattern or euphoria, elation, and mania alternating with physical collapse and depression. They are out of touch with aggressive impulses and hostility but tend to be irritable. They often show fear of aloneness, fear of abandonment, and jealousy.

---

meaningfully arrested, they cannot be met currently and a realization and mourning of that fact is necessary. However, at the same time, the individual typically can have more of his needs met than ever before. I have often said to clients with this issue, "You can't get all that you really want, but you can get much more than you have ever had." Even those of us who are very needy can get a lot of those needs met if we go about it properly. Denying one's needs, meeting them vicariously or only when collapsed, or, alternatively, expressing them in a demanding and entitled way are not among the strategies that work very well.

The oral character, whether compensated or not, needs to learn that his needs are alright. If his needs are exaggerated, he comes by that honestly, and he must realize that his needs cannot be met vicariously, that intimate relationships can exist outside his historical experience of them, that needs can be reciprocally met, etc. Furthermore, he needs to experience, understand, and work through his own natural reactions to deprivation and unreliable caretaking. He comes by his "oral rage" honestly, and the same is true for the grief he experiences around that insufficiency and the fear that is a natural consequence of caretakers who could not be counted on when, literally, his life depended on it. The extended treatment of the schizoid and oral characters was the subject of my first book in this series, *Characterological Transformation: The Hard Work Miracle* (Johnson, 1985).

CHAPTER 3

Characterological Issues of Self-Development

THIS CHAPTER IS DEVOTED to those characterological issues that underlie the development of a firm sense of a separate self. Though vastly different in expression, "self disorders" have in common the individual's alienation from his or her real self. For such a real self to develop there must be an environment that encourages a full range of self-expression, accurately and sympathetically mirrors that expression, and provides optimal frustration to such expression when necessary. All of the characterological issues reviewed in this chapter show the common etiology of environmental failure of the preceding prescription.

The symbiotic, narcissistic, and masochistic character structures essentially derive from a history in which children were used to fulfill the agendas of caretakers. There is, then, a resulting confusion in identity wherein the externally imposed identity agenda is consciously accepted while remaining somehow ill-fitting, inauthentic, or incomplete. Simultaneously, the more natural forms of self-expression that are discouraged remain undeveloped and the source of internal conflict. Finally, the traumatic constriction of real self-expression yields developmental arrests, which require recognition and maturation.

THE SYMBIOTIC ISSUE

This characterological issue revolves around separation from the matrix of interpersonal life, which surrounds the human child from the earliest days. Stern (1985), whose work is perhaps best known for challenging Mahler's concept of early symbiosis as a universal illusion in the early months of life, writes of the child of one year that "most of the things the infant does, feels, and perceives occur in different kinds of relationships. . . . The infant engages with real, external partners some of the time and with evoked companions almost all of the time. Development requires a constant, usually silent, dialogue between the two. . . . This subjective sense of being with (intrapsychically and extrapsychically) is always an active mental act of construction, however, not a passive fear of differentiation" (Stern, 1985, pp. 118–119).

All of the developmental research already reviewed attests to the young child's exquisite social sense, attunement, and responsivity to social contingencies. It is at about the one-year point that the child begins to develop the ability to stand upright and walk. The latter ability gives him the capacity to initiate separation and engage in autonomous activity at a far higher level than ever before. The development of speech, which also occurs at about this time, introduces another very powerful individual function, allowing differentiation at a symbolic level.

Mahler has called the period between 10 and 15 months the practicing subphase of individuation and characterizes it as a period during which the child has a love affair with the world and with his own emerging abilities. It is during this period that the child is observed to wander further away from the parent with far less apprehension than before and is relatively impervious to falls and other frustrations. It is called *practicing* because the child is practicing these new, exciting abilities, which open new opportunities for experiencing the world. The characterological-developmental theory that I espouse and develop here contends that this is an especially important period for the development of autonomy, particularly as it relates to autonomous adventure, initiative, and the development of a sense of agency and self-efficacy.

The experimental, developmental research indicates that, as early as 12 months, a child will look to his parent to signal whether adventurous moves are dangerous or safe (Emde & Sorce, 1983).

Early and, I believe, critical incidents that discourage separation, initiative, and adventure, occur when these parental signals err in the direction of danger, where the caretaker is threatened by this "practicing" of autonomous functions and this early exercise of self, or where these moves are actively punished because they are experienced as contentious or inconvenient. Such incidents may be even more powerful during the subsequent "rapprochement" period of 15 to 24 months when the observational research shows that the child particularly appreciates the implications of his separateness, vulnerability, and dependency on parents. It is at this same time that other researchers have witnessed an increase in the imitation of conventional social behaviors (Kuczynski, Zahn-Waxler, & Radke-Yarrow, 1987).

Whether or not a child in these circumstances has the illusion of symbiosis or fusion either through a natural tendency to make that error, à la Mahler, or on the basis of his ability to construct reality, à la Stern, the child's experience is one of intense involvement, indeed enmeshment, with another. But, at about 12 months there is enhanced ability and impulse to move out of that symbiotic orbit at times and to become one's own person by walking, talking, exploring, etc. When that impulse is blocked, the child learns that he must restrain himself in these respects and develops a compromised false self, which maintains contact with the parents through continued dependency and enmeshment. This leads to a kind of false self where, as in all other such adjustments, identity is found in the relationship with the other at the expense of the identity established through the exercise of autonomous functions.

Levy and Bleeker (1975) outlined the five steps of character development for each of the five classic characters described by Alexander Lowen. I reproduced these in *Characterological Transformation* (1985) with slight modifications and added a similar outline, which I derived for the symbiotic character. I reproduce this latter outline here to enhance understanding of the process in general and this structure in particular. This outline (see Table 5) presents a quick summary of what will be presented in greater detail later in this volume.

This description and etiological schema of character apply to structures from the low level borderline patient, who experiences extreme fusion states, panic, or acting-out at abandonment or engulfment, to symbiotic character neurotics, who are extraordinarily conflicted and tormented about their exaggerated responsibility and obligation to others, to those whose character style is less subject to neurotic conflict, but who have some difficulty finding or owning their autonomous identity and who overly define themselves by who they are with instead of by who they really are. Even in those of the latter character type who function rather well in the world, there is often a limited sense of self and self-agency, which can express itself in the lack of truly self-initiated preferences, tastes, and abilities. Even though there may be a very high level of competence and apparent self-expression, it is often not fully owned and integrated into a unified self-concept. In more technical language, the self is more likely to be formed through the incorporation of others or through the idealization of or identification with others rather than through a more fully developed process of internalization. Separation guilt and survivor guilt (Modell, 1965, 1971; Niederland, 1961; Weiss & Sampson, 1986) are often very useful concepts in the process of liberating the symbiotic character.

Among the more common themes in the psychotherapy of the symbiotic character is permission for the expression of natural aggression, which is a central part of the separation process as well as for the natural hostility that these individuals harbor as a result of being blocked in many forms of self-expression. Concomitantly, the therapy usually has to deal with the natural fear that will be aroused as the individual begins to separate from the fused relationship and identity. A common interpretive theme with this structure involves the many and intricate ways in which the person preserves the underlying, original relationship with all its limitations. The affects, behaviors, cognitions, and symptoms of these individuals may often be best understood for their preserving function. Neurotic compromises, which allow some expression of autonomy but simultaneously negate or deny it, are common.

Successful therapy with the symbiotic character involves breaking the bonds of restraint that fuse the individual and his identity to others. It may very well involve withstanding aggression and hostility in the transference, and in the higher functioning cases it will typically involve pulling for just that aggression and hostility and working through its disavowal. Successful therapy will also involve eroding the disavowal of whatever real, autonomous sense of self has been developed. Finally, to the extent that a real self must still find

Table 5
THE SYMBIOTIC ETIOLOGY

Self-affirmation: I have the right to separate and be myself.
Negative environmental response: Withdrawal, panic.
Organismic reaction: Panic.
  Chronic environmental frustration impels a squelching of the organismic reaction.
Self-negation process:
  —Retroflective attitude: I don't want to separate.
  —Muscular holding pattern: Holding still, holding breath, maintaining an undeveloped, undercharged body.
Adjustment process:
  —Ego compromise: I will live through another.
  —Characteristic behavior: Dependent, clinging, complaining, afraid of separation.
  —Ego ideal: I will be loyal.
  —Illusion of contraction: I am safe as long as I hold on to you.
  —Illusion of release: I will be abandoned and helpless.

Table 6
SYMBIOTIC CHARACTER

1. *Etiological constellation*: Parents block self-agency, adventure, and self-control by anxious, withdrawn, threatened, or punitive responses to those behaviors, which serve to produce distance, establish difference, demonstrate aggression, or establish a self-determined identity. Concomitantly, merger, empathy, and identification with and dependency on parents are overvalued. This yields an adopted, accommodated, other-determined self based on the overuse of incorporative introjection and uncritical identification. Identity formation relying on the more mature transmutative processes of assimilation and accommodation are underutilized.

2. *Symptom constellation*: Deficient in a solid sense of identity, self-concept, and behaviors that define a unique self. Identity found in relationship to intimate others with whom the individual merges. This lack of firm boundaries can lead to confusion about responsibility, susceptibility to invasion by the affects or thoughts of significant others, and, in borderline functioning, to actual fusion states. This propensity to be taken over by others can lead to fears of loss of autonomy and to fears of total engulfment, which prompt rigid distancing. These maneuvers,

Table 6
(*continued*)

---

in turn, lead to fears of abandonment and identityless isolation. Many other symptoms serve to preserve the original merged relationship, rebel against it, or, more commonly, both. The actual preservation of family pain going back generations is not uncommon. Separation guilt, survivor guilt, and weakened aggression are common.

3. *Cognitive style*: Boundary confusion results in poor reality testing with regard to who is responsible for what. In lower functioning individuals (i.e., borderlines), this leads to overexternalization of responsibility and blame. In higher functioning individuals, this results in excessive responsibility for others leading to the cognitive errors of separation and survivor guilt. These individuals often have difficulty discriminating their own likes and dislikes, beliefs, opinions, etc. Except at the lowest levels of structural development, aggression is denied and projected and is thereby unavailable for use.

4. *Defenses*: Merger, denial, projection, identification, coercion, manipulation, externalization, omnipotent responsibility (an expression of grandiosity), turning against the self, projective identification, splitting.

5. *Script decisions and pathogenic beliefs*: "I am nothing without you. You are taking me over or swallowing me up. I owe you myself. I am responsible for you, and/or you are responsible for me. I can't be happy if you aren't happy. I can't tolerate difference between us. I can't tolerate being too close. My happiness, success, survival will hurt you or is at your expense. Your separateness, success, or happiness that does not include me, hurts me and is gained at my expense. I can't survive without you."

6. *Self-representation*: Depends on connection with the other but is otherwise unclear with varying degrees of boundaryless features. Based excessively on incorporative introjection and identification. An independent, assertive self is denied or split off.

7. *Object representations and relations*: Others experienced as exceedingly important with blurring of self-other differentiation. Others often experienced as engulfing or abandoning (i.e., split). Particularly at lower levels of structural development, these individuals are experienced by others as manipulative and coercive.

8. *Affective characteristics*: At lower structural levels, the affective instability is characterized by panic and rage at abandonment and/or engulfment. At higher levels, guilt is common and associated with excessive responsibility for others. Anxiety may be stimulated by anything that leads to separation (e.g., differences of opinion, success, freedom from symptoms, etc.).

---

true expression and receive attuned support, this self-building must occur, and, to the extent that real internalization of relevant abilities such as self-soothing, responsible limit setting, etc., have not been acquired, this internalization process must also be initiated and supported. In general, at lower levels of ego development, there will be a longer process of therapy devoted to this self-development. At higher levels of development, there will be more real self available for the person to own, and a greater proportion of the therapeutic task will center on achieving that ownership, dispelling unconscious, pathogenic beliefs having to do with excessive obligation and responsibility, and eroding neurotic compromises which express yet deny the true self.

THE NARCISSISTIC ISSUE

Narcissism is the issue of self-esteem (see Table 7). The characterological-developmental theory espoused here asserts that this character structure comes out of the nonoptimal frustration of self-expression, just as does the symbiotic's. Here, however, the frustration is somewhat more complex and variable. It is not the separation per se that yields the unattuned or negative response from the caretaker. Rather, it is some form of the child's self-expression that is "not enough" or "too much" for the other. The reconstruction of narcissistic cases often yields the fact that the individual was repeatedly put down or "narcissistically injured" in the expression of his ambitious self-expression, or he was idealized, and therefore expected to provide far more gratification, excitement, or meaning for his parents than was possible, or both. It is not uncommon in the reconstruction of these cases that one parent was more idealizing, and that the narcissistic injury initiated by that parent came from the child's inability to live up to the inflated expectations. Simultaneously, the other parent can be threatened by the child's real magnificence and the spouse's extravagant attention to the child. Unable to deal with all that, the other parent may humiliate and shame the child, narcissistically injuring him more directly.

All narcissistic individuals live with the unresolved polarity of grandiosity and worthlessness. The true expression of their real magnificence and limitations did not bring accurately attuned recognition and praise as well as optimal frustration. Rather, it brought disappointment, humiliation, or, at best, it was ignored. The environmental block was then reinforced, as always, by the individual, who restricted those parts of himself that were not reinforced and inflated those parts that were so highly valued. This latter adjustment process constitutes Winnicott's "false self," which, in the narcissist, is experienced as more false or inauthentic, both by the self and others, than in any other character structure. But the false self is the individual's only source of self-esteem and is therefore typically guarded with intense vigilance. He doubts himself, because his real self has been undervalued, if not humiliated, and he easily projects or finds disapproval in the environment where he is exquisitely sensitive to slight disapproval or failure. When well-defended, the narcissistic person aggrandizes and adorns himself, plays to the audience for superlative approval, manipulates, objectfies, and devalues others in service of his grandiose, false self, and seems to believe in his own grandiosity. Everyone becomes part of the audience that is manipulated for the desired effect, but the inevitable frustrations of life will elicit the opposite pole of worthlessness, self-depreciation, and self-inhibition of activity. This will elicit again the defense of the grandiose false self, which is typically an even more desperate and sometimes unrealistic version of that compensation than existed before the threat.

Again, there has been controversy among developmental theorists as to when this issue initially arises and, therefore, at which point it can be earliest arrested. In many ways, this question is of little importance clinically. It is more the process than the point at which it happens that is important. Still, much evidence suggests that this process could happen fairly early. It is around the activities of Mahler's practicing period (10 to 15 months) that a great deal of self-expression is first seen, and the child obviously has the powers to discriminate and participate in attuned interaction at this point. Children have been consistently observed to be quite taken with themselves and their new abilities at this time. More recent research on children indicates that they become self-reflective at about 18 months of age, indicating that at this point they can at least begin to have some capacity for a self-concept (Stern, 1985). It is also between one and two years of age that children demonstrate that they react to activities in terms of standards of performance that could affect self-esteem (Gopnik & Meltzoff, 1984; Kagan, 1981). Even at this "late date," children would presumably base that construction on prior, as well as continuing, experiences, and, to the extent that these events were narcissistically injuring, the issues of self-esteem would likely arise.

Perhaps more than any other theorist, Kohut (1971, 1977, 1978) has been the most definitive in suggesting both ambition and idealization as inborn vicissitudes—ambition requiring accurate mirroring and idealization requiring idealizable others for optimal development. According to Kohut, it is the mishandling of these needs that prevents the optimal frustration and results in the narcissistic character formation.

At the low end of the ego development continuum, one sees those blatantly narcissistic individuals whom most laymen could diagnose after a couple of minutes of casual conversation. These people show the gross levels of entitlement, grandiosity, manipulation, devaluation, and objectification of others, which are definitional to all as narcissistic. Some of these people can be relatively effective in life in spite of all this, because they are able to mobilize a good deal of their aggressive self-expression and, particularly when they are bright and talented, may be quite successful in some areas. Interpersonally, they are a disaster, and if the "false self" fails, they break down into serious forms of void and fragmentation, often becoming truly dangerous to themselves and others.

In narcissistic character neurosis, these traits and issues are far less obvious, but this personality is at war with itself around the issue of self-esteem. There is typically more rapid vacillation between the poles of what I have termed the symptomatic self and the false self in the second book in this series, *Humanizing the Narcissistic Style*. The individual at this level of structural development is typically far less obvious in his expression of the grandiose false-self features such as entitlement, omnipotence, and the narcissistic use and devaluation of others. But self-esteem is fragile and is typically propped up by perfectionism and an extreme reliance on achievement. There is some awareness of a real self and a desire to express it, enjoy it, and have it well received. The narcissistic neurotic will say, "Why can't I relax, why can't I accept myself, why can't I let myself enjoy things, why do I always have to be number one, why do I procrastinate on important projects until the last minute and then pull them off in an anxious frenzy, etc., etc., etc.?" The war with self produces the neurotic symptoms, which usually have strong components, of course, of anxiety, depression, and the self-involvement of rumination about self-worth, physical symptoms, procrastination, and feelings of worthlessness.

At the level of narcissistic style, there is typically less torment, a less severe history of narcissistic injury, and more effective defenses, particularly if the person is capable. Still, there are threads of narcissistic issues of all the types mentioned earlier, including an exaggerated commitment to the persona or public self, which, often very gracefully, hides any aspect of the real self that would lead one to be seen in less than the most positive light. One feels, perhaps consciously, perhaps not, that if "they" knew all there is to know about me, they wouldn't like and admire me as much as they do now. In short, there is *something* about me that is bad or not enough or too much and that must be hidden. Though there is less symptomatology at this level, there often is still a measurable amount of it, and, more often, one's loved ones or family have a sense of missing something in the relationship, which is not quite real or authentic. The person at this level is often a bit "too good to be true" and, in that, is not.

As with the symbiotic character, the treatment of the narcissist involves the resurrection and development of the true self, including the injuries, the arrested development, the pathogenic beliefs, and the disavowed aspects of the "self." Those disavowed elements usually involve the less agreeable, narcissistic features such as entitlement, grandiosity, and objectification of others. It is the injured and undeveloped real self of the narcissist that needs an advocate in the psychotherapy, and this is why Kohut was so correct in his emphasis on the greater need for empathy in the treatment of this structure. The empathy is also required here, of course, for the tender fragility covered by the false-self mobilization. When the narcissistic person is really *understood* (seen, heard, recognized) for who he really is, he experiences the safety to discover who he is and to reexperience the injury to that real and often young and vulnerable person. Then, he can experience the necessary therapeutic shift where he begins to use others for the discovery and development of his real self rather than to bolster and aggrandize his false self.

With what I have termed the "borderline" narcissist, this treatment process is longer, more repetitive, more supportive, more "reluctantly indulgent" (Kohut) of both the grandiosity of self and the idealization of the therapist or others. And this therapy must be more de-

Table 7
NARCISSISTIC CHARACTER

---

1. *Etiological constellation*: Parents narcissistically cathect the child and disallow the child's legitimate narcissistic cathexis of the parents. The child is used to mirror, aggrandize, or fulfill the ambitions and ideals of the parent. The child's real magnificence and vulnerability are not simultaneously supported. Rather, the parents need the child to be more than he is for self-fulfillment and idealize him or need him to be less than he is and humiliate him, or both. This results in a deep injury to the experience of the real self and a consequent deficit in self-esteem regulation. The natural system of feedback and correction affecting the balance of ambitions, ideals, and abilities fails to mature such that ambitions and ideals remain grandiose, while corrective negative feedback about abilities must remain rigidly disavowed.

2. *Symptom constellation*: The individual harbors a grandiose false self characterized by omnipotence, pride, self-involvement, entitlement, perfectionism, and excessive reliance on achievement for the maintenance of self-esteem with manipulation, objectification, and devaluation of others. When this compensatory false self breaks down, the individual shows great vulnerability to shame or humiliation, feelings of worthlessness, difficulty in self-activation, and work inhibition. This low self-esteem dominated depression may be accompanied by hypochondriacal preoccupations, psychosomatic illness, anxiety, and loneliness. An even deeper real-self crisis includes the deeply felt enfeeblement and fragmentation of the self; emptiness, void, and panic at the realities of an arrested development; and long-suppressed real affects relating to the original narcissistic injuries.

3–4. *Cognitive style and defenses*: In the grandiose, false-self state, the narcissistic demonstrates cognitive errors that will maintain the grandiosity, e.g., externalization of responsibility (i.e., blaming others), denial of negative input, disavowal of his own negative attributes, devaluation of positive contributions from others, unrealistic identification with idealized others, etc. In the symptomatic or collapsed state, there is a preoccupation with symptoms, defensive rumination on self-worth, physical symptoms, procrastination, or other preoccupations that keep the demands and affects of the underlying real self at bay. Splitting keeps these two states separate and unintegrated. Feeling his real self, the narcissist always experiences at least some disorganization, vulnerability, and unfamiliar but vital affects. Here the individual may feel he is losing his mind, but, if managed correctly, it is here that he begins to find himself.

Table 7
(*continued*)

---

5. *Script decisions and pathogenic beliefs*: "I must be omnipotent, perfect, special. I must know without learning, achieve without working, be all powerful and universally admired. I must not make a mistake or I am worthless, nothing, and disgusting. I must be a god or I am nothing. If I am vulnerable, I will be used, humiliated, or shamed. I can't let anyone really matter to me. All that I own, including my friends and family, must reflect and confirm my perfection and superiority. I will never be humiliated again. Others are superior to me. Others are inferior to me."
6. *Self-representation*: Split — grandiose or worthless as outlined above.
7. *Object representations and relations*: Object representations are best understood using the four basic narcissistic transferences suggested by Kohut: (1) *Merger* — where the individual achieves a sense of security and worth through fusion. Here the individual will freely use the other without recognizing the actual self-other boundary; (2) *twinship* — where the individual achieves a sense of enhanced identity and self-worth by assuming exaggerated similarity between the self and other; (3) *mirroring* — where the individual relates to the other solely as one who enhances self-esteem by serving as a prizing, understanding, acknowledging "part-object;" and (4) *idealization* — where the other enhances self-cohesion and esteem by being perfect in one or more respects and serving as a source for emulation. Idealization may also serve to create the perception of the perfect merger, twinship, or mirroring object. Others typically feel used by the narcissistic, but if he is effective in his false self, others are attracted to him for his charisma and talent. The use of others to discover the real self, rather than aggrandize the false self, is pivotal in the desired maturation of the narcissist's relationships.
8. *Affective characteristics*: Narcissists are frequently noted for the "as if" or artificial quality of feelings, the inability to feel for others, and their extremely easily wounded pride. At lower levels of ego development, acting-out and impulse control disorders are common. At higher levels, there is great intolerance for most feelings, although a high level of affective responsiveness is held in check. Silently born shame and humiliation are common.

---

voted to the real development of a true self rather than working on its simple uncovering and ownership.

At higher levels of ego development, where many false-self abilities have been finely honed but not really experienced as one's own, as the source of pleasure for oneself, or as an authentic gift to others, the therapeutic problem is easier because it represents more of a shift in orientation and experience than a "redo" of the essential developmental processes.

At the middle or neurotic level of this issue, there is relatively more emphasis on helping the person to enjoy the exercise of his autonomous functions, which are indeed grand at times and which can be experienced and enjoyed without the neurotic entanglements that give achievement its typical pain for these people. In a sense, successful treatment of the narcissist involves reclaiming the healthy or normal narcissism that is the birthright of every human being — exercising it, enjoying it, and liberating it. Yet, to be human is to be in some ways vulnerable, limited, needy, dependent, weak, and even stupid at times. We all need to accept that part of humanness in ourselves and others. We need to be loved and to love ourselves when we are vulnerable in these ways. When there is a taming of normal narcissism, there is a self-directed object constancy in which the self is loved in all its magnificence and in all its humility.

THE MASOCHISTIC ISSUE

Masochism involves the issue of control (see Table 8). As Lowen (1958) has suggested, an understanding of this structure can be gained by simply imagining what an animal such as a dog or cat would do if it were forced in the natural processes of food intake and elimination. However docile the animal might be, intrusion in these natural organismic responses would undoubtedly elicit strong aggressive responses, and, if this highly intrusive intervention continued and aggressive responses were eventually eliminated, one can imagine highly pathological consequences for the animal. Such is often the case with the masochistic human, whose history is often replete with intrusion, control, and humiliating subjugation of the will.

Lowen (1958) reports these historical memories from one of his masochistic clients: "To my mind, as I look back, it's not that I didn't eat as much as it was that I didn't eat enough. My mother forced enormous quantities of food into me. . . . I remember at the age of three to four, running around the kitchen table, my mother running after me with a spoonful of something I didn't want in one hand a belt in another hand, threatening to strike me, which she often did. . . . One of the worst things my mother did was to threaten to leave me or to go up on the roof and jump off and kill herself if I didn't finish my food. She actually used to step out of the apartment into the hall, and I used to collapse on the floor in hysterical crying."

In relation to "toilet troubles," the same client recalled, "My mother forced me under pain of hitting me to sit on the toilet for one or two hours and try to 'do something,' but I couldn't." This same client recalls that after the age of two, he was constipated, and his mother inserted her finger into his anus, stimulating it. He received frequent enemas through age seven and was plagued with horrible-tasting laxatives (Lowen, 1958, pp. 196–197).

The individual's innate need or disposition to exert some control over these bodily functions appears obvious, as does the nature of the innate response to their excessive frustration. According to Reich, Lowen, and the contemporary analysts, the masochistic character is the result of this kind of relentless intrusion and control, which very naturally expresses itself most profoundly in the parents' attempts to socialize the child but not exclusively nor always in the very basic processes of food intake and elimination. In cases as serious as the one I've just reviewed, we can assume that these intrusive parental tendencies expressed themselves very early on and continued throughout childhood and beyond. What is often critical in the understanding of masochism is the point at which the child capitulated—the point at which the will was broken. It is at this point, when the self-negation is expressed as a self-imposed block against organismic reactions, that it is most fully imposed. It is due, I think, to the fact that many character analyses have uncovered these memories of intense parent-child battles prior to such capitulation that the formation of this structure is often seen as occurring at or beyond the second year.

The clinical picture that this character label is invoked to summarize and explain is represented by those seen as long-suffering, self-depreciating, self-defeating, and often self-torturing individuals who seem to have a need to suffer and, in their suffering, torture others. There is, in these unfortunate people, a strong tendency to complain, a chronic absence of joy, and the kind of chronic stasis in behavior and attitude that was labeled by Reich the "masochistic bog or morass." This hopeless immobility is highly frustrating to anyone who tries to help. Others typically experience being defeated by this hopeless, helpless person who can't be helped, and they sense her underlying passive aggression.

It is as if the intense rage at intrusion was turned against the self, leading to a bind in self-expression. In these individuals, there is a noteworthy absence of trust in others, and that absence of trust is expressed in hopelessness for the self and, for that matter, the world. Related to this dynamic is the oft-noted "negative therapeutic reaction" with these individuals, such that any improvement is often quickly followed by a relapse. Such return to suffering may be seen both as an expression of the underlying distrust, a justification for it, and a spiteful retaliation against the helper, who, because he is in the more powerful role, is associated with the injuring parent.

The bound negativity of the masochistic person is extremely virulent. To release these bonds, to really ask for help from another, to accept that help and even enjoy it, severely threatens a structure held together by a great deal of conflicting energy. To open oneself to trust and hope opens one to the possibility of being tricked, humiliated, and overpowered again. The resistance to all of that is legion and is reinforced by the individual's attachment to the self and "bad object" forged in the crucible of all this pain. Hence, the masochistic client frequently returns to the maddening position of burdened suffering in which complaints and self-depreciation are directed at whomever would help or offer real support in his exit from the hell of this particular "closed system of internal reality" (Fairbairn, 1958, p. 381).

It is in this that others usually feel the masochist's held resentment or spite, which is not very far below the surface of his self-effacing and pleasing nature. Indeed, it is thought that this pattern, which in therapy is represented in the negative therapeutic reaction, serves to provoke the retaliation and hostility of the other which justifies the distrust and, when that retaliation is sufficient, serves to release the expression of the held-back aggression and hostility of the masochistic person. Like a beating in a sexual context, it is not the beating itself that is desirable but the intensification of the physical charge, which provokes a sexual release that is, in fact, satisfying. And it is the release that the masochistic person desires most profoundly — a release not only of the pent-up hostility, but also of the overcontrolled impulses of love and tender expression. Yet, it is the release that opens the masochistic structure and the discouragement and hopelessness of the original position. The recycling and progressive understanding of this pattern comprise the primary theme in the masochist's treatment. Pleasure is a sin, trust is to be distrusted, hope leads to disappointment. If you expect the worst, you won't be disappointed or, worse yet, tricked.

It appears that this structure may be relatively less prevalent now than it was at one time, certainly in the western United States. This kind of very intrusive, dominant, and punitive parenting may well have been more typical of earlier generations where cleanliness training was more valued, where women had fewer forms of self-expression, etc. Those who work with battered women and incest survivors report seeing many of these features currently, but there is reason to believe that this structure, in its predominant and severe form, may be waning in the general population.

Whatever the validity of this speculation I certainly have seen relatively few cases of clearcut, severe masochistic pathology. Rather, I have seen a number of cases where the central issue seems to be symbiotic, but where the adopted identity replicates the more masochistic adjustment of the parent — particularly the mother. I think the understanding of the masochistic issue is important not only for itself but also for the treatment of many symbiotic individuals, because it is with this kind of parent that the phenomena of separation guilt and survivor guilt can be quite paramount. It is very difficult to enjoy life when one comes out of the matrix of the masochistic parent. Even though that parent may have the sense not to deliver the same kind of abuse to her offspring as was visited on her, the masochist's self-torture is torturing to others — particularly to the offspring, who are prone to take responsibility for their parent's suffering. In view of this, it is important in the process of diagnosis to distinguish between the process of characterological adjustment, which is essentially symbiotic in nature (more prevalent, I believe, in our time), and the truly masochistic disorders, which typically come from a more severely invasive etiology.

Table 8
MASOCHISTIC CHARACTER

---

1. *Etiological constellation*: Control-oriented, dominating parents are intrusive and invasive of appropriate boundaries. These experiences of being overpowered, which often occur around the child's food intake and elimination, are finally recapitulated by the individual's overpowering her own aggressive, hostile, and retaliatory impulses. To maintain contact and receive the necessary support, the individual typically develops a compliant and servile personality, which may often contain passive-aggressive features that are out of awareness.

2. *Symptom constellation*: Long-suffering, self-torturing, self-depreciating, and self-defeating behavior often suggests a "need to suffer." A chronic immobile depression that has been termed the masochistic bog or morass is common. Bound self-expression is accompanied by hopelessness, distrust, and passive-aggressive behavior. In therapy, resistance of a passive nature and "negative therapeutic reaction" are more common and obvious than in many other structures. The residuals of the masochist's considerable life energy often appear to exist only in her spite, which is tightly bound. Interpersonal difficulties of the kind outlined in other sections of this outline are common.

3. *Cognitive style*: Plodding, unimaginative, burdened cognition. Chronic, low-grade depression dulls cognitive functioning. There is an expectation of the worst and a distrust of the positive in life.

4. *Defenses*: Denial, projection, and disavowal, particularly of aggression and hostility, identification with the aggressor, reaction formation, and chronic holding back, often in the musculature, of unacceptable or distrusted impulses.

5. *Script decisions and pathogenic beliefs*: "I give up. I will be good. I'll never give in. I'll show you. I can punish you by withholding from both of us. Deprivation will hurt you more than it hurts me."

6. *Self-representation*: The individual experiences himself as being obligated to serve and as trying to live up to that obligation. The masochistic patient is usually aware of her lack of spontaneity, difficulty in aggressive movement, and her comparatively stuck and uninspiring life-style. Often she wishes for more adventure, release, etc., but she can't seem to marshall the energy to achieve this, or she will plead that she simply doesn't know how. However, she often sees her ability to endure pain and deprivation as an admirable quality.

7. *Object representation and relations*: The masochist seeks to make contact with others through being of service and complaining. But the service is tainted by its suffering, joyless, guilt-inducing quality, and the

Table 8
(*continued*)

---

complaining, which brings attention and suggestions, never ceases. "Why don't you, yes but" is a typical masochistic game. Through these actions and other passive-aggressive maneuvers, the masochist provokes retaliation and can then occasionally get some release of the pent-up spite in response. In particular, the masochist can be seen as one who deprives himself of satisfaction in order to punish another by depriving them of satisfaction. Since the masochist is used to this form of deprivation (i.e., of satisfaction) she is better than most at tolerating it, and it doesn't *appear* to punish her as much as it punishes the other.

Intrapsychically, others are seen as those who should be served at one's own expense. Unconsciously, others are the object of a great deal of pent-up hostility which can only be passively expressed, except with extreme justification.

8. *Affective characteristics*: Restrained, muted, depressively tinged affect. Guilt at obligation failures is common. The individual is out of touch with aggressive or hostile feelings, but others may be well aware of them. The masochist often feels she is the victim of others or of life itself and feels victimized.

A successful therapy with a masochistic client must involve a therapist who does not get too irrevocably trapped in the web of repeated failure and discouragement which typically motivates any helper's retaliation. A therapist who has a comprehensive understanding of the masochistic issue and who expects this course of events will be far less likely to take it personally and to react in the usual ways. This same analytic understanding will, of course, help the client as well. Both parties can be greatly assisted by reviewing the many similar circumstances involving defeated helpers of the past. These historical and contemporary analyses will be most useful where they elicit the masochist's underlying hostility and distrust of the helper. As Fairbairn (1974) pointed out, it is with these clients, who most exemplify the "negative therapeutic reaction" and who led Freud to hypothesize the "death instinct," that the theory of internalized, unconscious, bad objects can be most easily seen to fit.

In these cases, the therapist is needed to assist in releasing those internal negative forces from repression, while interpreting them as natural consequences of intrusion, invasion, and suppression of the individual's healthy inclinations. At the same time, the therapist must offer a real and good relationship to replace the closed inner reality of the client, which contaminates all of his interactions with others. To quote Fairbairn (1974, p. 74), "the appeal of a good object is an indispensable factor in promoting a dissolution of the cathexis of internalized bad objects, and . . . the significance of the transference situation is partly derived from this fact."

The therapeutic tests (Weiss & Sampson, 1986) of the masochist can be tough because they pull eloquently for seeing him as bad, hopeless, inferior, and deserving of retaliation. The therapist will find that passing the tests, and there may be many, is greatly facilitated by understanding the internal self and object structures of the masochist and consistently and supportively refusing to become a participating part of them.

CHAPTER 4

Characterological Issues of the Self in the System

CLASSICAL PSYCHOANALYTIC THEORY traces all neurotic symptoms to the oedipal conflict, and, where personality disorders have been considered, these have typically been seen as pre-oedipal in origin. The position taken here, which is consistent with many contemporary psychoanalytic theorists, is that this dichotomous view is not only oversimplified but is incorrect. It seems clear now that "neurotic" psychopathology can revolve around a number of basic existential life issues, which exist throughout the life span, though they may be differentially important in the early years. Furthermore, the constellation of symptoms or problematic situations for people struggling with the oedipal etiology may, in general, be defined with far greater specificity. Finally, the characterological-developmental theory would place importance both on the child's sexual and rivalrous impulses, including the internal struggles that these impulses provoke, *and* on the environment's ability to optimally frustrate and indulge around the child's expression of early sexual interest and rivalry.

In this way, oedipal impulses are not essentially different from any other basic, inborn forms of self-expression that require appropriate environmental responses. The symptom constellations that derive from the oedipal issue can be complex because both sexuality and rivalry are involved and because the issue is triadic, involving a system rather than a dyad. Such complex interactions can occur with other issues as well, but they always occur with oedipal ones.

The oedipal issue is that classic complex involving love, sexuality, and competition, originally delineated by Freud. Understanding of this complex of issues is immeasurably enhanced by simply viewing it as similar, in most essential respects, to all other developmental challenges shared by the individual and his environment. The oedipal complex, like the schizoid, narcissistic, or masochistic complexes, comes out of the environment's inability to optimally indulge and frustrate these existential demands of the individual. Specifically, I believe that psychopathology of an oedipal nature is related to either the exploitation of or the anxious, threatened, and often punitive response to sexually related love and competition that children receive. This was certainly Freud's original position, and both social history (e.g., see Miller, 1984) and a century of clinical case reports give us every reason to return to it.

Of course, it is true that the oedipal issues are, in many ways, more difficult to handle optimally than some of the simpler issues presented thus far. Oedipal issues typically involve three or more people, and they can interact easily with other issues that precede them developmentally, thus yielding more permutations and combinations of etiological factors. But, what essentially happens in the oedipal case is that the child's sexuality is not lovingly permitted and supported by the optimal frustration of clear boundaries. Rather, it is exploited or punished or both. For example, you may find one parent exploiting sexuality and the competitive urges that go with it, both for sexual satisfaction and for the indirect expression of hostility toward the other parent. Simultaneously, the other parent may be threatened by such behavior and, both directly and indirectly, act threatened and retaliate toward the child. A parent may also encourage and exploit the sexuality and competition, but when it becomes too much or when it threatens the relationship with the spouse, withdraw from the child, or humiliate or punish him for these previously encouraged behaviors. Where there is only exploitation, children may fear punishment and, in any case, will find such exploitation of their sexuality overwhelming.

Learning that it is unsafe to love sexually with an open heart and to experience natural human rivalry, these children will pull back, block off, and restrain these thoughts and feelings by whatever defenses are available. By the time these oedipal issues are salient, children have access to a very broad range of defensive maneuvers to ward off these troublesome thoughts and feelings. This is another reason why the oedipal constellations can be quite complex. Individuals can, for example, marshall affect as a defense and develop an ability to blot out their troublesome internal experience by the histrionic overdramatization of any feeling. Or individuals may keep themselves preoccupied by compulsive behaviors and/or obsessional thoughts. Children, too, have a large repertoire of abilities to enhance the process of adjusting to this particular type of narcissistic injury. It is not uncommon for these individuals to seek acceptance and avoid reinjury by trying to develop a perfect persona and achieve perfection in every area of endeavor.

Lowen (1958) has associated the oedipal etiology with a number of characterological expressions, including hysteric or histrionic, obsessive-compulsive, passive-feminine, and phallic-narcissistic. Some of these constellations involve the interaction of the oedipal issue with other pre-oedipal issues (i.e., the phallic-narcissistic character is an interaction of the narcissistic and oedipal issues, and the passive-feminine is the interaction of the oedipal and masochistic issues). It seems to me that there are two basic oedipal characterological adaptations, which provide the essential underpinnings for the other permutations and combinations: the *histrionic* (formerly hysteric) and the *obsessive-compulsive*. The histrionic represents the etiological pole characterized more by inappropriate encouragement and exploitation of sexuality and competition, and the obsessive-compulsive represents a preponderance of punishment for these same expressions. While the clinical literature classifies women as histrionic with far greater frequency, males can also receive this diagnosis. Males are the sole bearers of Lowen's phallic-narcissistic diagnosis, and, while the behaviors of this character differ from the histrionic, the etiological dynamics are often quite similar.

It is crucial to note here that obsessive-compulsive behavior, in particular, can derive from other etiological constellations. It is becoming increasingly apparent that obsessive-compulsive disorder per se as distinct from obsessive-compulsive personality may be a neurological problem. Obsessive-compulsive behavior as a strategy can keep many unacceptable feelings at bay and can provide a kind of artificial structure in the absence of authentic structure. But it is also a common neurotic compensation for unacceptable oedipal impulses and can derive from this etiologic constellation. Similarly, certain kinds of dissociation, denial, and affect defenses typical of the histrionic character can also be seen as a result of other etiological circumstances, but these defenses are commonly seen as sequelae of these etiological circumstances.

THE OEDIPAL ISSUE IN THE HISTRIONIC CHARACTER

Most histories of histrionic women in the literature are replete with rigid, cold, and rejecting mothers and seductive, emotionally infantile fathers (see pp. 313–314 for a report of my research on this observation). The following case (Horowitz, 1989) is archetypal:

Miss Smith's mother was rigid and moralistic. Her family found her joyless and often depressed. Devoted to the Catholic church, she served on its committee on pornography and was concerned throughout life with social propriety. . . . Mr. Smith was unusual . . . one of his greatest eccentricities was nudism. He insisted on practicing his nudism around the house, including taking his breakfast while naked. He assumed the function of waking each daughter and would lie undressed on their beds above the covers until they arose. During early adolescence, this so embarrassed and upset the patient that she begged her mother to make him stop. Her mother would cry and claim that she was helpless. . . . While the father overtly chided his oldest daughter for her sexual behavior, covertly he was interested and teased for details. Later when Miss Smith was in college, he wanted to visit her to flirt with her roommate. (Horowitz, 1989, pp. 202–204)

Paul Chodoff (1978) reports another typical case of histrionic personality:

The product of a family background of wealth and social position on both sides, O. had lived with her mother, whom she saw as cold, distant and ungiving, after her parent's divorce when she was age five. Her handsome, "perfect" father became the focus of her longings and fantasies, the summers spent with him the high point of her life. During these visits, she reported episodes when she'd wake up to find her father standing beside her bed rubbing her back under her nightgown. Twice in her life, she was in the course of achieving some autonomy—as a nineteen-year-old college student and later when caring for herself and her children after the failure of her initial marriage. The first period was terminated by a summons from her father to return and finish college while living with him, and the second by the promise of her present husband to rescue and take total care of her.

Very often in these cases, the isolation from the mother and the special, sexually charged relationship with the father persists well into adult life with continuing dependency of the daughter on the father and inappropriate sexual advances or sexually tinged interaction occurring between them. These fathers do such things as sharing their intimate lives with their daughters, telling seductive off-color jokes, or maintaining romantic symbols of the special relationship, which are more appropriate to lovers than to a father-daughter relationship.

Just as in families where the incestuous child abuse goes much further, the family of the histrionic is characterized by denial and rationalization. The child, of course, models these strategies, which protect everyone in the family from facing the uncomfortable realities of their existence together. The child, caught in the middle of this incestuous drama, must often go further to distance herself from all the overwhelming emotions and thoughts. This, then, can lead to what Shapiro (1965) has labeled the impressionistic cognitive style of the histrionic, wherein there is "an incapacity for persistent or intense intellectual concentration," a "distractibility or impressionability that follows from it," and a "nonfactual world in which the hysterical person lives" (Shapiro, 1965, p. 113). This more global cognitive orientation is accompanied by an emotional overreactivity, which can serve as an affect defense and often serves to coerce the environment into taking responsibility for her and perpetuating the dependency.

Histrionic people frequently see themselves as childlike and get into relationships where they play "baby doll" to "big daddy." Histrionic women often gravitate toward older men who can take care of them, thereby replicating the father-daughter relationship where caretaking is exchanged for a kind of sexual factor. Conversion hys-

Table 9
OEDIPAL CHARACTER

General etiological constellation: Caretakers exploit or react negatively to the child's natural sexuality and competition. These bipolar responses often occur together with one parent being seductive and exploitative, while the other is threatened, cold, or directly punitive. Or this ambitendency toward sexuality and/or competition can be promulgated by the same parent. This conditioning results in any number of affective, behavioral, and cognitive strategies for suppressing or keeping from awareness these instinctual responses. This suppression or disavowal results in the removal of these drives from optimal frustration and indulgence so that they fail to mature and become appropriately integrated into the adult personality. While the permutations of these triadic constellations are legion, two basic themes are apparent: (1) The symptomatic and personality constellations resulting from relatively more exploitation of sexuality and competition (e.g., histrionic and phallic-narcissistic characters) and (2) symptom and personality constellations resulting from relatively more restraint or punishment of these behaviors (e.g., obsessive-compulsive character). These will be outlined separately—histrionic below and obsessive-compulsive in Table 10.

Histrionic

1. *Etiological constellation*: At least one parent exploits natural sexuality and uses the child as a sex object. The other parent is often cold, distant, or directly punitive, particularly concerning sexuality and/or competition, or is seen as being so out of the child's guilt and associated projections.
2. *Symptom constellation*: Overly emotional reactivity, exhibitionistic and dramatic behavior, sexualized relationships with a denial of the sexuality, shallow emotional experience, global and imprecise thought processes, excessive attention to and toward the opposite sex, conversion reactions, dissociative episodes, high propensity to act-out, highly distractable with difficulty in sustaining concentration, sexual difficulties including difficulty with arousal, pre-orgasmic syndrome, dismeneuria, retarded or premature ejaculation, unsatisfying (superficial) orgasms, etc.
3. *Cognitive style*: Global, nonlinear, imprecise, and emotionally dominated thought processes that serve to keep "dangerous" affects and thoughts out of awareness. Thinking is often visually dominated and impressionistic resulting in fast and shallow judgments about the meaning of events, ideas, and feelings, and an absence of factual detail and reality based discrimination.

Table 9
(*continued*)

4. *Script decisions and pathogenic beliefs*: "Sex is bad. Competition and rivalry are bad. My worth depends on my sexuality and attractiveness. All gratification comes from the opposite sex. I can't love, be sexual, be competitive. I need to be more attractive. If I love fully I will (1) be exploited or rejected, (2) hurt my parents, or (3) be shamed."
5. *Defenses*: Denial, repression, acting-out, conversion, dissociation, externalization, impressionistic and global thinking.
6. *Self-representation*: Imprecise and fluid with self-concept tending to rely more on appearance, social acceptance, and immediate experiences than on accomplishments or other more stable grounds.
7. *Object representations and relations*: Relationships frequently sexualized, impulsive, and characterized by superficial "role playing" behavior. Individuals of the opposite sex are extraordinarily important consciously, but unconsciously they are the target of considerable hostility, which is frequently expressed after some stereotyped excuse has been created. There is typically unconscious competition toward members of the same sex. Themes of victimization and nurturing-parent to helpless-child role relations are common in often repetitive, "gamelike" relationships.
8. *Affective characteristics*: Shallow, "as if" affects that are overly dramatic. A high level of sexual titillation with an absence of deep and mature sexual feelings. The individual may be easily overwhelmed by affective states with thoughts blocked or largely controlled by impressionistic and affective experiences. There is a tendency to act-out in response to feelings. Hostile and competitive feelings are not conscious but are expressed in repetitive "gamelike" interactions.

terics were first identified by Breuer and Freud for their conversion reactions, which they typically relate to with "la belle indifference," exemplifying their cognitive style and belying the defensive underlying purpose of the symptom. Dissociative episodes can also occur when stress is too high to manage with more adaptive defense mechanisms.

The relationships of histrionics, like their thinking, are often superficial and have an "as if" quality in which it seems that the person is playing a role. There is also a strong underlying unconscious hostility to the opposite sex, which, on the surface, is so overvalued.

Their relationships are also marked by a repetitive, gamelike quality where sexual seductiveness is often followed by sexual submissiveness to a greater force at times, or by rage, outrage, or forceful rejection at other times. Another common symptom in relationships is a split between those who stimulate sexual arousal and those who stimulate more heartfelt affection. This split, in which sexual and affectional needs may be met but only in isolation from one another, protects the individual from entering the original vulnerable situation in which she was injured.

Successful treatment of the histrionic personality demands a genuine human connection where all of the affective, behavioral, and cognitive maneuvers used to avoid forbidden thoughts and feelings and feared intimacy are slowly melted away. The histrionic needs to learn of her sexual and competitive impulses, her history of being exploited and deprived of love, and her hostility that results from this exploitation and deprivation. She needs to relearn how to open her heart, to be real and vulnerable, and to mature sexually and relationally. Further, she needs to relinquish the false-self histrionic phoniness and the investment in her particular brand of perfectionism, and to reinvest that energy in reclaiming her birthright to deeply felt and sexual love. Finally, she needs to mature in her relationships with other women so that rivalry is neither dominant nor denied in her experience but becomes merely an evolved human proclivity.

As in every other structure, the histrionic will provide "tests" that encourage the therapist to become a participating figure in the "closed system of inner reality." When this gambit succeeds, therapists are seduced, either sexually or into inappropriate and countertherapeutic caretaking and authority roles, which perpetuate the existing adaptation. The oedipally derived histrionic character is summarized in Table 9.

THE OBSESSIVE-COMPULSIVE

The obsessive-compulsive was the first such personality constellation described by Freud, and, until recently, it was clearly the most well-described syndrome. It is also the most frequently diagnosed personality disorder and is more often attributed to men (Frances, 1986). Indeed, it is so commonly discussed and demonstrated in so many people, at least to some minimal extent, that we tend to give its study short shrift, because we think we know what it means. It really warrants more serious attention than this, particularly for professionals, because understanding the nuances of the typical history, phenomenology, and psychological processes involved can significantly impact our empathy for and effectiveness with people who suffer from this disorder.

David Shapiro (1965) has helped me to understand this disorder by emphasizing the role of distorted volition or will directed at controlling and prescribing what cannot be prescribed or controlled— namely, drives, spontaneous interests, and affects. In Shapiro's words, "willful directedness has been distorted from its most subjective significance as an extension, and, so to speak, representative of one's wants, to a position of precedence over wants, aimed even at directing them. Impulse in this order of things is not the initiator of the full stage of willful directedness and effort, but its enemy" (p. 37).

Shapiro also points out the extent to which the obsessive-compulsive experiences "his own overseer issuing commands, directives, reminders, warnings, and admonitions" (p. 34) as external to himself. The overseer's values and directives are accepted but are not the result of free choice. And, particularly as the obsessions or compulsions appear more neurotic or absurd, the individual is puzzled, annoyed, or troubled by them, and experiences them as truly alien to himself. This external or alien quality of the "overseer sitting behind and issuing commands" has all the earmarks of an unassimilated, introjected other. Further, it leads to the projection outside the self of this introject, as Meissner (1988) has so cogently pointed out, which explains why the obsessive-compulsive often claims that be hehaves in the way he does in order to satisfy an objective necessity or a social imperative, which the rest of us do not experience as so absolute.

This demanding overseer phenomenology is consistent with the repeated experience of clinicians, who find that these patients remember and often currently perceive their parents as stern, exacting, rigid, and rule-bound. Parents of these individuals are often found to have been particularly threatened or disgusted by the child's alive, animal nature and were interested in producing the perfect little lady or gentleman. Not infrequently, the reconstruction or even current experience of parents is that they are threatened by competition or success that would diminish them by comparison.

As with all other general etiological constellations, not all of these descriptors apply to all cases. Here and in the summary tables, including Table 10 for this character, I deliberately use a number of related but different words to describe etiological factors for their clinical utility. In one case, the words "stern" and "exacting" may be precisely descriptive for the client and, therefore, quite helpful to her. In another, the phrases "threatened by success" and "disgusted by one's animal nature" may be more precisely descriptive and helpful.

So, the characterological-developmental theory for the obsessive-compulsive is simply this: The child introjects and identifies with the parent and the parent's standards or values and, over the course of structural development, tries to use his willpower to meet these introjected standards and live up to these unusually rigid, life-denying, and body-alien values. The will is used to block the original organismic expressions as well as to promulgate a false self consisting of the correct attitude and behavior that is necessary for some semblance of positive contact with the very contingent and often not very positive parent. This is a clear-cut example of a characterological reproduction—i.e., obsessive-compulsive parenting producing an obsessive-compulsive child.

It is critical to point out that a person with obsessive-compulsive traits is not always best understood through this more "anal" and "oedipal" etiology as expressed in traditional psychoanalytic language. Even Lowen (1958), who gives the clearest argument for the oedipal etiology of this syndrome, acknowledges that these traits will often be seen in primarily oral and masochistic characters (p. 157). I would add that one can often see extreme rigidity exhibited in low-functioning individuals who have a poor sense of self. In these cases, the obsessive-compulsive behavior is not defensive in the classic sense but literally protects the person from the void and fragmentation of an enfeebled self. In other words, the individual actually finds himself in his orderliness or in his rigid moral, political, or religious beliefs, and organizes his life around living up to them. The rigidity, then, does not serve to defend against unacceptable impulses as much as it serves to organize a disorganized structure. What I am offering in this section is the development of an understanding of obsessive-compulsive behavior when it is based on a more oedipally related etiology and when it serves a more classically defensive function.

When that is the case, the behavioral compulsions, cognitive obsessions, and less symptomatic activities consistent with this personality can be best understood as the organism's attempts to ward off or keep in check these unacceptable impulses, which tend to be sexual, aggressive, competitive, and affectively spontaneous. These "activities" include the obsessive-compulsive's tendency to live "under the gun" of constant, pervasive tension and pressure to do, feel, and think the right thing. This constant pressure keeps him busy cognitively and behaviorally and keeps him in check so that any spontaneous expression, which may be potentially wrong or dangerous, is inhibited. Similarly, his intense and narrowly focused attention, particularly to detail, and his characteristic isolation of thinking from feeling keeps him busy and away from truly self-initiated behavior, thought, and feeling that might threaten, anger, or displease the other. Similarly, his well-noted doubt, indecision, and procrastination keep him from committing to a course of action that, in the final analysis, must reflect a personal commitment and choice.

Furthermore, the obsessive-compulsive's social behavior, which is often noted as being stilted, emphasizing the correct social role behavior, and his pedantic, self-possessed, and affectless way of presenting himself, keeps him distant from his own distrusted impulses and from any dangerous feelings toward and for others. Finally, the obsessive-compulsive's tendency to be very aware of and responsive to others along the dimension of submission-subjugation also can be seen to derive from this overall personality organization. Others are seen as the personification of the external imperatives, social rules, and objective necessities to which the individual must live up or as subordinates who must be set straight by these rules. Others may also be seen to be threatened or injured by the individual's competitive nature or successes as was the parent in the oedipal struggle. Again, the preoccupation with correct rules, the proper behavior, the proper attitudes, and the possible adverse effects of one's interpersonal actions keeps the individual busy and keeps the dangerous impulses out of awareness.

Symptomatically, the suppression, self-regulation, and life-denying holding back create depression. When the individual is really pressed by stressful events and/or the increased pressure of unresolved, unexpressed impulses, the obsessions and/or compulsions can take possession of the individual to such an extent that he is driven to absurd lengths in his obsessive preoccupations and compulsively driven behaviors. Not infrequently, the failure of the defenses to manage all of this leads to intrusive thoughts which are frequently of a sexually sadistic or otherwise hostile nature. These thoughts are, of course, extraordinarily ego-dystonic, because they are so far away from the good person that this individual is trying to be.

Frequently, the obsessive-compulsive is also perfectionistic. While there can be some similarity to the perfectionism of the narcissist, this is a good example of how characterological theory can be useful in yielding the most accurate and empathic understanding of people. The obsessive-compulsive's perfectionism is driven more by a determination to willfully do the right thing and avoid the wrong thing. It is as if he is trying to please or appease that external authority and avoid its punishment. The perfectionism is motivated to avoid censure, control what is bad in the self, and hold in check what will threaten or displease the other.

In the case of the narcissistic etiology and orientation, the perfectionism is better conceptualized as a developmental arrest in grandiosity. Trying to be perfect maintains the grandiose false-self illusion and protects one from dipping into a state of worthlessness or void. Here, a perfect performance, achievement, or self-presentation enhances self-esteem. On the other hand, with the obsessive-compulsive, the perfectionism is directed more to the individual's attempts to control his own feelings and motivations so that he is the right kind of person and does not offend. The latter is a far more passive and interpersonally defensive position than that of the narcissist, who is better known for being able to mobilize his aggression and impress others with behavior that he himself often experiences as shallow, hollow, or phony.

The characterological-developmental theory is important for clinical work because, among other things, it assists the clinician by suggesting what to look for in the history, belief structure, attitude, self-presentation, and symptomatology that will aid her in understanding what lies beneath the observed expression and in helping the client understand this himself. Once this is done, the developmental theory has some prescriptions about how issues may be resolved. In the case of perfectionism, does the individual need to learn that his sexual, aggressive, and competitive impulses are normal and human and all right and that they cannot be subjugated to his will, or does he need to learn that his perfectionism is an expression of an unresolved grandiosity in early development, which requires him to learn a more realistic, well-modulated, "constant" self-esteem based on the integration of what is marvellous and what is limited in himself?

Returning now to the problem of the obsessive-compulsive, we may ask, when does all this develop? It is not possible to answer that question as completely as we would like. Nevertheless, we do know that children begin to operate on the basis of standards at about two years of age (Gopnick & Meltzoff, 1984). The experimental, developmental research indicates that a number of the factors operative in this particular adaptation do not develop until quite a bit later than we have seen in the characterological issues heretofore reviewed.

For example, children cannot distinguish between mental and physical events (Wellman & Estes, 1986) until about three years of age. It is also about this time that they begin to be able to distinguish between intended and accidental outcomes in their judgments of stories and what happens to characters in them (Yuill & Perner, 1988). This research is relevant because it documents the long period of childhood existence during which there is confusion about the realistic relationships between causes and effects. Furthermore, it is not until six years of age that children begin to use purely mental strategies to regulate their feelings (Bengtsson & Johnson, 1987) and to take moral and conventional rules seriously (Tisak & Turiel, 1988). These findings would indicate that the strategy for living by such rules and the purely mental strategy of trying to regulate drives by will develops relatively late. Further, naturalistic observation tends to confirm Freud's original position that the sexual interest, seductiveness, and rivalrous behavior that children can display also does not come until about three years of age. So, when obsessive-compulsive behavior is the result of these oedipal events, all the available information would indicate that this adaptation develops relatively late to begin with and that it continues to develop over some period of time.

Parenthetically, it is probably also true that these strategies in service of other functions (e.g., to bolster an enfeebled self) are also mastered relatively late, even though they may be motivated by a developmental lesion occurring considerably earlier. This phenomenon of the later overlay of more sophisticated strategies to deal with a more primitive complex is quite consistent with the kind of characterological-developmental theory I am trying to integrate here.

The final piece of the theory, which needs to be emphasized, is the extent to which the obsessive-compulsive solution binds the individual to the parent, who is, particularly in this case, supremely contingent in his or her response to the child. When the child is very good, he may get praise or at least absence of criticism. When the parent is very exacting, however, the child will receive qualified praise, with notation of how she might have done a bit better. This latter response, of course, promotes the perfectionism of the child, who can nurture the illusion that if she could only be a little better, she could have a more unqualified positive contact with the parent. Be that as it may, the most critical point to understand here is that the child's adoption of and attempts to live up to the parent's standards provides the social connection and the self-identity within that connection that all of us require. This living up to the family standard and being the kind of child you're expected to be defines the self and maintains the needed contact. The rigidity of the pattern can be explained by the combination, in this case made so obvious, of the avoidance of the punishment, the maintenance of contact and, through contact and emulation, identity. Thus, it is the fear of a repetition of the punishment, as well as the fear of isolation, both from the self as defined and from the family, that maintains the pathological pattern that may otherwise seem so absurd even to the individual himself.

The therapeutic themes in these cases are, of course, the gradual challenging of these tight defenses and the gradual acceptance and expression of the disavowed drives, affects, and thoughts. Insight concerning the basis for these rigid defenses, which require so much safety, is usually very helpful. "Getting the story straight" about the history that motivates this extreme need for control and proper functioning in all realms can yield the kind of sympathetic understanding for the self that these individuals absolutely require. The individual needs to learn slowly that these extreme guarantees of safety are no longer necessary, and that novel patterns of thinking and behaving, while anxiety provoking, do not lead to anywhere near the danger that is affectively anticipated. Through all this, the individual needs to learn to tolerate the anxiety that the relinquishing of defenses and the release of underlying contents will provoke, and

Table 10
OEDIPAL CHARACTER: OBSESSIVE-COMPULSIVE

---

1. *Etiological constellation*: Exacting, rigid, persistent, rule-bound parenting occurs, especially around socialization training, impulse control, and the "taming" of sexual, competitive, and aggressive expression. There is not, in this control, the invasion and intrusion into the organism's natural processes nor the crushing of the will that occurs in masochism. Rather, the child is encouraged through punishment, reinforcement, and example to use his will to tame all aspects of his animal impulses, spontaneous behavior, competitive nature, tender feelings, etc. As the individual achieves this exaggerated self-possession and reserve, he acquires the kinds of rigid, judgmental, and driven behavior that characterize this personality. The obsessions and compulsions serve to maintain this emotionally restrained stance by warding off affects and drives.

2. *Symptom constellation*: Possessed by a driven, pressured tension to do the correct, necessary, or imperative thing. This imposition of objective necessity or higher authority is constant and pervasive resulting in a life of continuous effort related to sanctioned purposes. Spontaneous expressions, personal choices, or any genuine feelings are difficult to access. Rigidity in bodily posture, moral and other judgments, or routine activities is definitional. This rule-bound personality is uncomfortable with freedom, and release from one concern will lead to anxiety and quick replacement with another pressing concern as the subject for stewing rumination. Perfectionism and procrastination are often present and related to the fear of doing the wrong thing. Similarly, difficulty in decision making reflects fears of self-initiated expression, which may be wrong. Social behavior can be pedantic, affectless, and stilted, with an emphasis on correct social role behavior. Depression and intrusive thoughts, especially of a hostile or sexually sadistic nature, are often problematic along with troublesome obsessive thoughts and compulsive behaviors that, at this symptomatic level, are experienced as alien and as taking over the individual.

3. *Cognitive style*: Intense, sharp, focused attention to detail is associated with a tendency to miss the essential features of things. A related characteristic is the isolation of cognitive understanding from the emotional meaning of events, ideas, or behavior. Cognitive activity can persist in a rigid pattern in spite of repeated failure or observed absurdity of the process. Doubt, uncertainty, and indecision often plague even the simplest activities.

Table 10
(*continued*)

4. *Defenses*: Rumination, rituals, rule-bound living serve to eliminate the need for accessing impulses or desires. Doubt, indecision, procrastination, shifting attention, and rigid posture all serve to overwhelm the cognitive and affective accessing of warded-off contents.
5. *Script decisions and pathogenic beliefs*: "I must have done something wrong, I must do the right thing. I'll never make another mistake. I have to control myself or I will totally lose control."
6. *Self-representation*: Consciously, the individual sees himself as conscientious, responsible, hardworking, morally and otherwise correct, and trying hard to be the right kind of person. He experiences himself as duty bound to follow an externally determined set of rules or principles and not as a free agent with respect for his own wishes and judgment. Unconsciously, as the script decisions and pathogenic beliefs illustrate, he harbors the feeling that he has done something terribly wrong and must hold himself under tight reign so that he will not transgress again.
7. *Object representations and relations*: The individual tends to see others as the personification of authority, to which he is subject, or as subjects of his authority. This lends a one-up/one-down flavor to his relationships, which are often formal with much attention to the proper role behavior as parent, spouse, superior, subordinate, etc. Power struggles often characterize relations, particularly where role-relationship rules are at all unclear or where there may be disagreement concerning such rules. Others often find these individuals frustrating due to the lack of meaningful connection or real communication experienced, the rigidity of values and behavior, the deadened affect, and the seemingly unnecessary pressure and tension that they create in themselves and others.
8. *Affective characteristics*: Overmodulated affect leading to a restrained and constricted manner with little access to feeling. The person will experience anxiety, particularly if defenses fail to bind it effectively. Underlying hostility is expressed indirectly or through intrusive thoughts, which may be sexually sadistic or violent. The individual separates ideas and feelings such that disturbing or highly positive thoughts do not produce the usual affective impact. Tender feelings are also blocked and expressed indirectly, if at all.

a good therapeutic alliance, which is not exclusively abstinent, will often facilitate that.

In a sense, the obsessive-compulsive needs to be desensitized to his own feelings, and a gradual process of uncovering and optimal frustration is necessary for that to occur. Almost all experts on this syndrome agree that it is important to keep the client in the here and now in this process and encourage greater attention to feelings than to thoughts. In this regard, the therapeutic relationship — transferential, countertransferential, and real — is a particularly good choice for therapeutic focus because of its immediacy and potential realness. The most common therapeutic error in these cases is a collusion with the intellectualized, distant, affectless relation to events and others by a therapist who is himself obsessive-compulsive or whose method may easily err in that direction (i.e., cognitive and behavior therapies and pedagogic psychoanalysis).

PART II

CHARACTER STYLES

CHAPTER 5

The Hated Child: The Schizoid Experience

Jeanine: You don't want to talk about it?
Conrad: I don't know, I've never really talked about it. To doctors, but
    not to anyone else; you're the first person who's asked.
Jeanine: Why'd you do it?
Conrad: I don't know. It was like falling into a hole. It was like falling
    into a hole and it keeps getting bigger and bigger and you can't get out
    and then all of a sudden it's inside and you're the hole and you're
    trapped and it's all over—something like that. And it's not really scary
    except it is when you look back on it because you know what you were
    feeling, strange and new . . .

— Ordinary People

ETIOLOGY

As THE HUMAN infant awakens to the social world, she may not
be met by one welcoming, contactful, and responsive to such a totally dependent being. Indeed, the parents may be cold, harsh, rejecting, and full of hate, resenting the infant's very existence. The parental reaction may, of course, not be that extreme and it may not
be consistent. But we know that many human infants have been
unwanted, and those who have been wanted on a conscious level
are not always wanted unambivalently. Furthermore, many parents
who think they want children find out differently when the full impact of the totally dependent human being is thrust upon them,
when circumstances change, or when their resources to deal with the
reality of an infant are much less than expected.

Perhaps even more common is the situation in which parents think
they want a child but what they really want is an ideal reflection of

73

their own idealized self. They want a "perfect baby" instead of an alive human being with elements of animal nature. Every infant will sooner or later and repeatedly disappoint this ideal, and the parental rejection and rage which that elicits can be shocking. In every case, it is the real, spontaneous *life* in the child that provokes the parental rejection and hatred.

When one couples the common reality of the hated child with the understanding that the newly "hatched" human being has no *conscious* discrimination of the difference between self and care-taker, one can begin to speculate on the nature of the unfortunate result.* One can imagine that when the caretaker is sufficiently harsh, the infant may simply choose to go back where he came from—to detachment which is his only avenue of escape. The cold or hateful treatment of the caretaker may be total or partial, continu-ous or periodic. The infant's defensive retreat will be more profound as a result of repeated child abuse, for example, than as a response to occasional outbursts or periodic coldness on the part of the care-taker. This continuum of environmental failure will then be reflected in the resulting structural continuum presented in Chapter 1—per-sonality disorder, character neurosis, and character style.

Winnicott (1953) refers to the concept of "good enough mother-ing" to describe the requisite empathic caretaking ability that will usher a newborn into the state of symbiosis and keep her there until the process of differentiation leads to conscious individuation. Where mothering is not "good enough"—and indeed where it is abusive and punishing—distancing, detachment, and literal turning away from social contact result. Because of the very primitive nature of the neonate's cognitive processes at this point in development, it is difficult to understand exactly how this chain of events is interpre-ted at any mental level. Nevertheless, we may surmise that at a very primitive level of awareness, and then at increasingly complex levels of understanding, the infant experiences an intense fear, which some have labeled the fear of annihilation (Blanck & Blanck, 1974; Lowen, 1967).

The infant's natural initial response to a cold, hostile, and threat-ening environment is terror and rage. Yet, chronic terror is an

---

*I am not saying here that the infant is operating with a symbiotic fantasy, only that the infant is insufficiently conscious to conceptualize the I-thou distinction.

untenable position from which to lead a life, as is chronic rage. Furthermore, such rage invites retaliation, which is experienced as life-threatening and terrorizing. So, the infant turns against herself, suppresses the natural feeling responses, and uses the very primitive defenses available in this early period to deal with a hostile world. In addition to, or as part of, the retreat inward, the organism essentially stops living in order to preserve its life. The ability to do that is limited by the ego development of the infant in this period. However, through the months of symbiosis she can regress to the previous developmental period which Mahler called autism and later wished she'd called awakening. During this earliest period, the child is more withdrawn and less reactive than she will shortly be. The hatred of the caretaking parent will be introjected and will begin to suppress the life force of the organism, such that movement and breathing are inhibited and there develops an involuntary tightening of the musculature to restrain the life force.

Therapeutic experience with clients who share this type of history suggests that, sooner or later, they make two core feeling decisions: (1) "There is something wrong with me," and (2) "I have no right to exist." These cognitive representations may, of course, be conscious or denied, but at a core level of existence the individual has taken the environmental response personally and has incorporated it into her self-concept. Enhancing this effect is the fact that at this symbiotic point in development there is no conscious differentiation between oneself and one's caretaker. It is the preverbal assimilation of these damning "script decisions" that renders them so insidious and difficult to change.

One way to gain an appreciation for the initial dilemma of the schizoid person is to remember those times when in a supermarket, laundromat, or other public place you have witnessed the explosion of a mother or father at a young child. This often alarming public example of child abuse demonstrates the not uncommon loss of parental control, and one cannot help but wonder about the limits of this kind of outburst. Presumably, the child herself is not sure of those limits either, and on occasion the parent may have gone well beyond mere yelling or minor corporal punishment. In these public circumstances, you may have witnessed the child herself taking on the maternal role and doing whatever was necessary to get the parent to pull himself together and leave the situation. In parents with marginal emotional stability, these abusive outbursts often have very little to do with what the child has or has not done. As a result, the child will often develop rather profound vigilance, as well as the ability to parent her parents when loss of control is imminent or realized. Schizoid character neurosis or style can also be created by environments that are simply chronically cold though not neglectful of physical needs nor ever openly hostile. The "hated child" label then seems a bit of an overstatement. To appreciate the metaphoric truth of that label, one must put oneself in the place of that child who has an inborn need for a great deal of attuned holding. The absence of such required human warmth and caretaking results in a kind of disembodied existence and the same kinds of phenomenological steps that I am outlining here for the more openly abused child, though often to a lesser degree.

As will be outlined in greater detail with the exploration of the behavior, attitudes, and feelings of this character structure, the hated child begins to find a safe haven in withdrawal into cognitive and spiritual endeavors. "If mother doesn't love me, then God will," and if the world on face appears to be hostile, it is really a beneficent unity in which one's current life is a mere flash in the eternal pan and "life on this physical plane is really irrelevant." In these ways, life is spiritualized rather than lived. The hated child may be one who loves mankind but twists away almost automatically from the closeness required in an ongoing love relationship.

As the person matures, the sophistication and complexity of the defenses increase, yet at a core emotional level the defensive structure is very primitive and essentially reflects *denial* of what really happened in relation to the mothering person. That denial freezes the situation present in symbiosis—an unfulfilled wish for intimate union on the one hand and an automatic refusal to merge on the other. The frozen symbiotic condition yields a continuing propensity to *introject* whole the ideas, characteristics, and feelings of others, as well as a tendency to *project* both good and bad feelings and motivations onto others. In this character structure there essentially was never a completed symbiotic attachment leading to a later individuation with autonomous functioning. The hated child's experience is: "My life threatens my life." The seeming independence and detachment of this basically frightened and angry person are purely defensive, and there is developmental arrest in the humanizing process and an arrest of life before it really began.

The classic research of Ainsworth (1979) and all the work it has spawned is very relevant to our understanding of the patterns of character and adaptation formed in this first year of life. Like the work of Bowlby and Mahler, Ainsworth's research is relatively pure observation in minimally contrived situations and employs global and qualitative categories of observation. In her procedure, a mother and her child of one year are brought into a novel playroom. After a relatively brief period for adaptation, the mother is asked to leave and then return at a predetermined time.

Ainsworth and her colleagues found that they were able to reliably characterize the child's pattern or syndrome of behavior in this situation. Furthermore, the three patterns or syndromes they delineated showed remarkable predictability to future adjustments up to five years of age.

In the first pattern, called "anxious/avoidant attachment," babies showed little affective resonance with their mothers and had little preference for interaction with her over interaction with a strange examiner. They were able to explore the room independently and showed little or no disturbance when their mothers left. As in all cases, the most noteworthy behavior occurred on the mother's return. At this point, these babies actively ignored their mothers, and a good portion of these children turned away from their returning mothers.

In "secure attachment," the child appeared to use the mother as a secure base for exploration. The child easily separated from the mother to explore the environment but also freely shared her experience with the mother, and the pair was more affectively attuned. The child was readily comforted by the mother when distressed and could then quickly return to playing after such comforting. When distressed by the mother's departure, these children would go to their mothers for comforting and reconnection when she returned. If not distressed by the mother's departure, which also occurred in these securely attached babies, they acknowledged, welcomed back, and happily approached their mothers on her return. All of these behaviors suggest that a child is positively and unambivalently attached to the mother.

"Anxious/resistant attachment" is characterized by far more clingingly dependent behavior. Initially, these babies have trouble separating from their mothers to explore the novel environment and tend to be more apprehensive of the examiner as well as showing a definite preference for their mothers. They're more likely than the other two groups to be distressed by the mother's departure, yet, when she returns, they often are even more upset, oscillating from anxious contact to obvious "resistance." They may, for example, reject the mother's attempts to initiate play, kick, squirm, or otherwise display negativity or ambivalence. Occasionally, these children show an alarming degree of pacivity in showing no attempts to interact either with the environment or with the returning mother.

For our purposes, this research is important for any number of reasons. These attachment patterns seem reliably established by one year of age and predict well to the same types of attachment observed six months later (Main & Weston, 1981; Waters, 1978). These types of attachments also have proven to be excellent predictors of relating to teachers and peers up through five years of age, always with the advantage going to those securely attached at one year (e.g., see Easterbrook & Lamb, 1979; Lieberman, 1977; Matas, Arend, & Sroufe, 1978; Waters, Wippman, & Sroufe, 1979).

Consistent with our developmental model, then, crucial patterns of relating to others are established quite early. While some of this may be related to genetic factors, I believe a good deal of it is related to the parent-child relationship. If it is not already obvious, the anxious/avoidant attachment is virtually identical to what I am describing as schizoid, while the anxious/resistant attachment is virtually identical to what I am describing as oral. By the time one has reached adulthood, these patterns may be intermingled with other characterological patterns. Furthermore, they may be more effectively covered by defensive styles or social skills. Yet, the underlying phenomenology of the anxious/avoidant or anxious/resistant attachment remains and characterizes the individual's process.

EXTERNAL CIRCUMSTANCES AND
GENETIC ENDOWMENT

Some element of the schizoid structure seems apparent in many patients who present themselves for treatment. In understanding the prevalence of these failures in attachment and the associated results, it may be well to consider the effects of particular external circumstances during the symbiotic period that may have put considerable strain on the mothering figure and thereby further diminished her ability to be contactful and accepting. For example, a mother who may have been "good enough" under ordinary circumstances may not be if she loses her husband to divorce, death, or military service. The experience of early serious childhood illness and particularly early hospitalization can also severely disrupt the attachment. The child may experience the disruption of object impermanence during this sensitive period, together with agonizing and severe pain associated with the treatment administered by the caretaker or others. Similarly, war, economic depression, or environmental catastrophe may be involved in diminishing the parents' ability to be contactful and loving in this crucial period. Obviously, there are levels of hateful or contactless environments, and environmental events can either enhance or detract from the quality of life in symbiosis.

There is also considerable individual variation in the ability of infants to sustain a human relationship. The innate ability of the child to provide the mothering person with the nonverbal signals on which she bases her responses will differ. Some infants will seek to maintain proximity to a greater extent than others or be more motorically responsive to contact. Individual differences that affect the attachment process have been noted by those who have systematically observed these child-caretaker interactions (e.g., Bowlby, 1969; Murphy & Moriarty, 1976). It seems clear now that a good deal of serious infantile autism is the result of some processes internal to the child and not primarily the function of environmental influence (Judd & Mandell, 1968). While the focus of the present work will be on environmental influences, the effects of early external circumstances and genetic endowment should be taken into consideration in each individual case.

AFFECT, BEHAVIOR, COGNITION

Affect

The psychoanalytic concept of developmental arrest assumes that cognitive and behavioral resources, as well as the form of affective expressions, are in some very meaningful way *frozen* at the point of serious environmental frustration. Thus, in the classic case of the hated infant, there is an arrest in the attachment–bonding period, and in some cases even in the prior period, to which the infant may regress in defense. In the area of affect or feeling, the classic schizoid character can be characterized most meaningfully by underlying, often unconscious, feelings of terror and rage in response to a life-threatening environment. The terror may be expressed in a variety of symptoms, including anxiety or panic attacks in response to situations that are perceived as threatening. Such stimuli may not necessarily be consciously experienced as threatening and the individual may be totally unaware of the nature of the triggering stimuli. But, at an unconscious level at least, the stimuli release the terror response. The terror may be circumscribed in phobias; in more conscious individuals it may be perceived as generalized anxiety or tension specific to social situations or intimacy. There may be a general expression of discomfort or lack of belonging in the world and even a sense of unreality about one's connection with it all.

In those who share this schizoid condition, yet defend against it more completely, absence of any real spontaneous affect and a machine-like manner of self-expression will be characteristic. There may be a hyperrationality and a tendency to see those who are emotional as irrational, out-of-control, or crazy. There may be a concomitant "as if" quality in the expression of feelings, almost as if the person were badly acting an expected role. In some cases the person may express concern about what he or she "should feel" under certain circumstances.

In the widely acclaimed film, *Ordinary People*, Conrad enters psychotherapy under the strain of no longer being able to control powerful negative affective states in his adolescent years. In the initiation of that treatment he asks for more emotional control and in the course of it relates an incident after the funeral of his brother in which he does not know what to say or how to feel and wonders how the TV character John-Boy would feel and what he would say in that situation. Timothy Hutton's portrayal of Conrad in this film is one of the best current exemplifications of a person with this character structure. And, Mary Tyler Moore renders a good portrayal of one type of "schizoid-genic" mothering.

In sum, the hated child's most basic underlying feeling is that of terror associated with annihilation or, on an adult level, with failure to make it in the world. All defenses are marshaled to stave off rejection and failure. The more complete the defense against this fear, the more extreme the withdrawal into machine-like behavior and total absence of any apparent feeling.

To an even greater extent than with the terror, there is usually a denial and avoidance of the emotion of anger or rage. In infancy, the destructive rage would risk the destruction of the caretaker and therefore the infant himself and could provoke the caretaker's destructive retaliation. Thus, the repression of this emotion is life-preserving. What is encountered, then, in the adult patient, is typically an avoidance or withdrawal from conflict, an inability to get angry or to face anger in others, and the propensity to express it, if at all, in passive-aggressive withdrawal. The hated child has learned to leave rather than fight back and feels that anger is useless and accomplishes nothing. Very often the hated child denies completely his own anger and idealizes and spiritualizes his own loving nature.

As these individuals become more aware of the deep levels of rage in them, they often express considerable fear of their own destructive power. The fantasy is that they may let go suddenly and destroy everyone and everything in their path. The sudden explosions that result, for example, in that quiet, withdrawn, unassuming boy shooting down innocent people at random from the top of a building suggest that this fantasy is occasionally realized. In the course of a well-engineered therapy, however, where the capacity to tolerate feeling is systematically developed, the existing defenses are made conscious, fortified, and then gradually melted, there is little danger of anything so dramatic. It is not uncommon, however, for some socially inappropriate anger to spill over in the course of treatment; in fact, it is often useful for schizoid individuals to experience loss of control, which, while regrettable, is usually nowhere near the feared fantasy. Similarly, it is useful for these people to achieve a rapprochement with those to whom they have expressed the anger and experience that loss of control of this emotion does not result in anybody's annihilation and usually not even in prolonged disaffection.

The therapeutic context is particularly valuable, I think, in providing an atmosphere in which a good deal of this rageful affect can be literally dumped with no negative environmental consequences. It is important to caution, however, that this should not be done prematurely, before the capacity to tolerate this affective experience and self-observe its release is developed.

Whenever there is a death in the family there is sorrow and grief. When there is a death of the self, as in the schizoid experience, there is similarly a mourning for the self that could have been and for the loving relationship that was instinctively expected but not forthcoming. As a consequence, the affect of sorrow, grief, or depression is common in individuals with this characterological makeup. It is usually the least suppressed affect, though its active expression in deep crying or sobbing may be partially or totally absent. As with the other affects, it is not fully and deeply experienced by the organism; rather, it may be experienced as a long-standing or periodic chronic depressive state, characterized more by withdrawal and whining discomfort than by deeply felt grief. In order to get on with life, the hated child also had to deny this feeling and persevere in spite of a chronic underlying depressive condition. Such depression, particularly accompanied by suicidal ideation, the termination of self-caring functions, and the self-recognized inability to feel anything else, may well be the referral complaints of those with this general history and character structure.

Just as there is very little negative affect in this structure, there is a concomitant absence of positive affect. Possible exceptions to this include a not-uncommon ungrounded euphoria triggered by some philosophical or religious idea or artificially induced by drugs. In these situations, there may be a euphoria, which is fleeting and artificial in connection with the briefly experienced realization of some of the symbiotic illusion—that is, when *the* religion, idea, mate, or drug state that answers all prayers is briefly found. The high always ends, of course, and the person always returns to the essential affective state that characterized him prior to the illusory high.

Behavior

The behavior of the unloved or insufficiently loved child will vary on several basic dimensions. He or she will be able to function in the world based on how well the underlying powerful affects are controlled or held in. While the holding in may have other detrimental effects, such as psychosomatic illness, to be discussed later, or the diminished capacity for any kind of close relationship, it does allow the person to function. To the extent that this is unaccomplished, one is dealing with an individual who is extremely sensitive to any harshness in the environment, who has difficulty maintaining a sustained commitment to any work activity or relationship, and who will flee, often in a more or less dissociated state, from one thing to another. So, to the extent that the underlying affects are available, one may be faced with an individual who appears quite fragile and susceptible to breakdown into emotional states, confusion, and even loss of contact with reality. This tenuous reality relatedness may be expressed in fairly mild forms of being "spaced out" to more profound fugue states or periods of psychotic-like behaviors.

Where the individual's defenses allow her to be more effective in the external world, one is more apt to find an individual who withdraws into those activities that offer some worldly accomplishment while avoiding other areas of involvement. For instance, one might be a computer whiz, a renowned ballet dancer, or a workaholic attorney with a conspicuously absent, late, or damaged history of intimate relationships. In those less damaged, there may be a sustained relationship with a spouse or family but with little emotional contact or intimacy. There may even be the ability for the person to play the role of an assertive or dominant individual in a certain isolated context (e.g., in the classroom or courtroom), in striking contrast to shyness and ineptitude in other social settings.

The key to understanding the schizoid structure is the disconnection of the individual from life processes—from the body, from feelings, from intimate others, from community, and often even from inanimate objects such as food, nature, etc. Except in those areas where an individual may have attained exceptional achievement, there is a universal tendency to avoid meeting life head-on—to look away, to twist out of confrontation or closeness, to "space out" or migrate internally away from contact. The person himself may be unaware of that tendency, since it is often an automatic, unconscious response to threat. Even in areas of great accomplishment, there is almost always the existence of severe and often debilitating performance anxiety, in that the person's identity is so invested in that achievement that any hint of failure is tantamount to annihilation of the self. It is not uncommon for these tendencies to also be expressed in perfectionism and procrastination. As stated earlier, the schizoid person often discovers that the pursuit of mental processes and achievement is a safe haven from life. Since the schizoid character cannot identify with life in the body and develop a solid sense from that biological core, he needs to find that somewhere else. The defensive attempt to earn external approval and self-acceptance through achievement, often involving mental abilities, is common in this structure. This is often the only way in which he contacts the world, expresses himself, gains acceptance or recognition, and senses who he is and where he belongs. Failure in this area of endeavor can precipitate serious depression and suicidal thinking and behavior.

In the service of denying the hatred or coldness that he experienced, the schizoid character typically offers to others what he did not receive himself. That is, his ideal self is characteristically very accepting and understanding of others—he believes in letting others be. If the hostility toward himself or others begins to emerge, it is experienced as very threatening and cannot usually be acted out unless there is dissociation or an ego-syntonic excuse for that expression.

Paradoxically, some schizoid individuals will be experienced as quite controlling in relationships, particularly close relationships. These people, often in the personality disorder range, are keeping the archaic feelings of terror and rage at bay by maintaining a close watch on any circumstance that might trigger these emotions. Thus, they may carefully evaluate each action that involves another and insist on retaining control of it. In psychotherapy or other close relationships, for example, they may be continually regulating the amount and depth of contact to maintain safety. This will typically leave the other feeling controlled. The resulting control battles can be intense because the schizoid literally feels she is fighting for her life.

Concomitant with all of this, there is often the need, usually conscious, to be special. As a way of denying the reality of being unloved, even hated, rejected, and abused, there is the compensatory ideal of specialness, which is often realized one way or another. This may be through real achievement in science or art or through the delusional achievement of the kind so well portrayed in Robert De Niro's more narcissistic character (Rupert Pupkin) in the film *King of Comedy*. When the specialness, real or delusional, is threatened, there results a tightening of the defense and eventually a breakdown in the structure.

I am reminded of one of my clients, a successful 40-year-old doctor, who remarked poignantly, "I think I have worked so hard all my life in order to forget that I don't have the right to exist." The schizoid issue is literally existence and those who have to deal with this issue will try to find something that will justify their existence. Their right to exist is always on the line, and there is extraordinary anxiety in case the justification should fail.

Cognition

Any of the adaptive or cognitive functions that are developing during attachment-bonding may be seriously weakened or retarded by trauma. The extent and duration of the trauma, the genetic strengths of the organism, the availability of alternative resources such as extended family, and the nature of the available defenses or compensations will determine the extent to which adaptive functions or structures are over- or underdeveloped. For these reasons, it is probably more instructive to be aware of the cognitive abilities that one might assess than to describe any fixed way in which they may be represented in people with this character structure.

It is possible, however, to outline a number of internal belief structures, ego ideals, and "script decisions," which are usually operative in people with this kind of history. In this latter area, there will always, for example, be the underlying sense that "there is something wrong with me." And, there will always be the belief that the world is dangerous, hard, or cold. To the extent that the person has compensated or defended against this, these ideas will be denied and there will be a cognitive structure or belief system supporting that denial. The denial may well break down under stress, however, and this breakdown may be accompanied by suicidal ideation or behavior, depression, panic attacks, paranoid thought, and other symptoms. The more frequent and florid that breakdown, the more one is dealing with a person whose defenses are fragile and whose diagnosis would most likely be in the personality disorder range. The more a person is able to intellectualize or otherwise defend against these cognitions and their associated feelings, and the more intact the other adaptive functions, the more one is dealing with a more reliably functioning person who can tolerate more stress (character neurosis or style). The underlying dynamic, however, is similar in spite of these very important differences, and it is this core issue that must sooner or later be addressed for the person to realize her potential.

Because the issue of existence is critical in this structure, there will likely be some expression of this in a person's day-to-day life. For instance, the issue of security may be particularly important or obviously denied. Having enough money, holding on to one's job—in short, "making it" in life—may be a persistent concern. Alternatively, in an attempt to escape the anxiety associated with survival, the person may simply look the other way regarding these adult responsibilities and be defensively oblivious to security issues. There will be the polar opposite defensive idea or belief that "I am special." Similarly, there will often be the associated belief of a philosophical or religious nature asserting that the universe is benevolent, a unity, and supremely meaningful. In both cases, these beliefs will not be particularly well integrated or digested within the person. The specialness may be grandiose, at least at times, and the philosophical or religious beliefs may be such a part of the self-concept that contrary beliefs are experienced as threatening. Because these ideas maintain the denial of the original position, they may be held very tenaciously.

Whatever the quality of the schizoid cognitive functioning, one common characteristic is the dissociation of thinking and feeling. It is with these people that one can most readily realize the limitations of pure intellectual, affectless insight. It is perhaps this ability to dissociate, however, which is responsible for the fact that many with this kind of problem have been able to develop cognitive abilities to a highly sophisticated level, though often within a narrow range. It is as if the dissociation of feeling and thinking protects these intellectual functions from contamination. It is as if the intellectual functions are walled off from upsetting affects and thoughts and therefore protected. Like so many other defensive and compensatory moves, this one has its cost, but it also has obvious survival value for the organism, not only in childhood but throughout life.

In terms of an object relations view of the developmental arrest in early attachment-bonding, it is useful to note that a salient feature is the merged experience with the caretaker. There is the ability to imitate and the ability to engage in the primitive defensive functions of denial, introjection, and projection. There also is the ability to retreat to the more withdrawn state of the first few weeks of life. The development here is from (1) a relatively withdrawn state to (2) a state of merged experience or symbiosis to (3) a phase in which the self is consciously differentiated from others. While there will later develop other ways to defend against the schizoid's reality, in the early period all that appears to be available is direct denial of that reality and withdrawal as well as the mechanisms of projection and introjection. In other words, all the individual can do is to primitively block out the reality of his existence, while introjecting the bad object and then projecting aspects of it outward.

As the ultimate result of all the schizoid trauma and these early developmental limitations, the individual will freeze in his body in order to control the powerful negative feelings. He can then move on to develop, in relative isolation, the cognitive adaptive functions that will begin to emerge as a function of his natural growth. Because of the disruptions in this early period, there may be a continuing failure of the powers of discrimination, particularly in social contexts, and, at the deepest level, problems with differentiating between his own thoughts and feelings and those of others.

As opposed to those characterological problems to be discussed in later chapters, the hated child is really faced with a choice between involvement and withdrawal. Developmentally, he is not up to more sophisticated adjustments. Involvement hurts so withdrawal is chosen. The naturally desired attachment is foregone in the interest of survival. In reviewing the research of Harlow et al. (e.g., Harlow & Harlow, 1966), we may remember that while the monkeys raised by artificial mothers were generally not very happy, social, or well adjusted, they did, by and large, survive.

In every schizoid personality I have treated it has eventually been necessary to face the destructive, demonic force. This is typically experienced as completely alien and often completely beyond the control of the individual. Structurally, I believe it is useful to understand this as an unassimilated introject of the mothering figure, as well as the natural response of rage at this rejecting or cold figure. If this destructive force is experienced prematurely, before sufficient grounding, understanding, and the building of security in therapy, it can lead to a disintegration or decompensation. Where self-other discrimination is weak, as in the personality disorder, this disintegration can result in paranoid pathology. These signs of disintegration are most obvious not in the chronically mentally ill but in those persons who disintegrate in response to mind-altering drugs, encoun-

ter marathons, or psychotherapeutic techniques, which prematurely
overwhelm the defenses.

Summary

The schizoid experience basically involves a failure in the attachment process at or near the beginning of this process. This failure
occurs when the cognitive and structural resources of the organism
are minimal. As a consequence, the defense mechanisms which the
individual must use to deal with this fundamental assault are primitive—primarily denial, introjection, and projection. These mechanisms will be called upon again and again to deal with the persistent
issue of existence and survival, as well as with any subsequent situation that in any way triggers these more basic issues. So, while the
autonomous functions and other cognitive and ego abilities may very
well develop, often to an extraordinary degree, there exists this basic
structural vulnerability in the organism. In short, it is critical not to
underestimate the degree of damage and consequent vulnerability in
this character structure.

In spite of apparent strength, individuals with an essentially schizoid character structure must, at core, deal with the issue of survival
and the terror and rage around the threat to existence. It is important
that they not be overwhelmed by powerful therapeutic technique. It
is essential to develop their tolerance for aliveness in the body, to
solidify their trust in the therapeutic relationship, and to build a
well-grounded ego strength before they are asked to face this ultimate issue that will emerge when they melt their defenses and touch
the feelings that exist within them.

ENERGETIC EXPRESSION

Those who emphasize the physical dynamics of character structure simply assert that the organism will respond to environmental
frustration not only with a change of attitude and behavior but also
with responses in the voluntary and even involuntary musculature.
When the young organism comes up against continual and seemingly
immovable negativity and frustration, it will, in an attempt to survive, begin to inhibit or contract against the impulses that seem to
produce that negativity. This inhibition is represented in the organ-

ism by contraction of those muscles that inhibit the impulses. The contractions become chronic and as a result can produce rather dramatic changes in posture and even in the functioning of bodily organs.

The muscular inhibition of impulse is a concrete and visible manifestation of the parental or environmental prohibition. It is the physical manifestation of the process of introjection. This assumption of the prohibition or negativity initiates the loss of spontaneous movement, feeling, and behavior. It is chosen only because it is preferable to the pain involved in continuing the natural, spontaneous reactions to the chronic frustration. The decision to inhibit is experienced as a choice of survival over expression. The dependent infant cannot exist in a chronic state of war with the environment and the internal states of chronic rage, terror, and despair, which accompany the rejection of spontaneity. So, the organism turns against itself, restricts its impulses, and internalizes that battle between its innate needs and the prohibitions of the environment.

If we accept the proposition that adaptive self functions promote the survival of the organism in negotiating the demands of the environment and the organism itself, we can appreciate how the self becomes identified with the inhibiting process as a survival mechanism. The inhibiting pattern becomes a survival pattern, which in turn becomes a part of the individual's ideal self. The ideal self is, from that point on, threatened by an alive, spontaneous self-expression and maintained by control of those impulses. Thus, cognitive self-statements in the form of "script decisions" (e.g., "I am an understanding, giving, peaceful person," etc.) reinforce the muscular blocks.

There is the corresponding illusion that the release of the blocks will yield catastrophe, often both personal and environmental. In the case of schizoid character, the illusion of release is annihilation — often not only the annihilation of oneself but also the annihilation of others as the uncontrollable rage is let go on the environment. The essential schizoid experience is, "My life threatens my life." So, what is ultimately blocked is the life force itself. The organism freezes, stiffens, or clenches in tension, and twists away from the threatening environment. All of the bodily consequences that the body oriented therapists have noted in this character structure are a result of this process.

In listing the body characteristics of the schizoid, it must be kept in mind that they represent the observations of a number of somatically oriented therapists who have treated a variety of clients with, presumably, various mixtures of schizoid and other characteristics. The listing is more of what one may look for rather than an exhaustive or exclusive list of what will always be present. Furthermore, where these chronic muscular contractions have characteristic postural consequences, it must also be remembered that characteristics of posture, as well as other physical dimensions, can also be the result of genetic endowment. A well-trained body oriented therapist does not typically look at the body to classify the pathology; rather, he looks to see where and how the natural flow of the organism has been restricted by chronic contraction.

Perhaps the most salient thing to look for in a schizoid personality is the virtual cutting off of life in the body. Movements tend to be restricted, often mechanical, and lacking in natural spontaneity and flow. Cutting off the life flow is particularly accomplished through restricting the breathing and in this personality structure that is often done by a constriction of the diaphragm and shallow breathing in the chest. This may be accompanied by raised shoulders and a concomitant contraction of the chest. This breathing constriction obviously can affect the voice and accompanying constriction in the throat may yield a high-pitched and often young-sounding voice, due to the narrowing in the throat. Correlated with this, one often finds that the choke response is easily elicited if the person is asked to breathe deeply. It is thought that the schizoid's split in thinking and feeling is literally represented in this chronic tension in the neck—the area separating the head and the trunk. It is as if the natural instinctual impulses are blocked off there and not allowed to register in the head.

Together with this characteristic contraction in the upper chest and neck, there is typically severe tension at the base of the skull corresponding to the characteristic block in the ocular segment of the head. This ocular block may also be observed in the appearance of the eyes, which may, especially under circumstances of stress, appear disconnected or unresponsive. It has been hypothesized that this ocular block results from the attempt on the part of the organism not to see the painful truth of his state of existence. Under stress, the schizoid individual may literally go away from the current circumstances and that escape may be perceived in the eyes, which appear to be looking but not seeing, disconnected from the present reality. Occasionally, the experience of frozen terror may also be seen in the eyes of the schizoid individual, a terror that is not consistent with the rest of the facial expression and that does not systematically vary with the situation but is fixed or frozen.

The early twisting away from the threatening environment may be chronically represented in a twisting of the body, which may be represented literally in a chronic spinal scoliosis. Again, there are many causes of spinal scoliosis but the schizoid experience is hypothesized to be one of them, a function of a chronically frozen twisting-away. The freezing or stiffening of the body is believed to typically result in difficulty in the joints. To understand this, one can imagine the chronic tension that would result in the joints from a response of chronic stiffening of the body. To illustrate this, I often ask my students to assume a posture of complete stiffening, locking the knees, elbows, and lower back while opening the eyes and mouth wide in an expression of terror. I then ask them to imagine themselves going through life in that position, bracing against the threat of life.

Many somatic therapists have also noted a number of characteristics in schizoid patients that could be summarized under the heading of "disproportional body." That is, the body does not present itself as a unitary whole, as certain parts do not fit with the whole. For example, the head may not seem to fit the body or the arms may not be proportional to the trunk. Bilateral asymmetry has also been noted, such that the left side of the body is larger or smaller than the right.

Finally, a general deadness of the schizoid body has often been observed and reflected in the lack of color in the body, particularly a lack of color or even coldness to the touch at the points of chronic constriction—the joints, diaphragm, and points where the body narrows (i.e., ankles, wrists, and neck). The lack of aliveness in the body is also often seen in a thin, narrow physique with limited bodily movement. Personally, I have seen a number of schizoid personalities where the body is more developed than in this classic type, though some of the energetic blocks are still present.

While I have sometimes found my students to scoff and dismiss the bodily implications of characterological theory, I have continued to find the insights delivered by body observation extremely useful. Where the underlying characterological problems are well hidden and well defended, the individual may often be unable to report the reality of his etiological history. In this not uncommon situation, it will be the individual's characteristic behavior and the language of the body that will more reliably indicate the basic issues with which he is dealing. This is particularly true in the schizoid situation, wherein denial is the primary mechanism of defense and where the historical events may have occurred so early and been so traumatic that their remembrance is both less possible and more debilitating.

As is probably obvious, the combination of extreme bodily distortions and lack of physical and emotional awareness makes the schizoid a natural for the development of psychosomatic illness. The chronic tension in the upper body, neck, and ocular segment translates readily to the susceptibility to headache and difficulty with the eyes. The constriction in respiration results in a susceptibility to respiratory illness, just as the chronic tension in the joints produces a susceptibility to illness and injury there. The chronic but usually repressed anxiety and resulting twisting and holding in the body can render the normal organic processes, particularly digestion, susceptible to difficulty. Further, the generalized diminution of life's energetic properties can render the organisms generally susceptible to infection and injury. Indeed, it has been my experience that the better defended the character, the more likely the presence of illness.

THERAPEUTIC OBJECTIVES

In every case, the therapeutic objectives are to repair the deficiencies in structural functioning, to restore the flow of instinctual self-expression, and to integrate these behavioral and cognitive abilities into a life-supporting system, which is able to adapt to or modify the external environment. I see psychotherapy as beginning a process, which can last a lifetime. As life is a race between maturity and senility, effective psychotherapy is designed to aid the former and retard the latter.

The provision of a trusting and safe environment is, or course, necessary in all psychotherapy, but in the treatment of the schizoid patient its importance is enhanced. Essentially, the schizoid person was scared out of his body and cannot be frightened or confronted back into it. It is essential, therefore, that the therapeutic setting be safe, congruent, and human. Because of the history, the sensitivity, and extraordinary perceptiveness of the typical schizoid client, it is even more crucial that the therapist realize Carl Rogers' three prerequisites for an enhancing therapeutic relationship—accurate empathy, unconditional positive regard, and congruence. In short, the first objective with this patient is to restore trust—trust in the self, trust in the significant other, trust in the community at large, and trust in the life process itself. Once this therapeutic environment is achieved, the other objectives are possible.

Affective Objectives

Perhaps most basic to the schizoid problem is the need to reconnect the person with himself. Without this there can be no essential change in his relationship with the world. This may be begun by helping him regain a greater feeling sense of himself. An increase in the depth, range, and realness of one's feeling is an objective that can be accomplished by many therapeutic techniques, including movement, internal focusing, and physical expression. Along with this increased feeling and an enhanced identification with that feeling, we also wish to increase the individual's physical relationship to objects in the world. That is, the schizoid person needs an increased felt relatedness to reality—to food, work, nature, home, etc. Next, that reality relatedness needs to be expanded to the human world— to the therapist, loved ones, coworkers, and friends.

As a central part of increasing the client's sensory contact with the environment, it is particularly crucial to build the sense of stability or *grounding* in the world. This refers to the felt sense that one's feet are planted firmly on the ground and that one can stand one's ground in circumstances where it may be threatened. As a part and consequence of this work in increasing sensory awareness, the therapist must work in many ways to reduce all forms of chronic tension or spasticity in the affected areas of the body. Initially, this increased awareness and emerging letting go may be associated with physical pain, but eventually it will reduce experienced pain and affect any psychosomatic illness that has not already produced lasting physical damage.

As with all clients, it will be useful to increase the schizoid's awareness of and identification with his own defenses. It is always useful for one to be aware of how one has and does defend himself, to respect the survival qualities of these defenses, and to understand how they were appropriate choices under the circumstances of one's development. In the schizoid case, for example, it will be useful to help the person identify his tendency to "go away," to ask him to do that deliberately, and to assist him in monitoring its effects.

As one works on the emotional level with the schizoid individual, one will confront deep-seated and profound hostility and terror. As the person begins to trust his body and feelings, more and more of these feelings will emerge to be owned, expressed, and eventually integrated into the self. Although getting to the terror is essential, it is in the retaliatory rage that the individual often experiences the surest road to finding his true self. When he experiences the power and realness of that rage, he begins to have the power base for self-expression. There is at last, in that rage, a self to experience and express. The alternating of experience and insight around that emotion, as well as around the terror, will initiate the emergence of self. In the expression of the rage particularly, the schizoid person restates his right to live and to be in this world.

As with the rage, the schizoid's ability to experience the terror and to tolerate it is an empowering experience. He can discover that the terror, like the rage, is within him, that it can be expressed, and that he will not disintegrate with its expression. Additionally, he can have someone to assist him and be in contact with during and after the emotional experience. The increase in feeling through the body and contact with the ground, the environment, and others allows him to experience the intensity of these feelings without needing to "go away."

A central objective throughout this process is to increase the schizoid's tolerance for feeling and expression. He can learn that neither rage nor terror results in annihilation or disintegration. He can be asked to reach out and maintain contact with the therapist, thereby reinforcing the notion that he can be expressive, identified with his negativity, and still not lose himself or the support of others.

In simple affirmation terms, we seek for the schizoid individual to experience the following on a physical, feeling level: "I am welcome here. I belong here. I can trust life. I can trust my own feelings. I am a member of the community. I am capable of love and lovable. I can and will take care of and love myself. I can enjoy the movement in my body. I can run, jump, yell, express myself. I am safe. I am loved. I can relax."

Behavioral-Social Objectives

Since, in the schizoid problem, the main failure is in attachment, it will be the therapist's objective to establish that attachment. In some cases, the therapist may be the client's only meaningful human contact and it may be necessary to establish and then resolve a symbiotic attachment. In other cases, where there are relationship or attachment difficulties, the therapist will also work to assist in the development of those attachments and commitments. In general, growth in the schizoid character will involve an increase in commitments to love, friendship, and work relationships. Establishing or increasing involvement in some nonthreatening small group experience can often be very useful. In short, the individual needs to learn that he is a member of the group and equal to all other members, that he can take what he needs and give what he is able. Assistance in discovering that perfection or special performance is not required for acceptability will often be needed. Decreasing the perfectionism and need for specialness will usually result in decreasing procrastination and/or performance anxiety if these are problems.

To facilitate and expedite increased social involvement, it may be necessary to give feedback on, teach, or arrange for the teaching of simple social skills. The behavioral programs in personal effectiveness or assertiveness training may be useful in this regard, since these individuals may need to learn both verbal and nonverbal social skills.

While the aggressive impulses are almost always denied in individuals with this basic character structure, the aggression or hostility always finds an outlet in one form or another. Thus, it is an objective to help the individual discover the ways in which she unwittingly aggresses against others. Commonly, individuals with this character structure engage in passive-aggressive patterns such as withdrawal, or they provoke aggression in others to justify retaliation or provoke rescuing from others. The essential objective here is to discover the "games" that these people play, which in a very general way tend to operate by the presentation of the schizoid individual as understanding, accepting, and even weak, but which culminate in withdrawal, rejection, hatred, and the humiliation of others. The typical characterological pattern is expressed here with the individual offering what was not forthcoming to her but ultimately delivering to others what was earlier received. In other words, we offer what we didn't get and we ultimately give what we got.

As the aggressive impulses are integrated, the individual will begin to behave more aggressively and assertively in the social world. The therapist will serve to smooth out this transition so that aggressive and assertive expressions in the real world are relatively appropriate and effective. The direct expression of aggression and assertiveness in appropriate ways and contexts will be encouraged in therapy. Similarly, therapists can encourage and facilitate the smooth and appropriate expression of other affective experiences in the real social world—sadness, anxiety, laughter, joy, etc.

Cognitive Objectives

There are two basic areas of repair that need to be considered in addressing the cognitive problems. The first involves the client's attitudes, beliefs, and processes of self-identification. These structures are represented by the "script decisions," "ego ideals," "false self" identifications, etc. Here we are talking about beliefs, attitudes, points of view, etc. The second area involves cognitive abilities or, in psychoanalytic terms, structural functioning. Here we are discussing the individual's cognitive strategies in dealing with the external world, the defense mechanisms used internally, and the quality and robustness of cognitive abilities (e.g., assimilation and accommodation). In the first case, the therapeutic objectives center around the restructuring of internal beliefs, while in the second case they involve the literal repair of structure or cognitive abilities per se.

Just as it is useful to help the client identify how his compromise solutions have expressed themselves in his body and behavior, it is useful to do this in the area of cognition or belief. The first step, therefore, may be to help the individual to identify the usually simplistic and exaggerated precepts of the ego ideal. In this process, the individual may find that she is demanding absolutely, "I must be all-accepting. I must be special." Or believing dogmatically, "I am my ideas. I am my achievements." Once these notions are identified and experienced with their real intensity, it becomes relatively easy to explain their origins and assist the client through interpretation to develop further insight into their operation. Identification and understanding will initiate change in the ego ideals and false self identifications and more direct methods can then be employed to further those changes.

As the defenses at all levels are systematically relaxed, the therapeutic objective of uncovering the various "script decisions" about self, life, and others in general will be facilitated. In this character structure, these tend to be of the following nature: "Something is wrong with me. The world is a threatening place. I have no right to exist." In general, the "script decisions" in this structure will reflect self-hate and paranoia.

With the identification of the ego ideals and script decisions, the very basis for the false self will begin to erode and there will begin to be greater opportunities to strengthen a real self-identification. The therapist can begin this with strategies that strengthen the identification of the self with the body and its life processes. In this structure, that would amount to replacing the identification, "I am my ideas and accomplishments" with "I am my body and the life therein."

In the second area of cognitive or ego functioning, the therapeutic task, simply stated, is to assess and repair the areas of cognitive weakness. In relation to the perception of external reality, for example, the client may need direct instruction in the processes of assimilation, accommodation, discrimination, integration, and generalization. The therapist may serve not only the role of reality tester but also that of instructor in the strategies for accurately perceiving and testing reality. Just as the schizoid individual may need to be directly taught simple social skills, he may also need to be taught strategies for simple social perception. How does one know when one is liked, disliked, or responded to with objective neutrality? How does one know whether the negative behaviors of others is the result of their internal preoccupation or their specific response to us personally? Similarly, the schizoid individual may be helped to sharpen his cognitive strategies for discriminating internal affective states. How, for example, does one discriminate anxiety from excitement or sexual arousal from love? All of this becomes increasingly necessary as the person's structure is in the personality disorder range and is typically unnecessary at the higher end of the continuum.

The schizoid individual will usually also need to be taught better or more evolved defense mechanisms than the ones she already has. The schizoid defenses are primitive and few in number and most of these individuals are capable of learning far more efficient and less costly internal defense mechanisms. Particularly where used consciously and deliberately, such methods of internal defense are extraordinarily useful. A number of strategies are available from the cognitive wing of psychotherapy (e.g., rational emotive therapy, neurolinguistic programming) to teach such defenses. A part of this teaching, of course, would be the identification and strengthening of existing defenses, increasing appreciation of their survival function and rendering them conscious and under voluntary control.

The schizoid individual can benefit greatly from direct instruction in dealing with the harsh and anxiety-provoking parts of the real world. Much of this will involve behavioral instruction; however, on a cognitive level the therapist can assist with cognitive maps concerning how to approach and think about the demands of adult reality. Thus, the therapy may at times deal with strategies for managing one's time, dealing with the demands of others, or simple strategies for living life: how to clean the house, pay the bills, study for exams, etc.

Finally, a great deal needs to be done in the schizoid case on the integration of the "good parent-bad parent" and "good self-bad self" representations into a healthy, ambivalently experienced self-concept and view of others. The "good parent" is usually deficient in its representation in this structure and is particularly deficient in the nurturing functions. As a result, the schizoid individual is usually poor at self-soothing or self-nurturing. She may be directly taught to strengthen those self-soothing abilities that she does possess and to learn anew those that she does not.

In the course of the treatment, a central theme must be the identification of the unintegrated introject—the "bad parent." It is often so split off from the rest of the self that the person feels literally possessed by an alien and destructive force, which is aimed primarily at himself. The therapist's task is to assist the individual in identifying and taking responsibility for this negative force, in understanding its origins, and in beginning the process of integrating it into the ambivalently experienced self and other representations. In any person so hated, there will be hatred. To erode the denial of that hatred, to admit its existence, to aim it at its appropriate target, to accept it as part of one's reality, and to release its expression in a manner that will reduce tension without undue harm is perhaps the central therapeutic task with the schizoid character. As this is accomplished, an integrated representation of the self with all its real components will be established at a cognitive level. Such a representation may be facilitated by intervention directly at the cognitive level.

An appreciation of the need for strengthening the cognitive abilities yields a solid theoretical justification for methods of direct instruction or influence. The theory presented here does so, however, without the extreme oversimplification in theory characteristic of those who espouse an exclusively cognitive understanding of the complex human condition. With this knowledge, one can engage in very simple and direct cognitive restructuring with an understanding of how that fits into a broader perspective of what the human dilemma is all about. One can help another to think differently without having to believe that thought is all there is. For a listing of all therapeutic objectives for each character structure, see Appendix B.

It may be useful at this point to remember that there is no such thing as a schizoid character. This is merely an archetype in a model, which identifies basic human issues. Those who have been terrified early in life by the harshness or coldness of the environment they found then will usually still be operating with the adaptations to that reality formed by a weak and frightened child. Understanding this element of any person seeking psychological assistance can guide the therapist in a useful way. Imperfect and incomplete, this map of the invisible territory is worth having. For those wishing further guidelines on the treatment of the schizoid personality, I would particularly recommend the following: Guntrip, 1968; Johnson, 1985, and Manfield, 1992.

CHAPTER 6

The Abandoned Child:
The Symbiotic Withdrawal

There is no experience to which a young child can be subjected that is more prone to elicit intense and violent hatred for the mother than that of separation.

—John Bowlby (1960, p. 24)

Sometimes I feel like a motherless child . . . a long way from home.

—Odetta, *A Motherless Child*

ETIOLOGY

JUST BEYOND THE right to existence emerges the human infant's need for nurturance, sustenance, and touch. Where these needs are incompletely met, another set of core issues will be established, yielding a characterological adjustment traditionally labeled "oral."

Not all children consciously wanted are adequately cared for and even those who are given what they appear to need are not always provided the consistency of a single, emotionally available caregiver capable of eliciting and maintaining a firm, healthy attachment. Orality will develop where the infant is essentially wanted and an attachment is initially or weakly formed but where nurturing becomes erratic, producing repeated emotional abandonment, or where the primary attachment figure is literally lost and never adequately replaced. The symbiosis is begun but never fulfilled and therefore

100

never really resolved. The mothering anchor is not reliably available and thus secure "confident expectation" is never established. While the schizoid character structure revolves around the central issue of *existence*, the oral character's life will revolve around the core issue of *need*. There will be, in his behavior, attitudes, and perceived feelings, a polarity around this issue — tendencies toward desperate clinging, fear of being alone or abandoned, and poor self-care juxtaposed with a reluctance to express his need or ask for help, an overnurturing of others, and an independent grandiosity in elated or manic periods.

The case histories of individuals with severe orality are often characterized by maternal abandonment or serious illness in the mothering person. While the effect of the actual loss of a good mother figure has been documented to be most profound after seven months when "differentiation" has begun, the more common case appears to involve a weak or erratic symbiosis extending to chronic insufficiency in the need-gratifying ability of the mothering person. As opposed to the schizoid character, there is a "paradise lost" quality about the oral. She has experienced some adequate contact and at least begun an attachment when the caretaker is either lost or experienced as repeatedly unable to hold up her end of the attachment. Chronically ill, depressed, or alcoholic caretakers, who have relatively little outside support, are among the prime creators of the oral character. To understand this, imagine yourself the primary or sole parent of one or more very young children while you are dealing with the worst illness you have ever had outside a hospital. You might love your children and wish to give them every possible advantage, but you have barely enough energy to handle the illness and certainly you could not meet the demands of an active brood. Short of chronic depression, alcoholism, or illness, the parents of the oral character are often simply oral themselves. As chronically low energy individuals, they repeatedly fail to adequately meet the dependency needs of their children.

As in the etiology of the schizoid issue, the external circumstances under which the parent must live can contribute to or detract from the adequacy of early nurturance. A mother who may have the energy to be "good enough" for one child with the support of husband and/or extended family may be totally inadequate with two or three children, as a single parent, or when isolated from an extended family. Indeed, I believe that the vulnerability of the nuclear family in our highly mobile industrialized culture is largely responsible for the preponderance of both schizoid and oral issues in psychotherapy clients.

The young infant is, of course, oblivious to these sociological insights. He knows only that he hurts, physically or emotionally, and that the hurt is not being relieved. Bowlby (1973, p. 23) writes, "whether a child or adult is in a state of insecurity, anxiety, or distress is determined in large part by the accessibility and responsiveness of his principal attachment figure." In studying children separated from their mothers, Bowlby has observed a three-stage reaction process in which the infant first protests acutely, second, falls into deep despair, and third, finally gives up and becomes superficially adjusted but detached. In the third phase of the process, the child will respond to the mother's return by either not recognizing her or retreating from her. This will be followed by a period of marked ambivalence toward the mother for some period of time after the reunion.

We may extrapolate from these observations to hypothesize that the infant, repeatedly left or disappointed, will eventually do whatever he can to adapt to the disappointment or abandonment. Chronic upset, protest, and despair are too painful to live with. The infant will try to find a compromise solution to deal with the pain and heartbreak of abandonment or chronically unmet needs. As with every character structure, the self-negation begins when the natural response to chronic frustration becomes too much to bear. At this point, the child looks for ways to cut off his own natural organismic self-expressions to stop the pain. In the oral case this step very logically becomes, "If I don't *need* anything, I can't be frustrated." This stoic position, while somewhat satisfactory in lessening immediate pain, is not very realistic for a totally dependent being. Other maneuvers must be sought to complete the compromise.

The anthropologists of infancy have given us clues concerning the types of defenses available at various developmental stages. In summarizing this work, Blanck and Blanck (1974) have outlined the defensive concerns and functions available to children at six to nine months of age — the period when maternal separation seems to produce the full loss reaction just outlined. According to this summary, the child's primary anxiety response shifts at this time from the fear of annihilation to the fear of the loss of the caregiving object. Additionally, to the earlier available defense mechanisms of projection, introjection, and denial are added the defensive functions of identification, displacement, reversal, and turning against the self. With all of these abilities available at a primitive level, the oral child begins to develop his defense against the pain of needs unmet.

The first step, to repeat, is the denial of need. That is the central element in the self-negation process of oral character development. The person literally *contracts against* his own need. "If my need makes me hurt, I will stop needing." By limiting breathing, activity, and output of energy, the oral child will, in fact, need less input. This solution, which chooses depression over expression, will result in the low level chronic depression that is often definitional of the oral character. However, still more must be done because the needs still exist. The more evolved defense mechanisms provide ways for either bootlegging gratification while denying it or controlling the natural rage that the chronic frustration has created.

Let us briefly define these defensive functions.

> *Identification:* The process by which one either blurs or eliminates the distinction between self and others by extending his identity into another, borrowing his identity from another, or fusing identity with another.
> *Displacement:* The process by which the direction of feeling is transferred from one object to another—the substitution of one object for another as the target of feeling.
> *Reversal:* In classical analytic theory this is an instinctual vicissitude by which an energetic expression is reversed to its opposite. Through this mechanism, hate may change to love, sadism to masochism, longing for an object to rejection of that object, and so on. Reaction formation is a defense mechanism, which is based on this process.
> *Turning Against the Self:* Another instinctual vicissitude described by Freud (1915), which is used to explain the phenomenon often observed in obsessional neuroses in which a person directs his hatred inward against himself. The desire to retaliate becomes the propensity to self-torture.

You will notice that all four of these defensive functions rely on the individual's ability to substitute one object with another (identification, displacement, and turning against the self) or to substitute or replace one feeling for another (reversal). This ability to change the object or reverse the drive can explain many of the oral's defense maneuvers, which have been observed by the characterological theorists (e.g., Lowen, 1958). An understanding of these defensive maneuvers will do much in assisting your comprehension of the oral adult to be described presently.

Irrespective of the cognitive defenses chosen to resolve the conflicts, the child, unable to be satisfied in symbiotic attachment, moves prematurely to individuation. Typically, the oral child walks and talks early, embracing activities that will gain him attention and provide independence from one who cannot give what is really needed. The second subphase of individuation, practicing, includes some pretty high times during which many wonderful discoveries are made. The baby can do many new things and explore the wide world with a beginner's mind. This is a manic time and a time of natural grandiosity and narcissism. "So what if mama isn't here, look what I can do. I don't need her. Let the good times roll." The despair is escaped in the elation of individuating and moving out into the world. Such is the beginning of the manic defense, grandiosity, and narcissism that characterize many an oral character.

In a heretofore unpublished paper, Dr. Alan Levy has presented a most lucid description of oral character development. With the use of musical lyrics, he has delineated and illustrated the sequential development of this character structure by amplifying on the classic character analytic outline presented in Chapter 1: self-affirmation process, negative environmental response, self-negation process, and adjustment process in the oral case. With his permission I reproduce it for you here to enhance both your understanding and feel for the oral dilemma. To assist your understanding of the dynamics of the oral character, you might find it useful to see how many of the defensive functions you can find in the adjustment processes as outlined by Dr. Levy.

THE LOVE SONG OF THE ORAL*

Where do I begin . . . to tell the story that is older than the sea? . . .
the simple truth about the love she brings to me . . .

— "Love Story"

*A musically illustrated story of oral character development, presented to the Southern California Bioenergetics Society Basic Training Group by Alan W. Levy, Ph.D., September 15, 1975. More musical illustrations were contained in the original paper.

Self-Affirmation Process

The story starts immediately at birth. Contact with mother's warm, giving body is all that the newborn organism has to replace their confluence, the previous totally dependent, symbiotic connection. From its very core, the neonate says "I need you" by virtually sucking in all of the emotional and physical nourishment that it possibly can absorb. Research findings amply demonstrate that bodily intimacy is essential to the neonate's survival.

> I'll get by, as long as I have you
> Tho' there be rain and darkness too . . .
> I'll see it through
> — "I'll Get By"

Without the vital maternal closeness, the newborn would die. Such contact is more than vital to life; it is also pleasurable and is the prototype for the development of the capacity for affection and sexuality. There are many ways to express the relationship between pleasure at the breast and the experience of being loved. Here is but one:

> Warm . . . touching warm, reaching out, touching me, touching you . . .
> — "Sweet Caroline"

To the neonate, mother is the world. When she really is there, the experience of the contact verges on the miraculous, perhaps the closest event to paradise on earth!

> I have seen so many wonders . . .
> But I haven't seen anything to match the wonder of a mother's love.
> — "A Mother's Love"

Negative Environmental Response

But all too often, the paradise is lost. The environment deprives the baby of the vital contact. Mother is not there enough when needed, is there but ignores or can't respond, or leaves precipitously, and the infant is abandoned and helpless.

Close to my heart she came, only to fly away . . .
Now, I'm alone, still dreaming of paradise,
Still saying that paradise once nearly was mine.
                                   —"This Nearly Was Mine"

Organismic Reaction

Remembering the pleasure and experiencing the pain of the loss, the baby naturally cries out for mother's return.

When I remember every little thing you used to do,
I'm so lonely . . .
. . . and while I'm waiting here, this heart of mine is singing;
Lover, come back to me.
                                   —"Lover Come Back to Me"

When mother does return, the infant has some difficulty settling down and trusting that she is there as she is needed. Separation anxiety is heightened; the baby clings tightly, mistrusting and fearful of the next possible abandonment.

If you go away, as I know you must,
There'll be nothing left in the world to trust,
Just an empty room, full of empty space . . .
. . . and I tell you now as you turn to go,
I'll be dying slowly 'til your next hello . . .
                                   —"If You Go Away"

The next time mother leaves, the frightened, hungry organism reacts with rage.

Blast your hide, hear me call!
Must I fight City Hall?
Here and now, damn it all, come back to me!
                          —from *A Clear Day*, "Come Back to Me"

Repeated Negative Environmental Response

If the organismic reaction of hungry rage is met with acceptance and nurturance, the desperation of the loss is only temporary and growth can continue. But if, as is often the case, the deprivation of the contact is maintained to the point of exhaustion of the crying-out energy, a chronic form of despair develops. It is as if the organism lives in a perpetual state of mourning.

Self-Negation Process

The baby now is in a dilemma. The pain of the despair is too much to live with, and each time the need for contact is felt, the discomfort returns. Yet there is no replacement for mothering. Since the neonate cannot discriminate between the experience inside its body and its experience of the external environment, the hunger sensations are perceived as the enemy. To survive, the infant must negate its own needy feelings, taking the retroflective position: "I don't need."

> What a fool I was . . . to think you were the earth and sky . . . No, you are not the beginning and the end . . . I shall not feel alone without you. I can stand on my own without you . . . I can do bloody well without you.
> — "Without You"

And the developing person learns to *contract against* the need rather than *reach out* with it. This leaves him limited capacity to take in nourishment from the world, a state of chronic hunger and loneliness, yet caught between the despair of the unfilled emptiness and the fear of exposing it and being abandoned again for "being too needy." Limited intake and output of energy is part of the attempted solution; depression is a frequent consequence.

> Broken windows and empty hallways, a pale dead moon in a sky streaked with gray. Human kindness overflowing, and I think it's going to rain today . . .
> — "I Think It's Going to Rain Today"

Adjustment Process

The collapse into depression must be coped with in order to somehow adjust to the demands of the external world. It is as if the ego says to the collapsed, undercharged body, "We can't live this way." And, one popular form of compensatory maneuver is to act out the fantasies of oral fulfillment—the good life of overconsumption of food, drink, drugs, etc., an infantile attempt to recapture the sweetness of the nursing experience.

> Who can take tomorrow, dip it in a dream,
> separate the sorrow and collect up all the cream?
> The candy man can . . . 'cuz he mixes it with
> love and makes the world taste good . . .
> —"Candy Man"

Another ego illusion is the promise of fulfillment through material security, the ever-present "good life" fantasy.

> All I want is a room somewhere . . . with one
> enormous chair . . . lots of chocolates for
> me to eat, lots of coal making lots of
> heat . . . oh, wouldn't it be loverly!
> —"Wouldn't It Be Loverly," from *My Fair Lady*

The light of reality dawns, and it turns out that dreams of oral goodies or material security provide no real adult satisfaction.

> I have almost everything a human could desire,
> Cars and houses, bearskin rugs to lie before my fire,
> But there's something missing,
> It seems I'm never kissing the one whom I could care for.
> —"Something to Live For"

The fundamental attitude is one of dependency. The oral character knows how to wait, to long for someone to bring love to him/her, and to cling to the supplier when they find one, so as not to feel the loneliness. The result of the clinging is advertised as happiness, but the passive dependency wears through in the highly variable mood swings which are sometimes characteristic.

> Sometimes I'm happy, sometimes I'm blue.
> My disposition depends on you.
> I never mind the rain from the skies
> if I can find the sun in your eyes . . .
> —"Sometimes I'm Happy"

Another way to cope with the desperate longing for that "special someone" and the despair of his ever coming is to bravely resolve to "go it alone," to make an ego virtue of the self-denial.

> Easy to be a man alone,
> Just make the whole wide world your only home.
> Don't talk to strangers, someone might be kind
> And muddle up your mind.
> — "A Man Alone"

If someone happens to be kind and offers contact that confounds that brave resolve, the ego has to work out a creative compromise to deny the need to be loved and meet it at the same time. How? By taking an interpersonal stance of "giving and caring," a way to get vicarious mothering by ministering to others. And the target person had better respond well, or else the original loss and depression will return.

> Come to me, my melancholy baby.
> Cuddle up and don't be blue.
> Every cloud must have a silver lining,
> wait until the sun shines through.
> Smile, my honey dear, while I kiss away each tear
> Or else I shall be melancholy too.
> — "My Melancholy Baby"

In this "mothering" personality, happiness is perceived as the assurance of never being alone again—the avoidance of another abandonment. A preferred means of both guaranteeing the needed contact and avoiding being left alone is finding someone who truly needs them. But that illusion, as powerful as it is, eventually breaks down when the "melancholy baby" grows out of the dependency or is less than grateful and the vicarious feeding process no longer seems to promise fulfillment. The disillusionment is real; the sadness and longing of the inner child cry out:

> Sometimes I fell like a motherless child . . .
> A long way from home.
> — "A Motherless Child"

And, for the love story of the oral character to have a satisfying ending, it must come full circle—a return to the mourning process, reexperiencing the loss of the contact with mother and the resulting fear, longing, rage, and hard work to increase the body's capacity to reach, take in, and discharge the energy needed for the person's own adult loving to emerge.

BEHAVIOR, ATTITUDE, AND FEELING

Essentially, the oral character develops when the longing for the mother is denied before the oral needs are satisfied. The unconscious conflict, then, is between need on the one hand and the fear of repeating that awful disappointment on the other. The characteristic behaviors, attitudes, and feelings you will see in the person will depend on the severity of the oral issue and on the current effectiveness of the defensive structure.

Though depression occurs in other character structures and is not definitional of orality, episodes of depression always occur where there is a significant oral component. A history of major depressive disorder or dysthymic disorder is common and cyclothymic disorder and even manic-depressive disorder can occur. The depressions of oral characters can be distinguished somewhat from those of other character types in that they usually hit harder and are often accompanied by more exhaustion, despair, and longing. While some will present a chronic unipolar depression, these people usually show greater fluctuation than the other character types. They can often sustain a normal or even supernormal level of activity, which may extend to manic proportions. Sooner or later, however, they run out of the synthetic fuel that moves them and they crash deeply, sometimes for an extended period. The oral character is essentially an undernourished organism with a depleted life force. The mania is an attempt to deny this and to avoid confronting the underlying despair and longing. As one might suspect, abandoned children tend to get sick a lot for several reasons. First, they have not internalized self-caring functions very well, second, the ungrounded periods of elation or hypomania deplete their resources, and third, sickness is a socially acceptable and ego-syntonic bid for attention and nurturance.

The oral character also has real difficulty in sustaining an adult adjustment to work, family, and personal management. The oral person simply grew up too soon, and in every such personality there is an underlying *resentment* about having to grow up and assume adult responsibilities. Unconsciously, the abandoned child wishes to be taken care of and feels the world still owes him a living. Though he may jam his system into overdrive to accomplish an adult adjustment, he secretly wishes he could just stay in bed and be fed. The demands of a job, spouse, children, home, personal and financial matters are just *too much*. In part because he is working overtime to do what he can to meet these demands, he is often reluctant to accept responsibility for his failures. He often sees himself as misunderstood, persecuted, and unappreciated.

Because the oral person has essentially given up, both assertiveness and aggression are weak. He does not adequately arrange his life or aggressively set out to make it work. He does not reach out for what he needs and cannot easily ask for things. Nor can he refuse to give what is asked of him. He can wait and long for life to come to him, but he cannot reach out for it or seize it. He can resent that it does not come to him, but he cannot express the rage he feels. Consequently, the oral person often shows a hyperirritability. Lowen (1958) has likened this to the condition of an unripened fruit. Separated from the tree too early, it is sour, hard, and bitter, missing the juicy sweetness that maturity would have provided.

I have most consistently seen all of these characteristics represented in people referred to me for psychological evaluation after an injury, often job-related, which fails to heal or ameliorate as expected. In these cases, the attending physician suspects a "psychological overlay" to the original problem. Very often I find a history of abandonment, repeated loss of the original attachment figure, or chronic lack of nurturance in childhood. Coupled with this is often a history of overwork and excessive responsibility, dating back to adolescence or before. There is often a not entirely unjustified seething resentment of the people for whom the person has worked, as well as for the doctors who cannot heal the injury. There is usually a passive or unassertive stance with regard to the injury, such that the responsibility for it is given over entirely to the doctors and there is little or no pursuit of self-healing.

These people typically really do hurt a great deal, but because they are hard to help and because they are passive-aggressive and complaining, they are usually disliked by their doctors and are not given the sympathetic ear they require. Their referral to me is often a "dump" by a frustrated physician, which the patient in pain resents. Being able to really hear the patient's pain and frustration and acknowledge its reality has been the single most valuable response in negotiating this initially difficult contact.

All oral characters hurt and they need to be heard in their pain and despair. In this particular symptomatic expression of orality, it often appears that the person has overworked himself until he breaks at his weakest point, most often the lower back. The break or injury gives him an honorable discharge from the resented demands of adult life, which were always really too much. Because he is sick or in pain, he can get caring and nurturance without asking. Through workers' compensation and other programs, he may finally be provided the living that he unconsciously believes is owed to him. He has found a compromise solution, which satisfies many conflicting demands. All he must do to sustain that solution is to stall his recovery. But to maintain his self-respect he must really hurt, and he does.

The oral character has many problems in love relationships. When she is not well-defended, or when her defenses are not working, the oral will lose herself in love. When the hope of finding the paradise lost is rekindled, the person will dissolve into the symbiosis. Her mate will complain that he feels suffocated and annoyed by this clinging behavior. The person may complain of loss of identity in relationships and will discontinue those activities that cannot be shared with the mate. Even though the oral may superficially offer a great deal of nurturance, her mate will often feel drained or sucked by the implicit demands for attention.

Sexual problems are common. The sex drive, like the essential life force, is weak in the oral character. There is a much greater need for touching, snuggling, and contact than for genital sexuality. The symbiotic nature of the relationship, which the oral craves and produces, dampens sexual passion. When the differences between man and woman are dissolved in the symbiotic relationship and when aggression and assertion are muted, passion of all kinds is suppressed and sex virtually disappears. A symbiotic relationship is a relationship without difference. Sexuality implies a set of differences too threatening to the symbiotic attachment. Oral women are frequently preorgasmic, and oral men often show a diminished sexual urge or a sexual urge that disappears once the early seductive phases of a relationship are passed. In the oral, commitment equals symbiosis and symbiosis kills sex.*

The abandoned child brings with her the fear of future abandonment in love relationships. She usually has terrible problems with loneliness and out of loneliness may prematurely rush into inappropriate relationships. Her fear of abandonment may fuel problems of jealousy or frequent panic attacks at any sign of possible abandonment. A mate's harmless roving eye or his failure to appear on time or to phone frequently or as expected may precipitate panic for which the mate is often held entirely responsible. The oral may project her propensity to leave the relationship when it is troubled onto her mate and thereby see imminent desertion when this has not occurred to the mate. As in every other character structure, we are inclined to do to others what was originally done to us. Congruent with this formula, the oral character is prone to abandoning those to whom she gets close. Because she suppresses assertion and aggression, loses herself in the relationship, gives more than she really wants to, and finds the demands of an adult relationship "too much," she builds resentment and becomes irritable. She then either gives up and withdraws or arranges for her own desertion. In the words of Jackson Browne:

> When you see through love's illusion there lies the danger
> And your perfect lover just looks like a perfect fool
> So you go running off in search of a perfect stranger
> While the loneliness seems to spring from your life like a fountain
>   from a pool.
> Fountain of sorrow, fountain of light
> You've known the hollow sound of your own steps in flight.
>   —Jackson Browne, *Fountain of Sorrow*

Particularly when not well-compensated, the oral has great difficulty with aloneness and may panic when alone or separated from his primary attachment figure. He may be prone to problematic behavior—particularly drug abuse or dependent behavior—at these times. The vicissitudes of early childhood development give some useful insights for understanding and dealing with these problems. By the fifth or sixth month of infant development, the child has

---

*I would like to again credit Ed Muller for this most helpful insight.

formed a person-specific attachment. "Eighth-month anxiety" refers to this such that the infant, at about eight months of age, displays anxiety or curiosity and wonderment when he is shifted from the mother or the father to another adult for holding. At this point, he becomes more prone to separation anxiety than before.

At about this time, the infant begins to become attached to "transitional objects" (Winnicott, 1953). These objects, commonly teddy bears and blankets in this culture, tend to partially allay separation anxiety and to take the place of the mothering figure during her absences. Children tend to give up these objects as they become more secure in their representation of the constancy of the primary attachment figures in their lives. Thus, when "object constancy" is more or less achieved, they give up the transitional object.

Such object constancy is never really achieved for the oral character; thus, the nature and role of transitional objects in his life can help in understanding and treating him. Often, those with orality issues are prone to develop very strong attachments to transitional objects, particularly those which make them feel better. Thus, I believe that great attachment to drugs of any kind can be usefully understood as transitional object attachment. The fact that many drugs produce a physiological dependence, as well as a psychological one, will enhance this effect. This kind of attachment exists not only for obvious recreational drugs like alcohol, tobacco, marijuana, and cocaine, but also for less obvious, culturally approved drugs such as caffeine and sugar. Characteristically, the oral character is prone to addictions of dependency and helping him to establish and then forego more benign transitional objects can be of great therapeutic utility.

When the oral character is well-compensated or defended, you will see a superficially effective person whose basic needs are not being met. His own need will be *denied* and *projected* onto others. He will tend to *identify* with the other melancholy babies of this world, and take care of them. He will probably be perceived as nurturing, generous, and soft. Alternatively, he may *displace* and compensate by the overconsumption of food, drink, or drugs in an attempt to easily alter the internal experience of loss, emptiness, and despair. This solution is closely associated with the *displacement* of the need for love from other people to the need to be surrounded by those material objects that, particularly in this culture, are believed to offer fulfillment.

Alternatively, the oral may *displace* his need for love and nurturance to a need for attention. Many clinicians have observed that oral people are often verbally bright and talkative, using this facility to gain attention and recognition. But, as any star will tell you, the satisfaction to be had from this source is nonsustaining.

> A legend's only a lonely boy when he goes home alone.
> —Carly Simon, *Legend in Your Own Time*

Attention, in the liberal doses that the celebrities of our culture get, becomes an annoying burden. Prior to realizing fame, however, it is tempting to sustain the illusion that it will eventually fill the emptiness.

Through *reversal*, the oral person transmutes his essentially infantile, selfishly narcissistic, irresponsible, and bitter real self into a much easier-to-sell package. He often gets support for his exaggerated nurturing, which is unconsciously demanding, or for his exaggerated responsibility, which is unconsciously resented. Where this false self is well-established and highly supported, it may take serious illness or injury to uncover the real self, which has been rejected and suppressed. By contracting against his own need, the oral has turned against himself. He despises the natural neediness that is his real self. The anger, which really belongs to the abandoning or withholding parent, has been *denied* and *turned against the self*, maintaining the compromise that is the false self. Thus, the oral character's ability to reverse, displace or substitute one object for another or one drive for another is a key to understanding his defensive structure. In treatment, it will be an essential key to unlocking his real self and his real feelings. The oral's problems tend to be cyclical and he usually will shuttle back and forth between compensation and collapse in the course of treatment. For his therapist, it will be important to understand the nature of the cycles and to keep him in treatment when it appears that the compensation is once again working or when he is in the hypomanic phase of new or rekindled love when he is inclined to think that the promise of symbiosis will conquer all.

The accompanying table, though oversimplified, describes what

Table 11
EXPRESSIONS OF ORALITY

	Oral Collapsed	*Oral Compensated*
Affect (feeling)	Depressed or *Lonely, despairing, and longing	Conscious: Good to elated to manic euphoria. Unconscious: Resentful, enraged, despairing, and fearful of loss.
Behavior	Withdrawn, self-absorbed, irresponsible, dependent, complaining, lacking energy or *Reaching for help	Overly nurturing of others. Takes on more responsibility and independent action than can be sustained. Makes plans which are optimistic to grandiose or unrealistic. Charged with ungrounded energy. Cares for self poorly—poor diet and sleep habits, overworks, plays too hard, excessive drug use.
Cognition (attitude)	Helpless and victimized or *Motivated to change	Conscious: Optimistic to grandiose Preconscious: "I am sweet, soft, and entirely giving. I am needed." Unconscious: Self-deprecating; "If I need, I will be despised or abandoned."

*Position from which most dramatic change can be initiated.

one will see with the oral character in his collapsed versus his compensated condition. Though one may see a few individuals whose collapse is chronic or whose oral issues are so minor that they can maintain fairly reliable compensations, the more typical pattern is one of fluctuation between the compensated and collapsed conditions. This is, of course, most obvious in manic-depressive* patients or in those clearly demonstrating a cyclothymic disorder. Like all the rest of us, the oral character is attached to his defenses and is particularly enamored with himself in the elated phase of his mood swing. He is not easy to help in that phase, but analysis of his grandiosity and the pattern of his mood swings can assist in this part of any ongoing treatment. He is also not easy to help when he has shut off all feeling, become depressed, withdrawn, self-absorbed, helpless, and victimized, as summarized in the top section of the table labeled "Oral Collapsed." He can most reliably be helped when the real despairing and longing emerges, motivating him at last to reach for help and take responsibility for change. Helping him to reach this uncomfortable yet hopeful place is a central goal of treatment.

It is in the course of treatment that the oral's secrets will begin to emerge. As his own neediness, weakness, and self-centeredness are uncovered, he will experience the depth of his self-hatred. Unlike the schizoid, the oral experiences self-hate less as an alien force which overcomes him and more as a conscious loathing of the weak and dependent person he feels himself to be. The hatred is not so much an unassimilated introject, as in the schizoid case, but more a redirection of his own hatred for the mother to himself. He may admit to longstanding fear of "needing too much" and to the script decision, "If I need too much I will be despised and abandoned." Frozen in his response to the symbiotic withdrawal, he is still enraged, despairing, and fearful of further loss. That "intense and violent hatred for the mother" of which Bowlby (1969, p. 24) speaks has been denied and turned against the self. The oral character is in the classic depressive position in which feelings of love and hate have been directed at the same object (the mother). The hatred has blocked the love and the love has been instrumental in blocking the hatred. With the affect

---

*Manic-depression illness often has an organic basis, but may be affected by personality factors.

depressed, there is a consequent depression. Typically, the oral person, whose ideal self is invested in his loving, caring, and soft nature, is alarmed by the seething rage that he finds within. As with the schizoid character, uncovering these unconscious beliefs and feelings and releasing the physical and cognitive blocks to expression constitute the road home.

There is a good deal of similarity between the issues of the oral and schizoid character, as well as a tendency for those with oral issues to have schizoid issues and vice versa. Indeed, clinicians who use the character analytic approach will often refer to their "oral-schiz" cases in conference with their peers. It is obvious that a child who is unwanted or despised will often be poorly nurtured. Similarly, when a child is too much for the parent, as in the oral case, the child's very existence confronts the parent with his limitations. That child may then well be the target of the parent's rage as that unwanted limitation is experienced by the parent. Both oral and schizoid characters have their primary difficulty in the attachment process and experience consequent difficulties in later attachments. Both tend to be weaker, more vulnerable, and less well-nourished than the character types that are created later in the developmental process.

Because of these similarities and overlaps, it may be useful, for educational purposes, to summarize the differences in etiology, behavior, attitude, and feeling. Where the schizoid's issue involves existence and survival, the oral's involves need. In other words, the oral character has relatively little concern about his right to exist and less worry over survival issues, but is more concerned with his right to need and with finding or losing his major attachment figure. According to object relations theory, the primary anxiety shifts from the fear of annihilation in the initial developmental period to the fear of the loss of the love object. Because the oral has experienced greater attachment, he is more contactable and open, less distanced or detached. While the denial of aggression is central in both characters, the oral has more access to feelings. Even with the aggressive impulse, there is generally more accessibility to it in the oral through conscious bitterness and resentment.

Having evolved to a higher level of ego development before the character-shaping trauma occurred, the oral is more sophisticated in his defenses, employing more reversal, displacement, and identification. There is more poignancy and drama in his life and, except in collapsed depression, less deadness. Along with this, the oral is more prone to affective mood swings than is the schizoid. At a cognitive level, the difference is highlighted in the core script decisions: In the schizoid, "There is something wrong with me. I have no right to exist." In the oral, "I mustn't need too much. I must do it alone." In addition, of course, there are also the similarities and differences in energetic expression, which are dealt with in the next section.

ENERGETIC EXPRESSION

Here I will present the observations of a number of body oriented therapists on the bodily consequences of the oral etiology. The proposition is that, in the process of self-negation, the person will constrict those muscles that will restrain the natural, spontaneous, original self-expression, as well as the innate emotional reaction to the environmental negativity. For the most part, the bodily consequences of character development are a result of the self-negation process. To a much lesser extent, they may also be reflective of the adjustment process, such that the individual changes himself, particularly in the more developed character structures, to present the image of his ego ideal to the world in the form of an adjustment mask.

As you will recall, the oral, as a part of the self-negation process, must inhibit his awareness and expression of need. In addition, he must suppress all of his natural and spontaneous reactions to having his needs unmet. Thus, in order to get on with life, he must suppress his rage at being abandoned or unfulfilled, his eventual and profound despair at that reality, and his fear of being abandoned again, either literally or emotionally. One of the simplest ways to achieve the suppression of all feeling, as has been outlined for the schizoid, is to simply restrict breathing. Many bioenergetic therapists have noticed that those with oral histories tend to do this by pulling the shoulders forward, thereby effecting a constricted and sunken chest, with frequent actual depression in the region of the sternum. As a consequence, the oral appears to have a collapsed chest and rounded shoulders.

Beyond this generalized restriction in breathing, the oral character demonstrates his inability to reach out on a concrete body level. Characteristically, there is a great deal of chronic tension in the entire shoulder girdle region and accompanying tension in the upper back between the shoulder blades. If you assume this posture, collapsing the chest and rolling the shoulders forward, you will find that your head naturally goes forward so that you are "leading with your head."

Next, to inhibit the crying and despair even further, the oral person will tense the lower abdominal muscles to restrain the sobbing and tighten the muscles at the base of the neck and up to the jaw. These energetic changes also serve to suppress aggressive impulses and fear. The tension in the shoulder girdle, upper back, and pectorals inhibit striking out, as well as reaching out, as the constriction around the base of the neck and in the jaw inhibit the direct expression of aggression. The inhibition of breathing inhibits the experience of fear itself, as does the clamping of the jaw.

If you experiment by taking the position described, you will experience that the oral character is in a difficult and uncomfortable position. Intake of the most basic environmental supply has been limited and expression constrained and held in. Chronic tension and restraint take energy, yet little is being supplied. At the same time, in denying your need and dependence you must now stand up independently on your own two feet and get on with life. To do this, the oral person may well walk prematurely and brace himself in that walking by a chronic stiffening in the knees. Such stiffening will increase the already chronic tension in the lower back, thereby causing the pelvis to roll forward. Typically, then, the oral person is weak in his overall muscular development. While the basic bone structure may be normal or even elongated, the muscular structure is typically underdeveloped. His legs are typically not solid, healthy, and muscular-looking but rather weak and even thin. Like the schizoid, he does not feel in solid contact with the ground and that may be observed in the appearance of his legs. Given all of this, the oral is quite literally a "pushover" in the world.

The eyes, as the windows of the soul, betray the oral character's true nature. The expression in the eyes has variously been described as needy, sympathetic, soulful, even begging. As the eyes of the schizoid character betray his deadness and withdrawal from the world, the eyes of the oral betray his true neediness. However giving or strongly independent the oral character may strive to be, this dependent posture and obvious lack of strength in the body and longing expression in the eyes give him away. He is really a pushover, weak, needy, and self-centered. He hates himself for this, but is still looking for someone who will affirm and love him for this real self—a very tall order.

It usually proves instructive to compare the schizoid and oral body structure, in that there are a number of similarities as well as a number of differences. In both cases, you are dealing with individuals who are weak and vulnerable due to insufficient acceptance and nurturing very early in their development. Both harbor fearful expectations of the world and are dealing with very strong negative feelings about what was done to them. In both, there is an inhibition of the life force and in breathing, which sustains that force. There is a corresponding lack of firm grounding, concretely represented in weakness and stiffness in the feet and legs. Both character types tend to be prone to illness, psychosomatic or otherwise.

The classic oral energetic expression does, however, differ in several ways from that of the schizoid. The oral's musculature tends to be more flaccid and less defined than the schizoid's, which can appear contracted, compact, stiff, and dead. While the eyes of the schizoid betray the withdrawal and even shock of the hated child or the frozen terror with which he must deal, the eyes of the oral tend to betray his need, longing, and despair. The oral's eyes signal that he is more contactable—more able to establish and maintain attachment. The oral is, in short, more "there" than the schizoid. The distortion in the oral's posture, marked most obviously by the forward thrust of the head and pelvis, is more obvious than the schizoid's typical distortion. As mentioned earlier, however, these distinctions are often more academic than real, in that the oral and schizoid issues often coexist in the same person.

As mentioned in the last section, the oral character is, like the schizoid, prone to illness. Because of the general weakness of the person, deficiencies in self-nurturing, and the tendency to hypomania which overwhelms the already fragile body defenses, the oral person tends to get sick a lot. She is susceptible to infection and illness generally, yet there are areas of particular vulnerability. Because of the tension in the base of the neck and jaw, there is a susceptibility to headache. The constriction of breathing, as well as the general weakness of the person, makes the oral character particularly susceptible to upper respiratory difficulties and infection. Because there is chronic tension in the lower back and lower abdominal region, there is a propensity toward low back pain or injury and lower abdominal illness such as irritable bowel syndrome, spastic colitis, etc. Because of the chronic spasticity in the shoulder girdle and upper back region, there is a susceptibility to pain, injury, or spinal subluxation in this region. Finally, because of the weakness in the legs and tendency to lock the knees, there is an increased susceptibility to knee injuries. Because of all of this, and the additional secondary gain features of illness, the oral character is often perceived as sickly, hypochondriacal, and psychosomatic.

THERAPEUTIC OBJECTIVES

Affect and Sensation

In this section, I will discuss the therapeutic objectives for the oral character involving emotions and the body. It will be critical, in the case of the oral, to release for experience and expression both the denied needs and those suppressed emotions that resulted from a chronic frustration of those needs. To effect and support that, it will also be necessary to change the person's experience of his body such that, for example, he experiences his feet and legs as solidly supportive and his body as able to fully breathe, relax, and let go of the chronic tension.

The oral person will be threatened by the emergence of his own neediness. When experiencing it he will often say, "God, I hate that feeling. It is degrading and humiliating. No one wants a baby." The emergence of the real need threatens the entire compensatory adjustment with its associated self-concepts, philosophies, and coping behaviors. Working through the resistance at all levels to the real underlying need will be a crucial part of the therapy of the oral character.

Though the liberation of the neediness will be central, it is often not the place to begin because of the understandably massive resistance to its experience. Indeed, it is often in the process of liberating other feelings for experience and expression that the underlying theme of pervasive neediness will be realized. The abandoned child may most easily be reached affectively by hearing his complaints and sympathizing with his pain and sorrow, which will eventually grow in therapy to deep despair at the chronic disappointment of unmet needs. Very often he will suppress his complaining in other contexts, either because he has himself turned against such overt display of weakness or because others are simply sick and tired of hearing his whining. An accepting and sympathetic ear will be greatly appreciated and begin the process of affective expression, which will lead to reclaiming the self.

Although there is a great deal of resistance to accessing the deep rage in the oral character, its not-so-distant cousins, resentment and irritability, are usually readily available. These sparks can be judiciously fanned and the resulting flames of anger can be nurtured until a raging fire of hostility is eventually uncovered. Along this path, major resistance will also be elicited because of the deep denial of this affect and the person's great investment in seeing himself as benevolent, loving, and all-nurturing.

Throughout the release of all of these feelings, the person with an oral issue will encounter fear. The experience and release of the neediness, rage and despair will all elicit the fear of rejection and abandonment. Not without reason, the oral fears, "No one will want anybody who is this needy, hostile, and desperately unhappy."

The oral person is correct is concluding that he must "grow up." Yet to do that fully, she must not skip maturational steps, as she has before. She must not try to sprint before she can walk. She must be nurtured, learn to bring the nurturing of others to her directly and, of course, learn to nurture herself.

The oral, like the schizoid, must develop *understanding* — both literally and figuratively. On a sensory level, this translates into reducing the chronic holding in the body and establishing simple grounding and strengthening. Additional work to strengthen the general musculature and accompanying sense of solidity, strength, and reliability in the functioning of the body will assist in this growing-up process. This grounding and general strengthening will serve to enhance experience and expression of the natural hostility, as well as strengthening the individual's healthy aggression and assertiveness. As this strengthening is accomplished, a therapist working on a body level will endeavor to release the spasticity in the lower back and abdomen, shoulder girdle, base of the neck, and jaw. Further, there will be repeated work on opening the chest, the breathing, and the energy flow through the neck and throat.*

---

*These changes need not be effected by direct body therapy but may result from any intervention that liberates the oral character to experience his real self.

When the body is nurtured, strengthened, and grounded in reality, when the breathing and natural flow of energy are opened through the body, and when the suppressed affects are released, the real loving of the oral person may begin to emerge and take on a more adult form. The oral person did make an attachment and, once the abandonment is worked through, he may begin to really trust again, grow up, individuate, and direct his love from a *differentiated self* to a *differentiated other*. Then, and only then, his legitimate adult needs can be met. He can be cared for and genuinely caring, dependent yet genuinely independent, relaxed and genuinely enthused about life.

Cognitive: Attitudes and Beliefs

It is perhaps most evident in the oral character case that the conscious attitudes and beliefs are polar opposites of the unconscious attitudes and beliefs. At a cognitive level, the therapist's job is to assist the client in identifying this polarity and developing mental understanding, insight, and knowledge about the self. Thus, the oral character must eventually realize that she prematurely contracted against her own infantile nature and developed a compensatory false self, offering to others what she did not receive. Though highly developed, and often quite effective externally, her nurturing nature is psychically an attempt to obtain nurturing either directly or vicariously. Her nurturing in very close relationships is often experienced as a demand.

The oral person may be helped to appreciate how she engineers or creates her own loneliness and even abandonment in relationships. She may be led to develop insight into her own script decisions, "I don't need. I have to do it alone. If I need I will be despised and abandoned." Further, she can be helped to appreciate how these script decisions fuel the "games" that she plays, which repeatedly justify the reassertion of these basic life decisions. Though she typically offers love and nurturance and though she can typically deliver what she didn't receive for a while, her undercharged and basically infantile nature will eventually assert itself and cause the breakdown of any steady, solidly grounded, adult giving. The consequent collapse, dependency, clinging, and essentially self-centered behavior will eventually wear down the patience and affection of friends, colleagues, and lovers to the point where she may be rejected, abandoned, and frustrated again. Her demands, usually unconscious, for unconditional, total acceptance and love are inappropriate for mutual adult functioning. Just as she fears, the neediness and the collapse associated with it bring abandonment. Inevitably, they lead to a reassertion of the essential script decision and of the compensatory moves to grow up in order to be acceptable. The flight to compensation, then, sets up the progression toward collapse, and so on. This pattern is, of course more destructive, dramatic, and persuasive as one descends in overall structure. The fluctuations of a person with character style can be invisible while those of one with a personality disorder are profound.

Insight into the cycle will prove to be a very useful tool for the adult oral character. As this is done, the therapist can begin to work to dismantle those defenses that fuel the compensation: denial, projection, introjection, reversal, identification, turning against the self, and displacement. Always keeping in mind the oral's need for continued acceptance and support, you can explain, challenge, confront, interpret, or otherwise undermine the defensive systems, which keep the pattern going. These cognitive strategies related to insight about the cycle are particularly useful during the excited or hypomanic phase of the oral's process if combined with physical grounding strategies.

As all of this is done, and as these insights are complemented by affective and behavioral changes, the oral person will begin to be able to see herself as she really is. She will be able to admit to her infantile and needy nature, knowing that she came by it honestly and acknowledging that she does need to grow up. She will identify with her history of abandonment and chronically unmet needs. Knowing that these are the wounds to be healed, she can more realistically devote herself to the growing-up process. She will then not attempt to override her vulnerability, but realistically work within her limitations, building her strength, reality relatedness, and instrumental abilities.

Throughout this entire process, it will be important to repeatedly affirm the oral's right to need and to strengthen the identification of the self with those needs. In simple affirmation terms, we hope for the oral person to achieve this: "I have the right to need. I have the right to ask that my needs be met. I have the right to reach out and take what I need, respecting the rights of others. I can take care of myself. I can be alone. I have the right to mourn the losses I have sustained. I can be strong. I am whole in myself. I have the right to want love and to love another."

When any of us come from our true ground, there is a fundamental solidity and strength in that. Even when that ground is as infantile and despairing as it can be in the classic oral character, there emerges a certain peace at knowing just what we are dealing with. No more energy need be wasted in maintaining the illusions, the suppression of affect, the maintenance of false ideals and hopes, and the continuance of poorly integrated behaviors. It may take many years, and perhaps more than a lifetime to repair the damage and realize the potential that living affords, but there is no longer the despair of false hopes forever unrealized. There can then be reasonably steady movement, growth, and maturation. With the early disappointments worked through and accepted, the disappointments are no longer repetitive and unabating. Then one can reach out for what is available under the circumstances, however limiting they may be, and live life from one's own realistic ground, whatever that is. This does not constitute a resignation to life; rather it represents an acceptance of a resolution with reality—a rapprochement. From that position, one can really live and appreciate life's tender mercies.

Like the schizoid, the oral also suffers from the good-bad split in his representation of self and others. This split is, of course, exemplified by the polarities he exhibits in his representation and feelings toward himself and others. The good self is independent, nurturing, active, and in other ways compensatory, while the bad self is needy, longing, despairing, unenergized, hostile, and afraid. The good other is accepting, nurturing, attention-giving, and praising, while the bad other is rejecting, abandoning, and out to persecute the weaknesses. As with the schizoid character, a central cognitive objective will be to affect the ambivalent experience of the self such that the client is aware of his real assets and similarly cognizant of the difficulties with which he must deal. A related objective, of course, is ambivalent experience of the other, who can then potentially be truly loved as a differentiated person rather than merely as a source of narcissistic supplies.

Behavioral-Social Objectives

The behavioral-social objectives for the oral character derive directly from the affective and cognitive objectives and in some ways are repetitive of what has earlier been described. The difference, of course, is that in addressing yourself to behavioral objectives, you work directly to change behavior both in and, particularly, outside of therapy. This may, in classic behavioral tradition, be effected by direct suggestion or prescription or, in hypnotic tradition, through more indirect suggestion.

A number of discrete objectives can be derived from the simple knowledge that the oral person needs to be whatever he can to get his needs met. Because he has not internalized the self-caring functions very well, it is usually necessary to suggest and even prescribe the learning of self-caring behaviors. It may be useful to help him experience the fact that his "adult part" can care for, soothe, and nurture his "child." Together with this, a number of techniques can be used to strengthen his ability to reach out and ask for help or for what he needs in all relevant social relationships. He will probably need to be encouraged to develop his aggressive and assertive nature so that he may set up his life in a way that serves him.

A part of his growing up may involve the direct learning of various instrumental behaviors, which will allow him to get more of what he wants. Thus, acknowledging that he needs, claiming the right to need and to have his needs met, may not be enough. Because his development has been retarded, there may be many areas in which he has been waiting and longing to be given what he wants. Once his assertiveness is mobilized to solve his own problems, he may need to actively learn the skills he needs in order to achieve such a set of solutions. As he takes real responsibility for himself and his adult functioning in work, family, and personal management, he may need to simply learn strategies for coping with realistic adult demands. One of those demands will be to really face his own aloneness. Behavioral strategies may be used to increase his tolerance for simply being alone and being enough for himself.

One fundamental ingredient of all of this will be an increased constancy of commitment to work, relationships, child-rearing, personal projects, etc. As the oral grows up, he will need to develop simple "stick-to-itiveness." With regard to relationships of all kinds, but particularly close love relationships, he will need to work on developing mutuality and adult-adult forms of relating, which are individuated as opposed to dependent or co-dependent. Thus, he may need to learn very discreetly and behaviorally to give *and* take rather than to simply give *or* take.

The oral character will also typically need some assistance to smooth out the cyclic hypomanic-depressive pattern. Thus, when he is feeling good he needs to be discouraged from overwork, overexercise, excessive drug use, exaggerated responsibility and nurturing of others, and all other hypomanic behaviors, which exhaust him and propel him to collapse. He needs to learn to stay in touch with himself and recognize the real signs of increased fatigue or vulnerability and then to rest. The self-administration of body or relaxation techniques may be useful to him in smoothing out the cycles, such that he moderates his activity when feeling good and enjoys peaceful relaxation when fatigued or at rest. Teaching him to use direct techniques to experience his real feelings rather than collapsing into illness or depression will also smooth out the cycle and reduce the severity of his down times. Though this is an affective objective, it may be realized by directly teaching him the techniques for emotional access and expression. Thus, the therapist may give him something to do in order to *feel* and eventually *feel better*. A program of physical exercise may be particularly important for an oral person and constitutes a strategy of self-care and strengthening; further, exercise will discourage the driveness in manic periods and bring him back to life in depressive ones.

As with every character structure, the oral's existence is devoted to preventing what has already happened—abandonment. The very maneuvers engaged in to prevent it often recreate it, together with strengthening the characterological defenses to deal with the loss. The oral must learn to stop abandoning herself, denying her needs and her natural reactions to needs unmet. When this happens, she begins to grow up by acknowledging what is infantile in her and caring for her own abandoned child. By taking responsibility in this way, she stops looking for the lost mother and is able to receive adult love.

CHAPTER 7

The Owned Child: The Symbiotic Character

LIKE ALL OTHER CHARACTEROLOGICAL ISSUES, the symbiotic one is existential and lifelong. From walking and weaning to leaving home and retirement, there are recurring opportunities to master individuation and form a new identity. To the extent that any of us suffer from functional psychopathology, we must separate from the role we adopted in our family of origin to become ourselves and to know freedom. There are very important lessons to be learned from those whose problems in living are most clearly defined by their difficulties in separation and identity formation. The strategies found successful in liberating the "symbiotic character" can be of nearly universal significance. Becoming optimally integrated with others, yet remaining autonomous, is an accomplishment of only the wisest and most fortunate.

ETIOLOGY

The essence of the symbiotic's etiology is this: Natural attempts at separation are blocked, cause parental anxiety, or are actively punished. At the same time, the child's natural abilities for empathic mirroring are overvalued and reinforced by parents who require merger with the child in order to feel secure or worthwhile.

All developmental research, whether naturalistic or experimental, confirms the need of the child for the parent in the earliest months of life—for sustenance, relationship, and regulation. The developmental research reviewed by Stern (1985) documents the remarkable degree of mother-infant attunement typical of the normal child's first year. While Stern questions the psychoanalytic notion of the child's *illusion* of fusion with the mother, his work documents that the child's actual *experience* is indeed one of unique behavioral union with the mother and that the infant's sensitivity to others in general, and the mothering figure in particular, from a very early age, is truly remarkable.

Concomitant with the need for relationship and all that it brings, there is also a natural human need for individuation. When does the need for autonomy first emerge in the human infant? It seems to me that it depends on what kind of autonomy one is talking about. Even in the first days of life, a child initiates and separates from the caregiver through the visual gaze interaction over which he shows control. Patterns of parental neglect or intrusion can begin immediately if this channel is used as the vehicle for communicating excessive closeness or distance. The infant develops an enhanced ability to move out of the parent's orbit of influence when he begins to walk at about 10 months. Mahler has noted that in the "practicing period" initiated by this change, the child becomes more independent, more engrossed in his own activities, more impervious to difficulties, and generally more adventurous. Clearly, the child will develop differently if these early adventures are supported, delighted in, and freely allowed than if these initial trials at independence are met with fearfulness, punishment, or excessive restraint. Developmental research documents that a child as young as 10 months will look to the mother for signals about the safety of venturing forth (Emde & Sorce, 1983). An anxious, overprotective mother will consistently signal that such initiations are unsafe, and the child will inevitably introject that overly fearful perspective. As a consequence, the child's orientation to this kind of self-expression will not be one resulting from the direct experience of trial and error but rather an adopted standard, which is excessively conservative, constrained, and anxious.

This incorporative introjection of standard is prototypical of the symbiotic's entire identity. It is an identity swallowed whole as a function of experience with the parent, rather than an identity developed out of the entirety of experience in the interaction of self with environment. This fact lies behind a therapeutic theme that I have found useful with every symbiotic character. Stated simply, the theme is this: "That is not who you are" and "That's not you." This simple intervention repeatedly reminds the individual to reexamine his standards, beliefs, reactions, etc., on the basis of his actual experience of himself and the world and, in so doing, fosters individuation and the development of a real self.

Developmental experiments (e.g., Stern, 1985) indicate that children discover that there are other minds in the world and that others have changeable subjective states as early as seven to nine months of age. Mahler's more naturalistic observation of children shows that, at about 15 months of age, children evidence more noticeable behavior that indicates they understand the concept that their experience is both different from that of others and shareable. The rapprochement period (15 to 24 months) refers to the returning of the infant from practicing to a more intense relationship with the parent. Rapprochement is begun when the child starts bringing objects to the parent, presumably to get the parent to share in the child's experience of that object. While the developmental research indicates that the child has awareness of separate subjectivity prior to this time, it would appear that during rapprochement children begin to appreciate more fully the implications of this knowledge and begin to act upon it in these more obvious ways.*

At this same time, Spitz (1982) has noted that children make the discovery of the wonderful "no" word. Like the adolescent's loud music and radical haircuts, the rapprochement child begins to assert an autonomous identity through opposition. How the environment responds to these various assertions of autonomy and requests for a new kind of intimacy will determine the extent to which the child feels comfortable in asserting this form of autonomy and requesting this form of attention. During these crucial initial periods of individuation, we may ask: Is the child allowed some negativity with limits? Is negativity completely indulged or severely punished? Is the inter-

---

*I believe this delay between awareness and full appreciation of the implications of that awareness accounts for the fact that experimental research (e.g., Stern) shows earlier acquisition of abilities than naturalistic research (e.g., Mahler).

subjective experience available and if it is, is there a mutuality in who leads it and who follows? Is the intersubjective experience contingent on compliance or restraint on the part of the child?

These experiences are among the first that affect the individual's sense of independent agency — a sense that is weakened in every symbiotic character. Typically, the symbiotic looks outside himself for the agenda in his life. He has a poor sense of his own likes and dislikes, as they have not been allowed to spontaneously develop nor been given adequate support. In mirroring others, he finds a greater sense of security — his "security operation" is an accommodating false self. He experiences aggression, assertion, and particularly, opposition as dangerous.

As Freud has pointed out, another type of autonomy issue develops in response to the need of the environment to socialize the child. At about 24 months of age, toilet training as well as other socialization demands become more salient. Obviously, the child's sense of autonomy is affected by how all this is handled. Is the timing of these socializations geared to the child's abilities and emerging inclination to be socialized? Is there rigidity or flexibility in the parents' orientation to the problems? Is the child gently corrected or severely punished or humiliated for errors? Is the child allowed some self-control or is she symbolically or literally invaded (e.g., with food, enemas, etc.)? In other words, is there an interaction between the abilities, inclinations, and talents of the child with the demands of the environment, or do these demands overpower and otherwise injure the child? Is the child's willfulness allowed but moderated or is it crushed? When the will is crushed, the life issue is more one of overcontrol, and I think the characterological formulation is more properly differentiated from the symbiotic issue and labeled masochistic. As is probably obvious, however, the symbiotic and masochistic issues commonly exist together because they reflect different forms of autonomy frustration. I separate them, not from a commitment to any particular developmental model, but for reasons of clinical utility. There is a distinct difference in the constellation of symptoms and therapeutic themes in these two types, even though they have some similarities and can coexist in the same person.

We can characterize these three forms of autonomy as reflecting the individual's orientation to agency, adventure, and self-control. The remainder of the individual's life will contain experiences that give the opportunity for additional or revised learning in these areas, and change is always possible. Yet, the experience of the young human the first few times around is usually of paramount importance, particularly when his experience is of a traumatic nature and the abilities, strategies, and defenses used to cope with trauma are more likely to become fixed. This very real "developmental arrest" will tend to persist throughout life in relation to the affected form of autonomy. It is also often true that parents who have any real difficulty with the child's expression of autonomy at 10 months of age are going to have similar difficulties with later varieties of autonomous expression. So, the first time the issue becomes an issue is generally prototypic of future confrontations of that particular issue.

The combination of developmental arrest with the consistently frustrating environmental response to adventure, agency, or self-control can often combine to negate the potential effects of new learning experiences which might be corrective. For these reasons, then, an otherwise normal adult may still be operating with the defenses, strategies, and belief systems that derive almost exclusively from the traumatic experiences of a very young child. This fact, which we all find difficult to believe, becomes more believable for the therapist who sees this model of psychopathology compatible with the facts again and again. It is also believable to tortured clients who directly experience their symptomatic behavior, attitudes, and feelings as childlike and outside the influence of their adult, direct experience and knowledge. Particularly upon analysis, patients experience that part of their reality that is symptomatic as based on a model of the world and themselves that is clearly discrepant from current reality. Sometimes without psychotherapy and very often with only a little of it, they can begin to say, "This is not me. This is not how it really is."

In considering the symbiotic's essential lack of self, it is important to understand how a "self" is formed. This involves an understanding of how internal functions and structures are built as well as how external functions are internalized and modify the existing structures. I have found psychoanalytic developmental observation and theory, as well as Piagetian concepts, to be particularly useful in this understanding. Basically, that which originates from the inside requires an "optimal indulgence" of the emerging person with an attuned mirroring of developing abilities. The "gleam in the mother's eye" (Mahler) at the child's developing abilities to walk, talk, and individuate throughout childhood and into adolescence exemplifies this requirement. At the same time, the environment must allow an optimal level of frustration in the child's acquisition of abilities, concepts, etc. Thus, the self is developed through exercise of self. Classically, this has often been termed the strengthening of self through the "exercise of function."

Internalization, that process by which what is outside the self is taken in and made one's own, may be understood in a hierarchical way. At the lowest level of development, or consciousness, if you will, there is a process which I will label "incorporative introjection." Here, the individual seems to swallow the other whole, and there is no assimilation of the other into the self. There is no digestive process by which what is outside is transformed into what is inside. The incorporative introjection is in some ways similar to the Kohutian concept of a merger transference in which the individual sees the other as literally part of himself, failing to differentiate or perceive realistic boundaries.

In describing this, I am often reminded of the picture I once saw of a snake that had just swallowed a rabbit. Prior to the snake's digestive processes going to work on the rabbit, the snake no longer looks like a snake, but rather an odd configuration of snake and rabbit. In the psychoanalytic literature, this is often referred to as an unassimilated introject, or an example of incorporation. One can often observe this phenomenon in adolescents or other immature individuals who embrace whole a religious, philosophical, or political cult without developing a very complete understanding of the underlying belief structure. Such action is taken in the absence of a well-developed self, and the incorporative introjection shores up a defective self.

At a higher level of development is the process of identification, wherein the individual copies or borrows or fuses his identity with someone else. In psychoanalytic theory, the primary identification is presumed to occur in that period of infancy when the individual has yet to distinguish between himself and the other. Secondary identification is the same phenomenon but occurs with the recognition of the separateness of the other. While the work of Stern and others would call this theoretical distinction into question, it is still useful to recognize that identification can take place with varying degrees of awareness or consciousness of the process itself. Identification that is conscious and selective is more cognitively mediated and thus developmentally more sophisticated. This process is analogous to Kohut's concept of the twinship transference, in which the self and other are seen as identical, as well as in the concept of an idealization transference, where the individual tries to emulate a superior figure.

At the higher level of development is the phenomenon that I will label internalization, in which there is some process of assimilation or accommodation, such that what is taken in becomes one's own. There is, then, some work involved in internalization. Typically, there is an effort over a period of time to fit the externally derived idea, belief, skill, or function into the existing experience and expression of the self so that it becomes congruent and integrated with other expressions. This is assimilation. Even more effort is typically necessary when the Piagetian (1936) process of accommodation is required. Here, the individual must actively change some part of the self structure to congruently hold the new material brought in from the outside. In all of these "transmuting internalizations" (Kohut, 1984), there must be some tension or frustration to work through. This fact, I think, underlies the conventional wisdom that "hardship builds character."

So, how do these processes typically work in the formation of self for the symbiotic character? To one extent or another, the internal demands for individuation are not appropriately mirrored, echoed, and prized. In particular, ideas, abilities, ambitions, or behaviors that will make the person different from her caretakers or that will result in any kind of separation are not reinforced, but are ignored or actively punished. Furthermore, in the etiology of the symbiotic, caretakers often help the individual avoid experiencing the kind of frustration that would lead to the development of initiative in dealing with life. So there is a combination of overindulging dependency and undervaluing initiative. This, in turn, leads quite naturally to reliance on the more immature forms of identity formation; namely, incorporative introjection and identification. This results in "a self I can't call my own," with a diminished sense of agency, intentionality, initiative, and identity.

Therefore, a good deal of the symbiotic's life work involves the rediscovery and development of the self. This involves the rediscovery of innate abilities, capacities, and aptitudes that eventually can develop into interests, tastes, preferences, etc. This may involve the discovery of athletic, intellectual, or artistic propensities, which have gone uncultivated and therefore still require recognition, support, and reinforcement. Along with this, of course, is the requirement for a kind of individualized reassessment in developing one's identifications, idealizations, and introjections. It is necessary for the symbiotic to face up to his or her own indulgence in failing to adequately internalize functions and structures that to some extent, must develop from the outside in.

I believe that the real difficulty in treating the symbiotic character is in overcoming the natural ease with which this person will remain passive with respect to her own internal impulses while simultaneously borrowing an identity from others. These strategies are so well ingrained, so effortless, and so insidiously capable of providing temporary fulfillment and escape from uncomfortable frustration that they are often very difficult to overcome. For this reason, it is not surprising that the symbiotic characterological issue is so often found in those who compulsively overeat. This kind of incorporation soothes, fills a void, and often serves to blot out uncomfortable affects, obviating the necessity for some kind of discipline in one's social and intellectual life—a discipline that is all the harder due to the history of deficient support for individuation and overindulgence of dependence.

In sum, the essential message from the parent to the symbiotic is, "You can have the sustenance you require from me only if you deny the development of your self. You can have me or you, not both." Autonomy, in whatever form, becomes a danger situation. Consequently, the need for it is repressed, and with it, that natural aggression necessary for separation is squelched. Compromise solutions in the classic neurotic forms are then often developed and refined in order to achieve some semblance of autonomy while preventing the feared abandonment. Herein lies the conflict for the symbiotic character, which can be understood through the classic psychoanalytic model: the wish for autonomy and the fear of having it. The deficit for the symbiotic character exists in the developmental arrest around this issue and the failures in new learning that result from it. These include the symbiotic's failure to form good self-other boundaries, to develop a sense of safety in adventure, a sense of self-agency, and all these in aggregate—a good sense of self. Rather, there is the development of a chameleon-like false self in which the individual looks for his identity not in himself but in the other.

BEHAVIOR, AFFECT, COGNITION

Behavior

The symbiotic's life is exceedingly object related. There is no sphere of her life that is not almost continually involved with others, and indeed, activity that is independent, autonomous, or disconnected from others is experienced as dangerous, selfish, immoral, and injurious to others. The symbiotic experiences her experience only in relation to others and can have great difficulty in self-activation if another is not present in that activity somewhere. The needs of the other are necessary to initiate activity, and the other's responses are necessary to sustain it.

One client reported that, just as she began to become interested in reading a book, she would begin to think of other friends and family who would be interested in or benefit from the book. With these thoughts, her own self-determined interest in the book would wane, and she would fail to attend to what she was reading. She would then put the book down, never return to it for herself, and deny herself what she experienced as a great pleasure.

As the symbiotic person gains insight, he will confess to the fact that there is very little of intrinsic interest to him; he doesn't know what activities, hobbies, or fields of interest draw him personally. Typically, he will not have a very well-developed sense of taste in things, for his preferences and activities have been adopted rather than acquired. These phenomena are a reflection of the absence of any real developed sense of self apart from relationship. He molds himself to the interests and tastes of others and, in a sense, finds his only real sense of self in losing himself in the other.

This lack of self-other boundary makes the symbiotic person exceedingly vulnerable to the affective states of others. He can easily absorb or be invaded by others' affects, and his equilibrium can be easily affected by them. He is particularly vulnerable to a significant other's upset with him and may well be prone to interpreting such upset as a threat of abandonment or rejection. Thus, a disruption of the affective tone of important relationships in upsetting or even disorganizing, and a good deal of the symbiotic's activity at such times, both cognitive and behavioral, will be directed at restoring the relationship equilibrium.

Though these propensities can be highly problematic, the higher functioning symbiotic person can be particularly well attuned to the needs and feelings of others, and his empathic abilities may be quite profound. The ability to get under another's skin, as it were, can serve him in many ways as long as the relationship is relatively conflict-free and unthreatened.

Perhaps the most interesting aspect of the symbiotic's behavior is his tendency to engage in thought patterns and behaviors that serve the purpose of preserving the original, pathogenic relationship. Behaviorally, this involves such things as selecting friends, colleagues, and mates who replicate in some significant way the binding features of the original object or, through projective identification, recreating that in others. The symbiotic's life is often filled with people who require a good deal of sensitive mirroring, whose feelings can be easily hurt, who actively or passively demand attuned holding, and who are very difficult to satisfy. In short, the symbiotic picks others for close relationships who justify her projections, or she helps them to provide such justification. By so doing, the symbiotic character now has a role to fill, and thereby she has a self. The void and fragmentation of the real self are avoided by the immersion in the other. Such immersion can, at least at times, look compulsive in the behavioral realm and obsessive in the cognitive realm. Thus, the person with a symbiotic issue may go to great lengths to placate or accommodate the other, particularly where this may reduce the other's negative affect. The symbiotic individual not only absorbs the other's negative states but also takes responsibility for them.

In psychotherapy, the *interpretation of preservation* of the pathogenic relationship is usually a ubiquitous theme in the symbiotic's treatment. However, what is important is to anticipate that accepting such an interpretation, much less acting on it, will elicit anxiety, guilt, and even emptiness of the self. For, while the symbiotic can keep herself busy, either accommodating or resisting the needs of the other, to live without that kind of relationship may seem literally impossible, not to mention morally wrong. Fairbairn's (1974) work is particularly helpful in achieving an understanding of the role of this deep human need to preserve object ties in maintaining psychopathology.

The person who develops a symbiotic character often becomes the carrier of responsibility for the family pain. It is as if that pain has been absorbed by the individual not necessarily by direct experience but by a kind of assimilation or uncritical inheritance. The trap, of course, is in the assumption of responsibility for something so pervasive that it may well span generations, and the individual's power to affect it is virtually nil. The assumption of responsibility is executed by an innocently egocentric child who doesn't appreciate the magnitude of the burden assumed. The psychopathology of the symbiotic person often yields to understanding when seen as the expression of the family's pathology passed on, rather than as the direct result of trauma experienced directly by the patient. This accounts for the fact that the symbiotic's symptomatology is often experienced by him as alien in the extreme and is difficult for even an experienced analyst to understand in that it doesn't seem to derive from the patient's own history, but is a derivative of the family's history more generally.

Were there no conflict about the accommodation, enmeshment, or engulfment of the symbiotic character, there would be far less of a problem. But the individual's aggression and natural desire for self-expression cannot be so easily obliterated. Like all other characterological adaptations, this is a compromise solution to an impossible problem. There is always a deep reservoir of resentment toward the other for causing the dysphoric states of anxiety, guilt, depression, and burdening responsibility, as well as for the suppression of one's natural aggression and self-expression.

So, where do the aggression and self-expression go? They go into resisting the demands for accommodation, albeit conflictually and/or they are turned against the self. The resistance can take many forms. The most common form is passive resistance in which the person withdraws from the field, forgets, or in other unconscious ways refuses and frustrates the other. In these ways, the resistance is deniable, though it still may stimulate considerable guilt. Once the resistance becomes more conscious or active, it often takes on a kind of rigidity in which the person is extraordinarily sensitive to any possibility of invasion by another. This, indeed, is not an uncommon phenomenon in the psychotherapy of these individuals, because it is essentially the self-other boundaries that cannot be well modulated. The symbiotic, in the middle of such change, can be similar to the teenager who insists on defending her "rights," and the client can get stuck in such a position if the therapist cannot assist her in achieving smoother modulation. For resisting the other is just the other side of accommodating the other. In both cases, the self is found in relationship to the other, either in accommodating or resisting, but not in self-activation.

Even where a literal other is not in the picture, the symbiotic's behavior can be best understood in the accommodation or resistance of the "evoked companion" (Stern, 1985) who is demanding and often impossible to satisfy. In this activity, as well, the individual preserves the kind of role relationship to which she has become accustomed and, thereby, preserves a false sense of self. So, whether the original relationship is preserved by finding or creating others who justify the projection and living in accommodation or resistance, or is lived out purely intrapsychically (e.g., in ruminative worry), the preservation of original role relationship is at the heart of one's life. Where that relationship cannot be preserved, the symbiotic character experiences what Masterson has termed the abandonment depression, in which the individual experiences extreme difficulty in self-activation, panic, an empty terrifying loneliness, and fragmentation of the self. It is in this state that the person reexperiences the rapprochement crisis; again without the necessary connection and support, he is alone with an enfeebled self where in individuating, separating, and autonomous activity will only serve to maintain the desolate aloneness.

The corrective emotional experience of psychotherapy with this structure involves the discovery that self-expression can now receive support. Such self-expression constitutes a "danger situation," and, both in therapy and out, the client needs to experience a kind of desensitization to it. Further, the person needs to be sustained through the separation from the enmeshed relationships that sustain a false identity, whether they are intrapsychic, transferential, or actual.

Affect

Affectively, the symbiotic character is distinguished mostly in his disturbed relationship with aggression. The aggressive impulse that is separating has been at best discouraged and at worst severely punished, so that it has not developed into a healthy, well-modulated assertiveness. Rather, the symbiotic's aggression is denied or, in borderline states, is blown off or violently directed against the self. At the lower end of the ego development continuum, hostility can appear as freely expressed rage at the perceived rejection or distancing of others or, conversely, at the perception that others are engulfing or intruding. At higher levels of ego development within this character, there is typically more defensiveness around the hostility, and its expression becomes more passive or convoluted.

The hostility exists in response to the impossible bind to which the person has had to adjust: the threat of abandonment for individuation. Thus, it is particularly elicited by any threat of abandonment or any experience of engulfment. The problem is that the feelings about such hostility are, in a very meaningful way, arrested in the experience and belief structure of the very young child. He believes that his expression of hostility will either be exceedingly destructive and depriving to the other or that it will be completely ineffective. The undercontrolled, borderline symbiotic person will more often experience his hostility as ineffectual, whereas the overcontrolled symbiotic more often will tend to experience his hostility as destructive. But this tendency can be radically reversed, and the borderline patient can indulge in the often more conscious magical thinking that his hostility is destructive, and the higher functioning person can experience that his overcontrolled responses are indeed ineffectual. At both ends of the ego development continuum, there exists this polarity around the experience and expression of hostility, and, from the symbiotic character disorder to character style, there is a consistent lack of well-modulated, goal-directed, sustained aggression.

Winnicott (1971) has been particularly instructive in emphasizing the role of aggression in the individuation process. Winnicott seemed to literally believe that the child discovers what is *not* him by trying to destroy it and finding he cannot.

More recent developmental research would certainly challenge this more radical object relations position. Still, aggression is a separating force. It establishes the existence of difference. Furthermore, it is reasonable to conjecture that a child might easily fear damage to himself or the other as a function of his own aggression (i.e., retaliation or destruction of the object). To the extent that the child operates with the illusion of "omnipotent responsibility," he may believe that his aggression literally has the power to injure or destroy. So, what is necessary to separate can easily create a danger situation in the classic analytic sense, thereby providing a conflict. The impulse or wish to aggress stimulates a complex of fears. To the extent that the parental figures can withstand and sustain themselves through this aggression, they literally desensitize the child's fears and enhance the accurate reality perception that his aggression does not necessarily injure, destroy, or lead to traumatic retaliation. This is what Winnicott means when he writes, "In the unconscious phantasy, growing up is inherently an aggressive act. . . . If the child is to become an adult, then this move is achieved over the dead body of an adult (unconsciously)" (1971, pp. 144–145).

The problem for the symbiotic character is that the necessary aggression is disallowed, and the fantasy, that aggression is inherently harmful and dangerous, is either created or reinforced. The creation of the adult through aggression is thereby prohibited, and there is a resulting developmental arrest.

For purposes of clarification, it is probably necessary to underline the meaning of symbiosis as used here: This term does not refer to the illusion that "Mommy and I are one" (Silverman & Weinberger, 1985). Rather, it refers to the experience of this character structure that the self is essentially void without enmeshment in another.

In healthy development, the child's aggressive responses are both optimally indulged and optimally frustrated. He is allowed to discover that aggression is permissible and even encouraged, but within limits. As a result of this continuing process, he learns to modulate aggression appropriately and is thereby able to increasingly express it within a middle range and evaluate his aggressive responses appropriately. When this is not the case, a polarity response around the expression and evaluation of aggression will result. In the symbiotic character of the middle to high range of structural development, the aggression will typically be overcontrolled, with excessive fear of damage and retaliation as a result of even minimal aggressive expressions, together with the breaking-through of extremely aggressive fantasies, dreams, or even behaviors, which are quite alarming and ego-dystonic. At the low end of the structural development continuum, where a borderline pathology is exhibited, there will often be the episodic lack of control of aggressive impulses, which can indeed be both destructive and stimulate retaliation. Concomitantly, the borderline personality may often see the aggression as justified.

Where one's natural aggression is habitually repressed and resentment builds, the aggressive impulse is more and more accompanied by an increasingly savage hostility, which is destructive and which would, if expressed, stimulate retaliation. As this occurs, and the person loses the distinction between aggression and hostility, the illusion of danger is no longer an illusion. The child's illusions about aggression bolstered by the parent's reinforcement of those illusions, together with the progressive change in the aggression/hostility constellation, makes what once was an illusion a reality. And, short of intervention, this snowballing continues. Finally, to the extent that there is a developmental arrest in structure, the individual must deal with the high level of aggressive and hostile impulses with limited resources. This results either in the out-of-control hostile behavior of the borderline or the more adaptive denial and passive aggression of the symbiotic character neurosis or style. In treating the symbiotic character, a great deal of therapeutic direction can be gained by continued attention to the patient's relationship with his aggression and hostility.

When natural aggression is disallowed, normal individuation cannot occur and, as a result, a separate identity or sense of self cannot be established. A true identity is built through a combination of the discovery of self through its expression and the gradual internalization of external figures through optimal indulgence and optimal frustration. When normal aggression is disallowed, neither process can unfold as it should and, as a consequence, a real-self identity cannot be adequately established.

Identity formation, such as it is, occurs through a more primitive incorporative introjection of the self-regulating other. An identity formed in this way is not truly assimilated or owned and, in the case of the symbiotic character, there will always be the need for a significant other for the experience of self-cohesion. As Meissner

(1986) has so cogently pointed out, it is this unassimilated, unincorporated, alien, and implanted identity that may be projected so readily onto others, because it is not fully one's own in the first place. This is particularly true, of course, of the uncomfortable or undesirable aspects of that identity. In the case of the symbiotic character specifically, this projection often involves the controlling, guilt-inducing, and aggression-inhibiting aspects of the introjected identity.

Concomitant with the processes outlined above, the symbiotic character has not gradually internalized the abilities to care for the self and to self-soothe. These functions remain with the external object, so that the other is needed as a vehicle for projecting the negative aspects of the introjected self as well as an instrument for performing the functions of sustenance and regulation. Thus, in the lower-level symbiotic character, the other is absolutely necessary for any semblance of the experience of cohesion, stability, or firm relationship to reality. But, if the other gets too close, the symbiotic person experiences the engulfment of a controlling and hostile force; if the other is too distant, he experiences the panic of loneliness and abandonment with a poverty of internal resources. With this extreme polarization, it is nearly impossible to find, much less maintain, an optimal distance from another. Particularly where ego strength is also quite limited, as in the borderline case, one witnesses the characteristic pattern of extreme dependency alternating with enraged distancing (Masterson, 1976). This pattern exists ubiquitously even at higher levels of structural development in the symbiotic, although its expression is more subtle and more appropriately defended from the underlying feelings.

Etiologically, the symbiotic's difficulty in modulating aggression is related to her inability to modulate distance. Aggression is separating; the symbiotic cannot aggress and therefore cannot separate. The natural impulse to aggress and to separate constitutes a danger situation. So, the individual must create some compromise solution to handle the aggressive, separating impulse, the continuing need for contact, and the increasingly realistic fear of her own destructiveness and the environment's retaliation. This compromise is the symbiotic character expressed along the dimension of ego development from borderline or dependent personality disorder to a more neurotic-like symbiotic character neurosis and style. In whatever expression, this character structure will contain the failure to reconcile two important polarities and maintain a tendency to split along these dimensions. They are aggressive vs. passive and enmeshment vs. distance. These polarities are seen in almost every expression of the symbiotic character, whether they be in the affective, behavioral, or cognitive realms.

The impulse to individuate, which may express itself variously in the wish to explore, in the expression of exuberance, in the desire to succeed, or in the expression of difference, will elicit the internalized negative consequences. Then, the individual will feel anxiety or guilt or some other form of self-imposed prohibition. That prohibition, which interferes with one's natural self-expression, naturally elicits aggression and hostility. But, again, as an expression of one's impulse to differentiate, the aggression and hostility themselves elicit the prohibition, the anxiety, the guilt, etc. There is, then, a whole cluster of impulses and affects that are conflicting, each of which the troubled individual will attempt to avoid. Neurotic-like symptomatology is the typical consequence of trying to find some compromise solution to all of these conflict-ridden impulses. When these compromise solutions work reasonably well and are ego-syntonic, we observe characterological adaptations that are not experienced as problematic but that are nevertheless typical of the individual's overall functioning and might most easily be seen as examples of character style.

As the individual goes through a psychotherapeutic process focused on her symbiotic issues, she begins to experience more and more the various forms of the impulse to individuate, the prohibitions to such differentiation, and the consequences of such prohibitions (i.e., the anxiety, the guilt, the self-sabotage, etc.). There occurs, then, a typical conflict as to how to identify with or to make ego-syntonic the originally prohibited ideas and affects. At this stage of the game, the individual may become even more neurotic in that she represents a house more consciously divided—for example, one part being more interested in adventure or success and the other part more afraid of or guilty about such impulses and ambitions. As the individuation process continues, the individual typically becomes more aware of her anger and hostility at the prohibitive injunctions and affects and, at the same time, becomes aware of the anxiety that this anger and hostility engender. In the most highly developed individuals in which this pattern is typical, analytic and reconstructive working-through can be of immeasurable assistance.

The structural development continuum is useful here in helping us understand other problematic feelings of the symbiotic character and what to do about them. At the lower end of the continuum, there is more open access to the primitive fears that make the symbiotic so emotionally vulnerable. Because the defensive structure doesn't work very well, the individual can tell you of her rage at anticipated abandonment or her terror of rejection and loneliness. The problem is in the transference acting-out of all this in her life, as well as in the therapeutic relationship, and the extent to which the powerful feelings overwhelm and disorganize her.

The person functioning at the lower structural level needs the security of an interpersonal relationship in which the boundaries are firm and caringly set with a confrontation of the destructiveness of the acting-out. At the higher end of the continuum, where things are more neurotic, and person does not have full access to what his often mysterious symptoms are all about. He may feel obliged to be ever-caring and attentive to others yet, paradoxically, show an absence of normal thoughtfulness, an absence of spontaneously generous feelings, or evidence of clearly hostile dreams or fantasies. Because the impulses to distance, separate, or aggress are unacceptable, they have become unconscious and result in behaviors that are experienced as mysterious or dystonic. Similarly, preservation of dysfunctional relationships, attitudes, and even behaviors may serve the function of allaying fears of separation, but this is also a secret. In these latter cases, the interpretation of this underlying emotional pattern can be therapeutic because it brings these "irrational" feelings into the conscious sphere where they may be understood, evaluated, and directly experienced by a person whose ego resources are capable of a reordering. The person suffering the symbiotic character style needs to know what the symbiotic borderline knows all too well — the chaotic feelings of the immature child caught in the conflict of the fear of abandonment or the fear of engulfment.

The dysphoria of the symbiotic person often relates, in one way or another, to the fundamental void in the experience of self. In the more borderline individuals, this is often acted-out in blaming others for failing to provide that necessary direction or meaning or for taking over the weakened self. As one moves up the continuum, one finds a more responsible expression of sadness at the emptiness and meaninglessness of life, either chronically or periodically. In the process of psychotherapy, the person with a symbiotic character will encounter this grief at the void in his own life in the same way as does the narcissist. This realization and the grief it brings are important to experience as a true experience of a real self.

Cognition

Central to understanding the cognitive aspects of the symbiotic character is his confusion about self-other boundaries. The experience of the self and other as fused may be held consciously or may be totally disavowed or repressed. But whether conscious, partially conscious, or unconscious, the underlying assumptions of the cognitive errors in the symbiotic have to do with this self-other fusion. There is not a realistic perception of who is responsible for what in lower functioning "borderline" structures, so there is a greater tendency for the individual to hold others responsible for her actions or states of mind. The "borderline" tends more in therapy as in life, toward transference acting-out and "turning passive into active" (Weiss & Sampson, 1986). Transference acting-out refers to the pathological reaction in which the individual sees the other as the original frustrating figure but without acknowledgement of the transference process, so that, unaware of the projective nature of the stimulus, he acts-out as if the other were as truly frustrating as he is experienced. Turning passive into active refers to the process in which the individual frustrates the other in the way that he himself was earlier frustrated. For the present character structure, this might be manifested by the individual expressing extreme disappointment in and rage at the other for failing to adequately understand, anticipate, and remedy his needs.

At higher levels of functioning, however, the tendency toward merger more often expresses itself in the excessive responsibility taken for the well-being of others. For the symbiotic characters in the neurotic range and higher, the concepts of separation guilt and survivor guilt (Modell, 1965, 1971) will prove particularly useful. In these cases, the child's natural tendencies toward "omnipotent responsibility" have been reinforced rather than gently disabused, so that the individual believes that his individuation will literally hurt the one he loves and on whom he depends. The belief is that separation really hurts the other and that one is responsible for that hurt. Not far removed from this is the magical notion of survivor guilt: the belief that the positive experience of life itself will be purchased at the expense of the other. Having anything good in life is, in this inaccurate model of reality, the result of taking it away from someone else. Weiss (in Weiss & Sampson, 1986, p. 43), writes, "the child may develop guilt . . . not only about motives such as incest and murder, which are generally considered reprehensible, but also about reasonable and generally accepted goals, such as becoming stronger or deriving greater enjoyment from life. Indeed, a person may suffer from guilt or anxiety about relaxing, or about feeling healthy and happy."

Many individuals with this characterological issue were told discreetly and repetitively that they were indeed responsible for their parent's well-being and that separation in any form — from adventure to difference of opinion to self-expression in which the parent could or would not engage — was injurious to that parent. This "How could you do this to me, your parent?" message reinforces what appears to be the child's natural tendency to err in the direction of "omnipotent responsibility." Furthermore, this kind of conditioning occurs during developmental periods in which it is vitally important for the child to maintain solidly positive ties to the parent, and during which he will sacrifice almost anything to do so. So it is no wonder that the child will accept and identify with the parent's construction of reality and then see himself as bad to the extent that he does not live up to it.

If the symbiotic individual could have separated gradually and with support, the other would have become gradually less vital and central to her sense of identity. However, because that did not occur, the other remains vital to the symbiotic character at an emotional level, as is normal for a young child between one and two years of age. This is an extremely debilitating set with which to enter adult life, particularly in modern Western cultures. The solution constructed maintains symbiotic contact with the other while, at the same time, living an adult life with all its autonomy demands.

Underneath the complexity of highly neurotic solutions, one will often find the script decisions or "pathogenic beliefs" of the following nature: "I am nothing without you. I owe you myself. I don't deserve what you can't share. I deserve punishment for my success. I can't be happy unless you are. I am responsible for your unhappiness," etc. These beliefs are often unconscious for a number of reasons. They may have been verbally disavowed by the very parent who promulgated them nonverbally; they may have been disavowed by the individual in order for him to survive in the world, they may be seen by his rational conscious mind as inappropriate, etc. Underlying all this, one often finds the belief, often based on threats or on actual experience, that the assertion of one's autonomy will result in abandonment. Particularly to the extent that this is true and to the extent that one faces adult life with the emotional organization of a child, this is very effective in keeping the individual from truly emerging. As these sorts of beliefs are uncovered in psychotherapy, the intricacy of what Modell has termed "mental bookkeeping" can be truly remarkable. For example, an individual might pay for his success by not enjoying it or in some way sabotaging himself. Because of the internalization, it's often the case that the individual will replicate the more self-destructive patterns of his parent in this bookkeeping effort.

As with the other structures where the primary psychic trauma occurs in the process of individuation (i.e., narcissistic and masochistic), the central objective of psychotherapy is the resurrection and development of the true self. This process first involves the discovery and then selective removal or modification of those aspects of self that are solely the product of incorporative introjection, inappropriate indoctrination, self-destructive identification, and inappropriate decisions. While this "false self" is not as obviously false as in the narcissistic personality, it is, nonetheless, artificial, adopted, and imposed. The erosion of this malignant self will leave a void and an emerging need for the discovery and development of a true sense of self, a realistic self-concept, and a set of behaviors that defines the self. In higher functioning individuals, the void may be more easily filled, as the individual takes ownership of that part of his life with which he can truly identify and uses his considerable skills to develop additional areas of self-functioning. In lower functioning individuals, the entire process will take longer because there is greater requirement for the remedying of deficits and some substantial filling of a

real void. In either case, there will be periods of the experience of
the void and a need for the therapist to deal with this phenomenology
in the patient.

Psychotherapy of the symbiotic issue involves taking ownership
of the self and rebuilding it where it has been enfeebled. Fortunately,
however, the *feelings* of enfeeblement are usually more regressed
than the actual development of the self. Indeed, one popular compromise solution for the symbiotic character involves the development
of the capacities of the self while denying such capacities. Once the
right to ownership of the self is reclaimed, a relatively speedy recovery is possible for these individuals.

THERAPEUTIC OBJECTIVES

Affective Objectives

The central affective therapeutic objective with the symbiotic
character is to assist the individual in expressing himself more freely,
particularly expressing those affects that have been inhibited and
disallowed. Most often, this involves the expression of assertion,
aggression, and hostility, though often other more benign affects are
also involved. To effect this, the therapy for all those other than the
acting out borderline must reduce the individual's sense of obligation
to others, his generalized guilt at self-expression, and particularly,
his fear of hurting others through self-expression or succeeding at
others' expense. Somewhere along the way, the therapy will have to
involve accessing the client's real hostility at others, usually at the
imagined or real restraint or intrusion that they are seen to impose.

Frequently, the psychotherapy of the symbiotic character will involve dealing with affective states that grow out of identification
with the affective states of others—usually the parent. It is not uncommon, for example, to see individuals in this category who experience life as overwhelming, extraordinarily unfair, depriving, abusive, etc., not so much because this was their *direct* experience, but
because it was the experience of their immediate and even extended
family. These "adopted affects" need to be understood for what they
are and returned to their original owners. Often, the patient's family
has encouraged this kind of maladaptive identification and indoctrinated the patient with the notion that to be good is to feel for others,

particularly the family, in these ways. As all these negative affects and discriminations are elicited, the individual will need to be carried through the fears of her own destructiveness and the fears of abandonment and retaliation which all this can elicit. Such a patient can be helped to see that such fears are the result of earlier conditioning, the kinds of cognitive errors that are typical of young children, as well as of the accumulation of her own aggression and hostility.

A second common conflictual theme involves closeness vs. distance. Often, the therapist will need to normalize and give permission for the client's natural impulses—particularly those involving the need to distance. The therapist can also help the symbiotic individual understand similar impulses in others, thereby affecting the client's fear of abandonment. An overall theme of the therapy of the symbiotic character will be the modulation of the self-other boundary. Particularly as the person is developing the capacities for increased closeness, she will experience enhanced fears of engulfment, of "losing herself" in the needs and personality of another.

The personal growth of the symbiotic person will be suffused with loss—loss of the compensatory characteristics of the self, realization of the historical loss of the real self, and not infrequently, loss of significant others who have been, like the parent, burdensome to the patient. Furthermore, to the extent that the person has not completed grieving for the losses of loved ones, this empathic grief must be worked through.

Finally, the symbiotic individual needs permission for pleasure in life. In particular, he needs to develop the ability to enjoy and take pride in his self-expression and its results. He may need to learn that not only is it OK to be powerful, but it's OK to enjoy being powerful. Adventure, indulgence, and accomplishment are all a part of his birthright, and he is entitled to their enjoyment. In short, the symbiotic character needs to learn that it's OK to be himself; it's OK to be different; it's OK to have pleasure; it's OK to be proud of himself; it's OK to be satisfied, even if others can never be satisfied, and others' satisfaction in life is not his responsibility.

Cognitive Objectives

Perhaps the central theme of the psychotherapy of the symbiotic character will be the repeated uncovering and correction of patho-

genic beliefs, script decisions, and inappropriate introjects and identifications. Almost always, this will involve the uncovering of a belief
that self-expression will harm others—particularly parents or their
psychic equivalents in current life, and the belief that the good things
or feelings of life are acquired at the expense of these others. The
fusion of the symbiotic self with a significant other is typically maintained in numerous and often marvelously intricate ways. The analytic therapy of the symbiotic character will, to a great extent, involve interpretations that highlight the preservation of this kind of
internal fixed relationship. This can involve the incorporation of
affects, belief structures, and behaviors that are really authentic attributes of another. Repeated insight into this adopted identity in all
realms of experience will be necessary for the relinquishing of the
symbiotic's compensatory self. A well-developed understanding of
the symbiotic's history and arrested cognitive development will be
necessary to extricate him from the family of origin and his pathogenic role in it. Repeated help in reality relatedness, particularly in
the area of social obligation and responsibility, may be needed to
correct the symbiotic's tendency toward creating social enmeshment
and expecting it from others.

Insight into the particular nature of compromise solutions to essential symbiotic conflicts will be required. In other words, how has
the individual been able to solve the problems of being aggressive
while denying it, being successful while failing to acknowledge or
enjoy it, or being adventurous while being anxiety-ridden in adventure, etc. Uncovering the "games that symbiotics play" with particular emphasis on the passive-aggressive maneuvers they employ will
often be productive.

The symbiotic's arrested development in the issues of rapprochement often leads to the maintenance of splitting in adult life. Others
are typically seen as good when they are indulgent and bad when
they are not, while the self is seen as good when indulging others as
demanded and bad or guilty when not. Awareness of this ambitendency and maturation to ambivalence about the self and others is
often a very necessary aspect of the treatment, particularly at the
lower ranges of structural development. Finally, perhaps the most
basic theme of the symbiotic's successful psychotherapy will involve
the identification, development, and accurate labeling of a concept

of self. This involves finally answering the questions, "Who am I?" in terms of one's ambitions, abilities, aptitudes, skills, preference, tastes, etc. Sometimes the realization by the client that she really likes or dislikes something very simple but idiosyncratic signals or symbolizes the accomplishment of self-identification.

Behavioral-Social Objectives

It is really in the context of the client's current social environment that he must extricate himself from an identity based on fusion and establish an identity that is more his own. It is often the case that current relationships replicate and thus preserve historical, pathological ones. These must either be changed or dropped. Where the weight of a pathological history is compounded by the weight of a pathological interpersonal present, many changes will be hardwon. Yet, it is these very contemporary relationship problems that often enhance the reconstruction of the original ones. Where the patient's reactions are more purely transferential and the environment is not cooperating in the patient's current imprisonment, and particularly where the positive changes will be welcomed by the social environment, the therapeutic gains can be more easily and rapidly achieved.

As distinct from affects and thoughts, it is important in the behavioral-social arena for the therapist to support, encourage, identify, and even directly instruct the client in those social behaviors that express individuation and effectively modulate closeness and distance. Though more traditional psychodynamic therapists may have difficulty with such direct interventions in the social sphere, I believe that it is appropriate to assist the client in understanding and managing his social environment. This is particularly true with the symbiotic patient, who is likely to be required to deal with significant others who are intrusive and binding in their communications. It is not uncommon for these patients to need some more practical and concrete assistance in extricating themselves from these aspects of relationships, if not the relationships themselves. This means practical assistance in the behaviors required for mobilizing, expressing, and modulating aggression and hostility.

Finally, we define ourselves—we know who we are—by our behavior, by our social relationships, by those with whom we choose to identify, and by those qualities we choose to internalize and make our own. The symbiotic character is helped immensely by understanding all of that and orienting to those behaviors and those others who will, in these ways, help him define himself. The building of identity is an active process, and sometimes a very active therapy is necessary to assist in achieving it.

CHAPTER 8

The Used Child: The Narcissistic Experience

ETIOLOGY

THE KEYS TO UNDERSTANDING narcissism are the *narcissistic injury* and the *rapprochement crisis*. Appreciating the narcissist's injury yields an understanding of his underlying emotional experience. Much, if not all, of his surface presentation, both to himself and others, is in compensation for that injury. The rapprochement crisis yields an understanding of the developmental assets, the ego resources and deficits, and thereby the nature of his object relations, defensive structure, and the experience of self.

The injury is a deep wound to the experience of the real self. In the more extreme cases of narcissistic disorder, the injury is so deep and the compensations so tight that the person has no residual experience or comprehension of the real self. In the less extreme variations of this disorder, which are endemic to the culture, there is often a veiled awareness of the real self but a concomitant rejection of it. Even though narcissism comes from the Greek myth superficially understood to represent self-love, exactly the opposite is true in the narcissistic personality disorder character neurosis or style. The narcissist has buried his true self-expression in response to early injuries and replaced it with a highly developed, compensatory false self.

Narcissistic injury can take an infinite number of specific forms, but essentially it occurs when the environment needs the individual to be something substantially different from what he or she really is. Essentially, the message to the emerging person is, "Don't be who you are, be who I need you to be. Who you are disappoints me, threatens me, angers me, overstimulates me. Be what I want and I will love you."

As outlined earlier, every characterological issue could be seen in this general way. Essentially, the schizoid is told not to exist, the oral not to need, the symbiotic not to individuate, etc. As a result, there is narcissism in every characterological adjustment, and narcissistic characteristics will be found, to a greater or lesser extent, in every character structure developed before or during rapprochement.

This is true for several reasons. First, every characterological adaptation involves the development of a compensatory false self in which there is ego investment and of which there is considerable defense. Second, the tasks of the rapprochement subphase of individuation are truly difficult ones that demand an intact ego structure and a sympathetic, understanding, respectful, mirroring, echoing environment. The environments that create the schizoid and oral structures are, by definition, far from adequate and any preexisting ego wounds can be substantial. So, a number of the difficulties in self-representation, object relations, reality relatedness, and defensive functions characteristic of the more obvious narcissistic personality will often be found in these other characterological adaptations.

Concomitantly, it is often the case that those showing the most serious narcissistic adaptations have had clearly deficient parenting in the prior periods requiring holding and nurturance. Parents who produce narcissism often cannot relate to their children as real, human, living organisms. This yields a kind of underlying schizoid unreality in object and reality relatedness — an ideal breeding ground for a highly narcissistic adaptation when the issues of self-formation are confronted. Particularly if there is then parental idealization and/ or humiliation of the child as she attempts to form a self, the impetus for narcissistic resolution becomes overwhelming.

This more generalized view of narcissism is not a novel one, but is reflected in the work of Adler (1985), Blanck and Blanck (1974, 1979), Miller (1981, 1984), and Lowen (1983). A good deal of clarity has come to my own thinking about narcissism by recognizing it as a generalized difficulty that cuts across all character structures formed before or during the rapprochement subphase of individuation. Thus, I am alert to narcissistic features in other character structures, though the most important presenting life issues may not be clearly narcissistic. At the same time, I have come to see narcissism expressed in a more specific etiology and resulting in a specific characterological pattern. This "narrow narcissism" constitutes a very valuable diagnostic category. In short, individuals may be viewed as narcissistic in the narrow sense when they have had very little trauma prior to the narcissistic injury sustained in the rapprochement period. As a result, they show a pattern of adaptation in which the integrity and esteem of the self are very much at issue but in which basic security is not fundamentally a problem. I refer to this pattern as "pure" or "narrow" narcissism so as to distinguish it from narcissistic adaptations overlaying other structures.

In what follows, I will be discussing narcissism in this narrow sense for its heuristic value while realizing that narcissistic injuries and failures in self-representation and object relations cut across other categories. This is consistent with the approach of these volumes, in which character structures are viewed as expressions of central life issues. Within this framework, any given individual may manifest difficulty with any or all of these core issues. This is only more true of the narcissistic injuries and adaptations because of their position in the developmental sequence and the fact that all traumas in that sequence are ultimately to the real self.

In the narrow sense then, narcissistic pathology represents those difficulties in self-representation and object relations arising out of difficulties in the rapprochement subphase of separation-individuation. It is at this difficult juncture when the individual first fully appreciates his separation, deals emotionally with the impact of that reality, and is called upon to integrate his magnificence with his vulnerability. This rapprochement with reality represents the individual's first attempt to reconcile an idealized dream, which includes the experiences of *symbiosis* and *grandiosity*, with the realities of existence, which include *separateness* and *limitation*. If the environment can accept and nurture both sides of this polarity, love the wonders of an emerging person and the beauty of an open, dependent baby, the realness of the individual is bolstered, reinforced, and actualized. Then, the individual can be as magnificent as she was born to be and as weak and vulnerable as she was born to be. When the environment lets her be, she is, and there is no disorder of the self. But, when what you are is too much or too little, too energetic or not energetic enough, too sexual or not sexual enough, too stimulating or not stimulating enough, too precocious or too slow, too independent or not independent enough, . . . you cannot freely realize yourself. *That* is the narcissistic injury.

Your attempt to be who I need you to be is the false self. And the pathologies labeled "narcissistic" are simply the result of (1) your being who you were needed to be rather than who you really were and (2) your developmental arrest at that point when you needed supportive mirroring to really grow to be yourself. A very significant proportion of the resulting pathology will be from your rejection of yourself. You will mirror your environment by rejecting in yourself what was rejected by others. You will try to hide that which has been rejected and you will work diligently to compensate for it. Very likely, you will shun or be angered by those who display what you have rejected in yourself.

The narcissist's object relations will consistently reflect his or her attempt to deny the rejected and suppressed reality and to achieve and present the false compensation. The pattern is most obvious in those narcissistic personalities in which there is an almost compulsive commitment to *having* the right clothes, home, car, and mate to display to the world the false self compensation. Yet, it is important to remember that compulsive forms of self-denial and self-effacement can also be narcissistic in the way we are discussing it here. When one's vulnerability or humanness was threatening, that was denied; by the same token, when one's magnificence was too much, that too will have been denied. Narcissism is simply the promulgation of the false self over the expression of the real self. Successful therapy involves a resurrection and then expression of the real self.

I find it useful to think of Mahler's rapprochement subphase as the one in which two basic human polarities are first presented to the young child for eventual integration. These polarities are (1) unity-individuation and (2) grandiosity-vulnerability. Even under the best of circumstances this integration is not simple. Significant human psychopathology arises out of those familial situations in which any part of either polarity cannot be freely experienced and then integrated. Obviously, the symbiotic character arises more out of blocking the integration of the first polarity, whereas the narcissistic character arises more out of blocking the integration of the second. This dichotomy is, however, perhaps more heuristic than real, in that the narcissistic character in a sense never really individuates because he never truly becomes himself. Rather, he tries to become what the environment wants, and as a result his individuation is false. Still, he appears to be individuated and is typically capable of active, apparently individualistic, behavior in the real world.

It is particularly helpful in understanding people with narcissistic issues to remember the great vulnerability the child experiences during the rapprochement subphase. The child is threatened by his emerging awareness of his own vulnerability and powerlessness, as well as by his emerging awareness that he is separate from the mothering figure and does not own her magical powers. As he comes out of the rather manic-like practicing subphase, he requires particularly attuned understanding, sympathy, echoing, mirroring, and respect. This is the subphase in which it appears to be the most difficult to be a "good enough" mother. To be good enough means to allow the emerging individual to narcissistically cathect or use the parents in negotiating these difficult internal conflicts.

Understanding of the term *narcissistic cathexis* is necessary for true appreciation of the narcissistic development and eventual expression in adult life. An object is cathected narcissistically when it is the target of one's investment or attachment but not viewed as having its own life center or activity. Rather, it is viewed as significant only as a part of one's own life, seen as valuable only as it relates to oneself and, in a sense, expected to serve one's needs unconditionally. In other words, it is an archaic *selfobject* perceived only as one needs it to be, rather than a *real object* perceived to be as it really is.*

For the child in the rapprochement subphase, this is a legitimate developmental vicissitude. The mature parent will assist her offspring by allowing this narcissistic cathexis and permitting herself to be used by the child to define the emerging and separate self. The understanding, respect, mirroring, echoing, and love of which the analytic developmental psychologists speak are rather analogous to Carl Rogers's concepts of "prizing" and unconditional positive regard in psychotherapy. While the "good enough" parent must set

---

*Kohut does not make this selfobject/real object distinction, which I believe is heuristic.

limits for her child, there will be in her ministering the underlying message that the child is all right, acceptable, and lovable as she is. The unconditional positive regard will be for her essential humanness, with all of its magnificence and all its vulnerability. It is the same kind of acceptance that truly loving mates are able to give one another as adults when they attach as real object to real object and appreciate one another's magnificence while assisting one another with accepted vulnerabilities.

Alice Miller (1981) has been particularly helpful to me in my understanding of narcissism by outlining how narcissistic parents breed narcissistic children. When the parent has been narcissistically injured in childhood, she looks to her child to provide that narcissistic understanding and mirroring that she herself did not receive. As a result, she cannot be used by the child in negotiating the powerful issues of rapprochement; rather, she uses her child for the mirroring she still requires. In a highly accessible work, Golomb (1992) presents powerful stories of narcissistic parents and their children and explains the consequences of narcissistic parenting.

The classic archetypal mothering figure who narcissistically cathects her own child is the "stage mother." This typically pathetic character lives through the artistic expression of her offspring and loses her boundaries in that identification. Typically, the child of the stage mother is used in hope of remedying the disappointments and deficiencies in the mother's life; as a consequence, there is a desperate quality to the overseeing of the stage mother. In the film *Fame*, the character Doris Finsecker is accompanied by a classic stage mother. Her mother periodically intervenes and interferes as Doris auditions for the New York School of Performing Arts. When she is later called with the audition results, the mother says anxiously, "Well, is she in or is she out?" Upon receiving the answer, she turns from the phone and says passionately, "Doris, we made it."

When the child fails to provide the necessary echoing or fails to live up to the exaggerated expectations, the mothering figure may withdraw her love or display the kinds of outbursts of temper that characterize the child's rapprochement subphase. The child, vulnerable and dependent, will then deny his real self in order to hold onto the mother. Living up to her idealized expectations and ministering to her narcissistic needs, he denies and loses himself. He invests in the idealized, false self, trying through it to regain what he lost—the love, respect, echoing, and mirroring which were required for him to discover, accept, develop, and love his true self. In this etiological formulation, the narcissistic injury exists in the parents' inability to accept, understand, and love the child with all of his real conflicts, vulnerabilities, and magnificence. To feel again that rejection of one's real self is to reexperience the very chaotic and overwhelming emotions of the rapprochement period without the necessary parental support to negotiate the crisis. A confrontation of that state, labeled "abandonment depression" by Masterson (1976), emerges in every treatment of the narcissistic issue.

There exists a related etiological picture involving a narcissistic parent who is threatened by and envies the emerging magnificence of the young child. Such a parent—usually put down and humiliated himself in early life—does not want to give his child what was denied him. Particularly where he sees the other parent idealizing the child, he will act out to humiliate the emerging individual in his child.

I have often seen the combination of these etiological factors, usually occurring along predictable sexual lines. I have often seen the case, for example, in which the mother of a male child, disappointed in her mate, idealizes her son and requires him to take care of her and live up to her idealized image. Often the mother had previously idealized the father before becoming disillusioned with him. Narcissistically cathecting her boy-child, she reinvests her idealization in him and sets the stage for a doubly painful narcissistic injury in her son. The jealous father responds by humiliating his son as the boy develops the narcissistic false self in response to the mother's cathexis. In this case, the child's real self is injured twice: first by the mother's inability to accept his vulnerabilities and idealizing him, and second by the father's need to retaliate and humiliate him.

The desperation with which the classic narcissist holds on to the promulgation of the false self can be understood if one appreciates the intense pain experienced in this dual rejection of the real self. When this side of the polarity is experienced in or out of therapy, the person experiences intense lack of support and understanding, profound worthlessness and humiliation, and a desperate need to have these overwhelming feelings stop. It is at this point that the narcissistic person may attempt to marshall every possible defense to ward off these feelings. Such defensive maneuvers include an intensified reinvestment in the false self, ungrounded grandiosity, acting-out in violence, suicide, or drug abuse, and a splitting of the external social environment such that others are seen as entirely supportive or completely threatening. It is the working-through of the abandonment depression and the eventual integration of the grandiose and vulnerable selves that will pave the way for the narcissist's characterological transformation.

Thus the narcissistic compensation is formed in response to the injury. That compensation involves an arrest in grandiosity, which, because it is completely unrealistic, is extremely vulnerable. To live with this extreme vulnerability, the narcissist employs two basic strategies: (1) She tries to live up to the grandiosity by the accomplishment of perfection, and (2) she disavows and thereby renders unconscious the truly absolutistic and primitive nature of her grandiose nature. The more successful is her compromise, the more difficult it will be to ever give it up.

The child in rapprochement legitimately uses the parent in order to find himself. His identify is forged out of the symbiotic orbit as he uses the identification with and idealization of the parent figure to help define himself and discover his own identity in the mirroring that that adult provides. By contrast, the narcissistic adult uses others to bolster, fortify, and aggrandize the false self. This, unfortunately, continues the dependency because the false self can never become autonomous and self-gratifying. A central and necessary shift in the narcissist's healing comes when he turns to use others once again for the purpose of discovering and strengthening his real self. Initially, as with the infant, this becomes a more obviously dependent position. But as the person admits the paucity of his real self and looks to others to help him discover and nurture it, there emerge the seeds of eventual independence, because finding the real self ends the search and, with it, the desperate need for perpetual adoration. When the narcissist shifts from the use of others to perpetuate the false self to the use of others to discover the real self, he has begun the journey home.

BEHAVIOR, ATTITUDE, AND FEELING

The narcissist may be understood through the polarity he presents around the issue of grandiosity-worthlessness. While most descriptions of narcissistic personality focus on the compensated side of this polarity—his lack of humility, inability to accept failure, fear of helplessness, manipulativeness, a striving for power and a commitment to will—many a narcissistic character will display, often in the first session of therapy, the polar opposite. He will confess to his deep sense of worthlessness, his nagging sense of never being or having enough, his constant need to earn provisional worth, and his deep envy of those he perceives to be successful and healthy. In this confession, he will often admit to the feeling that he only fools others with his presentation of strength, competence, and happiness. In this state of mind, he knows that the self he presents to the world is false, that it gives him no pleasure or sustenance, and that he does not have a solid experience of himself as a real human being.

Although the compensated false self is more typical of his social functioning, he may well enter therapy when the compensation breaks down for some reason and the overpowering feelings of disintegration require him to seek out some assistance. Like the oral character in his collapsed phase, the narcissist in this crisis of existence wants something to stop the pain. Typically, he comes to therapy not for characterological transformation but for assistance in maintaining the viability of the compensation. It may be necessary to engage in therapeutic maneuvers that accomplish that goal, at least initially, because the lower functioning narcissist can be very dangerous to himself and others in the panic of decompensation. He can, for example, become very blaming of those "bad" others whom he perceives to be causing the pain, and he may act out violently against them. Alternatively, in the depth of his worthlessness, or in the realization of his falseness, he may become seriously suicidal.

Emotionally, he is at these times a 15- to 24-month-old child dealing with the crucial issues and consequent despair and tantrums of that period. Prior to the establishment of a very trusting therapeutic relationship and some critical ego-building, the narcissistic patient may be completely unable to work through this rapprochement crisis. Respect for the intense level of his pain and desperation is warranted, as is respect for how dangerous an adult can be in the throes of the rapprochement crisis. A true therapeutic transformation can be begun when there is sufficient relationship and ego strength for the narcissistic individual to experience the depth of his worthlessness, falseness, and desperation. That is the essential experience that needs to be released for the eventual transformation.

The narcissistic character in his compensated phase is a person who simply manifests those behaviors, attitudes, and affects that defend against that crisis of desperate feelings. Most typically, these include grandiosity, pride, entitlement, manipulation and objectification of others, self-involvement, and great reliance on achievement to sustain a fragile self-esteem. Although blown up in his self-presentation, he is extraordinarily dependent on external validation for the worth of his qualities and achievements. Typically, those who do not share or do not support such qualities are excessively devalued or overvalued. Any source of negative feedback can seriously reinjure and evoke rage or the defenses against it. His polarity around worthiness is mirrored in his evaluation of others. Some are seen as exceedingly worthy and are idealized in the extreme, while others are seen as exceedingly unworthy and contemptible. Paradoxically, others who approve of or buy the false self he is selling are often devalued. Because he knows at some level of awareness that his self-presentation is false, he feels he has fooled those who give him the approval he so desperately desires. Thus, he loses some respect and trust for anyone who rises to the bait of the false self he presents.

As with any person who idealizes, he is prone to disillusionment when the idealized others fail to live up to his unrealistic expectations. This pattern of idealization and disillusionment is particularly common in the psychotherapeutic interaction. Indeed, all of the narcissist's interpersonal relations are characterized by the narcissistic cathexis of others. In other words, the narcissist sees others not as they are, but as he needs them to be. So, they are admirers, idealized models, examples of what he rejects and considers bad, etc. People are split into categories, good and bad; they are used but not related to for the people they are. Others are seen not for the gifts they have to share, the limitations they face, and the pain they experience. They are related to only in relation to the narcissist's needs. It is with the narcissist that the term *object relations* has a particular poignancy. We are objects to him, and to the extent that we are narcissistic, others are objects to us. He doesn't really see and hear and feel who we are and, to the extent that we are narcissistic, we do not really see and hear and feel the true presence of others. They, we, are objects.

If you can get how that objectification feels from both sides, the object and the objectifier, you have gotten the essence of the narcissistic experience. I am not real. You are not real. You are an object to me. I am an object to you. We use, manipulate, and play with each other. We do not connect, we do not feel, we do not love. We are machines who use each other in the mechanical process of getting through the day and night.

It is so easy in seeing the narcissist's disagreeable qualities, which he often suppresses in depression, to objectify him, to lose touch with his painful internal experience, and to forget that he is often of great service to others in his compensatory activities. In a very real sense, he has sacrificed himself for others, and he often comes close to being the hero or savior he feels he must be to be worthy. Particularly in the more prevalent cases of narcissistic style, which are endemic to our culture, these more grandiose and manipulative aspects are effectively disavowed and thereby largely unknown to the self and others. What remains in consciousness is only the more egosyntonic requirement to earn worth by accomplishment. That that worth is a substitute for the love that is really wanted, that he has sacrificed himself for the booby prize, and that he is missing life in his struggle are too painful to realize.

And yet, there is that nagging sense pressing for awareness, evergreater with age, that there is more to life than this. In those moments when the defenses are dropped, the narcissist sees that others do see and hear and feel one another—that there is real joy and love in the experience of some others—that there is realness in human experience. In that realization, and in that envy, are the seeds of the narcissistic transformation.

The narcissist's salvation is not in his accomplishments, specialness, or uniqueness. The "drama of the gifted child" (Miller, 1981) is in his discovery of his human ordinariness. In that ordinariness is his ability to feel real human feelings unaffected by his internalized parents' acceptance or rejection of his feelings. Once his ordinariness is realized, he can express his gift as just that—a gift. His gift is not who he is; his humanness is who he is.

The hard work of psychotherapy for the narcissist is to assist him in relinquishing the compromise that has often felt bad but that has provided some gratification and often looked very good. In turn, he must invest in a reassertion of self, which risks reinjury and brings up all the old feelings of hurt, but promises eventual fulfillment.

The narcissist can be most clearly described by his pathology in self-representation and object relations. Additionally, to distinguish him from the other character structures that contain narcissistic components, it is useful to focus on the differences in his forms of psychological defense. For these reasons, I will begin the description of behavior, attitude, and characteristic affects by using the structural categories of functioning: object representations and relations, identity formation, and defensive functions.

Object Representations and Relations

Using Mahler's object relations theory, the narcissist is developmentally arrested in the rapprochement subphase of separation-individuation. As a consequence, there is a basic pathology in his being able to differentiate himself, at a psychological level, from significant others. Unlike the symbiotic character, the narcissist, as narrowly defined, differentiates himself clearly and does not have the same kind of diffuse body-ego boundaries seen in the symbiotic structure. At a psychological level, however, there is a confusion about boundaries. The extent of that confusion, and the degree to which it is perceived as ego-dystonic, represents the extent of the structural impairment. At the extreme low end of this continuum, Kohut (1971) has described the object relations as *merger through extension of the grandiose self*. In this extreme case, the client sees himself as psychologically merged, at least with significant others, and "entitled" to use them completely and exclusively.

This is the type of person who will become indignant or enraged with a therapist or spouse who is not unconditionally available for his unlimited use. He will typically be jealous of his spouse's work, hobbies, or other relationships, which in any way interfere with availability. In extreme cases such a client will openly resent his therapist for seeing anyone other than himself. Further, he will expect free and unlimited access to his therapist or any significant others and be enraged by any limitations set by others to define their own boundaries. Where the arrest is this early developmentally, there will usually have been severe deficiency in the nurturing-holding functions of the parents and associated pathologies of a schizoid-oral nature.

All narcissistic characters tend to idealize, but at this extreme pole of merger the person bathes in the "narcissistic glow" of any positive attributes of the cathected other. A beautiful wife makes him more physically attractive, a brilliant therapist reflects on his brilliance, a talented son makes him similarly talented. Recall the example of the stage mother merged with her talented offspring. Frequently, the objects merged with are those that most clearly represent an aspect of the self about which there is doubt or recrimination. If I feel ugly, I will seek to merge with someone who is beautiful. If I feel stupid, I will seek to merge with someone I perceive as intelligent. If I feel boring, I will attempt to merge with someone exciting.

Although this merging transference represents the bottom of the developmental continuum in narcissistic object relations, I have experienced differences in clients' ability to employ a more or less "adult observing ego" in being aware of and syntonic or dystonic with this adaptation. In other words, some clients are able to see that they engage in more or less merging transference relationships with spouses, children, and therapists and view that as unfortunate. So, in my experience, there can be a fixation at this level of development concurrent with development of thought processes and reality relatedness that serve to inhibit the extreme manifestations of the merger transference outlined above.

Kohut (1971) posits that the "twinship" transference is somewhat more evolved developmentally than the merger transference just outlined. Here, the separateness is acknowledged but the individual assumes that he and the object have more or less identical psychologies with similar likes, dislikes, philosophies, etc. The maintenance of this illusion is necessary for the maintenance of significant relationships. The discovery that another is not "just like me" even in some insignificant respect is enough to threaten the relationship. The twinship attachment, together with its fragility, is often seen in early teenage romances, where part of the function of the attachment is the discovery of self. It is not uncommon for narcissistic characters who exhibit this form of transferential relationship to find essentially oral or symbiotic characters who will indeed fulfill this twinship expectation. The currently popular literature on "soulmates" seems to me, at times at least, to perpetuate this transferential relationship based on the search for the perfect alter ego.

Kohut's (1971) most evolved form of narcissistic transference is the "mirror transference." In this form of relationship, the other is *used* primarily for the purpose of acknowledging or aggrandizing the false self. Here, the need for attention, "prizing," respect, and echoing is the focus of the relationship. This form of transference is more mature, in that it is directed more at the development of the separate self. In this transference, the false self has been somewhat more developed and others are narcissistically cathected to help support it. The tragedy, of course, is that others are used to aggrandize the false self rather than to help discover and accept the real self. Examples of this mirroring transference would include a client's upset at a therapist's forgetting a minor detail presented in an earlier session, a therapist's neglect to praise a current accomplishment, or a therapist's failure to remark on a new hairstyle or other significant change in personal appearance. The internal experience of this need for mirroring reduces to a more or less constant need for others to notice, confirm, and bolster the insecure self presented to the world. Narcissists with this level of development often have some insight into their narcissistic character, even though they may not know this pejorative and unfortunate label. Too, they may be much more aware of the negative and insecure polarity of their self-concept. As such, they appear more "neurotic" in the classic sense; yet, it is in their failure to negotiate the task of rapprochement and their history of *being used* that will be most helpful in engineering their therapeutic progress.

I find Kohut's categorization very useful in describing various forms of narcissistic transference both in and out of therapy. On the other hand, I have observed that all forms may be represented in the same individual. Particularly, I have seen regression to lower developmental forms of transference (i.e., merger transference) under extreme stress and milder forms of the need for mirroring when the therapeutic relationship is sound and stress is at a low level.

As is obvious from this outline of the narcissist's object relations, he is the ultimate other-directed individual. The self is defined almost entirely by the other or by the other's response to him. In the absence of the other, or in the absence of the favorable response, there is emptiness, despair, depression, or agitation, which is the narcissist's underlying emotional state. In defense of that state, the narcissistic personality will go to extreme lengths to find mirroring objects or to coerce those he has into the desired response.

The idealization of others that narcissists exhibit may be usefully conceptualized along the developmental continuum — merger, twinship, mirroring. In the merger transference, the individual will seek out and then misperceive the other as the *perfect* object with whom to merge. In ordinary life this perfection is most often sought in the *potential* mate — potential because it is nearly impossible to maintain idealization at close quarters. Where merger idealization exists there are always etiological difficulties with the nurturing-holding functions of the original caregivers. The individual is still looking for the symbiosis that was either insufficient or prematurely lost.

The perfect twinship is the idealization of the alter-ego transference, as seen in many adolescent love affairs. The perfect role model is the idealization of the mirroring transference. In this later developmental arrest, the individual needs someone to look up to, believe in, and emulate.

In each of these idealizations, the individual is looking for the self in the other. To an extent, this is a fruitful place to look, in that these kinds of relationships do provide the social context in which we come to know ourselves. But, unless the infantile, absolute character of the idealization is neutralized, there will be no maturation through internalization. Instead, the narcissistic person will endlessly circle from idealization to disillusionment.

Identity Formation

The narcissistic etiology leads to a basic disruption in the *sense* of self, the self-*concept*, and the self-*image*. I use each of these labels deliberately to highlight the fact that the narcissist's self-representation in all three basic sensory systems (visual, auditory, and kinesthetic) will suffer some pathology. The etiological circumstances lead the person to decide, "There is something wrong with me as I am. I must be special." This basic "script decision" is similar to that of the schizoid, although it does not involve the issue of the right to exist and is not concurrent with the schizoid's extreme fear of others and terror of life itself. Rather, this decision involves more the concept of the self in all channels of representation. At the point of self-formation, the narcissist is led to reject some part of himself, to suppress the feelings of sadness and rage that accompany such rejection, and to invest his energies in the promulgation of that false self that will meet with the environment's approval. It takes the exertion of considerable will to suppress the real pleasure demands of the organism and embrace the idealized functioning demanded. Yet, the exercise of this will gives the child power in an environment that is adverse in some important respects to his real self expression. In the narcissistic situation, the normal parent-child relationship is in some important respects reversed, such that the child is used to gratify the narcissistic needs of the parent. In this reversal, the child gains considerable power to manipulate and control at a developmental period when manipulating and controlling the environment are of central importance. So, the child learns to forego the pleasures of the real self in exchange for the power and control realized by the exercise of will required to actualize the demanded false self.

In the foregoing scenario, the child cuts himself off from a real sensory based experience of self and invests more exclusively in the self as it is seen or conceptualized (the self-image or self-concept). In other words, the self begins to be experienced not as the organismic whole it is, with the needs and pleasures it has. Rather, the self is an ideal, an image, a concept, an abstraction. The developmental arrest at grandiosity is then reinforced by the power the child experiences in meeting the parents' needs through the development of the false self. In a sense, the false self represents the ego's best shot at actualizing grandiosity in the real world. In this, the child makes the inevitable tragic decision of choosing power over pleasure. So, the self-representation at a kinesthetic level is often positively represented only by those feelings of elation and euphoria that come out of success, achievement, or the hollow joys of controlling, manipulating, or impressing others. As a result, the integrity of this "self" is extraordinarily dependent on those external sources of reassurance, yet the resulting sustenance is only temporary and unfulfilling. One is always craving more of what may taste good but is never filling or lasting.

As indicated earlier, the representation of self is far more consciously visual and conceptual than it is kinesthetic. It is more important to look good and think well of oneself than it is to feel good. In other words, "I am the one who lives up to my self-image and my self-concept." I derive good feelings only secondarily and artificially as the environment confirms the image or concept. The pride, euphoria, or elation that you see in the narcissist around his positive experience of self is often very mental and ungrounded, not truly representing a connected kinesthetic experience of pleasure in the body or even real pleasure in accomplishment. The downside of the narcissist's polarity around self-representation is far more kinesthetic in nature. When the false self fails in some way or the willpower becomes exhausted, the narcissist will collapse or compensate into ego-dystonic symptomatology.

I have found it useful to use Kohut's concept of the vertical and horizontal split to describe the three types of presentation of the self characteristic of the narcissistic patient. In Table 12, I have presented this outline using the concepts of false self, symptomatic self, and real self. The false self includes the behaviors, attitudes, and feelings of the compensation, including the developmental arrest in grandiosity with all its associated immaturity in ego functioning. The conscious awareness of the attributes of the false self by the individual is highly variable. Thus, the person may be aware that his self-esteem is very dependent on achievement or that he is perfectionistic, but he will not be aware of just how extreme these tendencies are. Similarly,

Table 12

THREE EXPRESSIONS OF NARCISSISM

False Self	*Symptomatic Self*
Reliance on achievement	Vulnerable to shame, humiliation
Perfectionism	Hypochondriacal, psychosomatic
Grandiosity-omnipotence	Worthlessness, self-depreciation
Pride	Isolation, loneliness
Entitlement	Depression, inertia, work inhibition
Self-involvement	
Manipulation and objectification of others	

Real Self

Feelings of emptiness, void, panic with enfeeblement and fragmentation of the self

Archaic demands of rapprochement: Merger, twinship, mirror and idealization transferences

Feelings of rage and hurt at the empathic failures of the archaic demands

Searching for, discovery, and development of the real self: Innate capacities, identification, ambitions, and ideals he will be able to admit, at times, to the less attractive attributes of feelings of entitlement, pride, and self-involvement but will be understandably even more reluctant to admit to the true depth of these qualities. Kohut has been particularly helpful in labeling the unconsciousness of the false self as due to *disavowal*. This helps us differentiate and conceptualize its partial and variable conscious awareness. Also it assists us in understanding how the narcissist's self-involvement may be so obvious to us yet so apparently invisible to him.

This highly fragile compensation is difficult to sustain, and its breakdown will result in symptomatology represented on the right side of the vertical split. In this state, the person is extremely sensitive to slight or criticism, prone to depression and hypochondria, bothered by thoughts of worthlessness, imperfections, etc. These symptoms are conscious but their relation to archaic grandiosity is largely unknown.

These symptomatic defenses are usually polar opposites of those qualities that produce the elation, euphoria, and pride in the false self. If the compensation is bolstered by a beautiful self-image, the narcissist feels ugly in the extreme. If intelligence is the bulwark of the false self, she feels incredibly stupid. If energetic strength is the compensatory quality, he becomes weak. If material possessions provide the necessary positive projective identification, those possessions become hollow or inadequate.

The well-defended narcissist will spend his time primarily on the left side of this vertical split, but with dim awareness of its true depth and falseness, actively engaged with life in a frenetic attempt to keep this active disavowing defense structure in place. As long as this ego-syntonic compensation is working, there is really no reason to seek out any therapeutic intervention; indeed, if he ever does, he will be interested in therapy only to reinstate that compensatory state. The less well-defended narcissistic character will spend more of his time on the right side of the vertical split in a chronic state of self-absorption, which may be cognitive and/or physical in nature, or in the crisis that occurs when all defenses fail. This, of course, is the condition in which most patients with a narcissistic issue will present themselves for treatment. Almost all seek the alleviation of these symptoms; only a few have a dim view of the underlying emotional reality that exists in the unconscious, below the horizontal line. This reality, which anyone would certainly avoid, includes the archaic crises of the rapprochement subphase and the affects associated with the failure of their resolution. Included here are the injury and rage of legitimate narcissistic demands chronically unmet and, perhaps most frightening, the sense of void in the experience of any real self.

The vertical split then relates to the experience of the polarity around self-worth. The characteristics outlined above the horizontal line describe what you will see in the narcissist. Some of the characteristics of the false self will be consciously and ego-syntonically experienced but most will be at least partially disavowed. The horizontal split covers the underlying unconscious demands and feelings and the essential absence of self. Perhaps the most difficult aspect of psychotherapy with all character problems involves the fact that it results in the very uncomfortable experience of the underlying emotional reality on the road to characterological transformation. The experience of that reality is quite understandably resisted, often at an unconscious, body level, making the discovery process long and painful.

Because the pure narcissist is generally better defended than the character structures developed earlier in the developmental process, it often takes massive, cumulative failure coupled with supportive therapeutic intervention to pull her toward that most uncomfortable underlying emotional reality. The key to any successful treatment of this tragic personality is in accessing whatever real self there is and furthering the development of self from arrest to transformation. As the compensations, both syntonic and dystonic, are dissolved, the person will begin to experience that very primitive and vulnerable self, subject to overwhelming affective states. As outlined in Table 12, the person may experience those extremely aversive feelings of panic, emptiness, and void associated with feeling there is no substance to the self. This direct experience of nothingness, of enfeeblement and fragmentation, is probably the most overwhelming affective experience and, for those narcissists who have any propensity to act out, the most dangerous.

Particularly at the lower or borderline end of the continuum, these feelings will be accompanied by deep experiences of rage and injury, demanding current empathic perfection to immediately gratify the archaic demands of the original rapprochement subphase—the need to merge with the perfect idealized other, the need to be attached in an experience of symbiotic twinship, the need for constant and perfect mirroring.

These patients may at these times launch vociferous attacks on the therapist and significant others in the environment. There is a very real danger of violence either to the self or others.

At the higher end of the continuum—the narcissistic character neurosis to style—there may very well be some rather extreme experiences of panic, void, and emptiness, together with a more controlled experience of those archaic demands and the associated narcissistic rage and injury. In other words, the higher functioning narcissist may experience but still be in wonderment at the extent to which he seems to want idealization or mirroring, and he may become alarmed at the depth of his hurt and rage. While he is easier to manage clinically because of the strength of his observing ego, the depth of his affective experience must be appreciated.

The silver lining in these very dark clouds is the beginning of the experience of reality. In the higher-functioning narcissist, there may even be expressions of relief and gratitude at the profundity of the reality of this experience. Even though it is bad, it is real, and that realness is to the higher-functioning person encouraging and, in a way, enlivening. It really requires this deep emotional experience to actualize the crucial shift from the *use of others to aggrandize and support the false self* to the *use of others to find and nurture the real self*. When that shift is made, the person can then devote his energy to that mission, which is at once human and heroic, simple and grand.

For me, it is the polarity around the self-representation in the vertical split that is clinically most definitional of the narcissistic presentation. But, it is the individual client's *particular* collapse into the underlying emotional reality that reveals the nature of early developmental injuries and resulting characterological issues. The false self compensation is the ego's best adaptation at the time of original injury to survive, maintain contact, retain love, and formulate the self. When the compensation fails and symptomatic defenses dissolve, the primary anxiety of the developmental period at which the false self was begun will resurface.

For the schizoid character, this will be the literal fear of annihilation. For the schizoid, if the false self dies, the being will die or be killed. The schizoid individual who has achieved a moderate level of observing adult ego abilities will experience the irrationality of this fear. Yet, she will still experience the extreme threat to survival and frequently have conceptual and imaginal experiences of actual annihilation when the false self is threatened. By contrast, the oral character will, in periods of severe depression, experience himself as extremely needy, weak, and distasteful and fear the desertion of any attachment objects that are significant for him. The collapse of the false self compensation will lead to the core fear of the loss of the object.

For the symbiotic character, the collapse of the false self will trigger similar fears of the loss of the object and, concomitantly and frighteningly, the loss of the emerging self. The symbiotic character knows who she is only in relation to the attachment object, so the loss of the object triggers the fear of the loss of the emerging self. In the narcissistic character, where the self-object discrimination is further along, the primary anxiety triggered is the loss of the love of the object. But since the love of the object is still intimately related to the existence of the self, that very existence is similarly threatened. Furthermore, for the narcissist the loss of the false self amounts to the loss of the ability to manipulate the environment and be in control. So, this loss also brings up the fear of being manipulated, humiliated, and used again. As a consequence, the "pure narcissist" (one who suffers from relatively little injury in prior phases) is more concerned with the loss of self-esteem and power to control the environment than all other character structures.

The characterological transformation of any pre-oedipal structure will involve this collapse into archaic, often overwhelming, feelings. In his treatment of the borderline and narcissistic character disorders, Masterson (e.g., 1976, 1981, 1985) has referred to this as the *abandonment* depression. Adler (1985), on the other hand, has emphasized the seeming threats of *annihilation* that come up for borderline patients. In his theoretical structure, these are the most essential core issues having to do with developmental arrest in the nurturing-holding phases of growth. Masterson sees borderline and narcissistic pathology as primarily coming out of developmental arrest in the individuation subphases, due to abandonment for individuation, whereas Adler and others see *borderline* pathology, particularly, as coming more out of failures in the parental nurturing-holding functions in the earlier developmental periods. I tend to agree with Adler's conceptualization with respect to the more serious manifestations of *borderline* pathology, although I acknowledge, with him, that the later abandonment for individuation issues are also often present in borderline individuals. Similarly, the earlier issues of nurturing and holding are very often present in individuals with narcissistic pathology.

I think, however, that the "depression" label is somewhat of a misnomer when applied to these archaic, chaotic feelings. Though there are often depressive features in this reactivation of infantile feelings, and people certainly don't feel very good when they experience them, there is a good deal of creative expression in these times of emotional crisis. This expression may be shut down by depression, but depression is not the essence of the experience, but rather a defense against it. For all of these reasons, I will henceforth label this most critical therapeutic step for all pre-oedipal characterological transformations the *annihilation-abandonment crisis*. This label acknowledges the dual and often mixed role of the activated fears of annihilation on the one hand and abandonment for individuation on the other. In addition, it highlights the essence of the experience—a crisis—a healing crisis, which may be either resisted or worked through.

The narcissist will be more easily reachable and treatable to the extent that he possesses an adult observing ego and to the extent that he has some ability to identify with the real self. That real self exists in the person's real feelings in the annihilation-abandonment crisis, in any vestiges of natural human pleasure, and in the positive feelings of relatedness that derive from constructive past relationships.

As the real self is developed in the course of psychotherapy, both extremes of feeling will be tapped. Often, the pleasure is more difficult to reach than the pain, because the experience of real body pleasure elicits guilt and fear and the experience of relatedness elicits the fear of humiliation and the realization of all the human contact that has been lost. The fear involves letting go of the false security provided by the false self and embracing the life in the body, which is relatively unknown and is therefore anxiety-provoking.

Accessing the real self through pleasure and relatedness opens the person to accessing the pain of the annihilation-abandonment crisis.

Still, many narcissists will remember or appreciate simple good feelings that can come from the ordinary experiences of life. These are the vestiges of the real self and represent the eventual rewards of finding that reality. Thankfully, the exaggerated forms of the narcissistic character presented in textbooks are rare. Most individuals with narcissistic issues can at least remember real pleasure and relatedness and either spontaneously or through therapeutic intervention be led to experience real pain. Both are necessary for the discovery and development of the real self.

The Nature of Real Self Formation

This search, discovery, and development mission cannot be done solo. Rather, it must be done in a social context in which the input and support of others are authentically used to form a better reality experience of the self. Though the transition from symbiosis to individuation has its very real difficulties, there is in the human being an innate push to differentiation, autonomy, and individual self-expression. In the unspoiled condition, the most natural self-expression exists in the realization of those innate capacities that develop spontaneously. We do not know how specific those innate capacities are, but we can be sure from observation of children that they at least include such variables as activity level, strength, and intelligence. At least a part of what Kohut has termed the "nuclear self" or what we may call the "real self" is the unfettered realization of these innate capacities.

At the same time, that expression of real self needs to be contextualized within the culture that surrounds and shapes the individual. It is clear from the observation of children that they seek to identify with and mimic the significant others in their environment and begin the creation of a unique self in this early identification. Furthermore, Kohut has offered the interpretation that the self is also the ultimate product of the child's natural and healthy grandiosity, which ultimately matures into ambition and natural and healthy idealization, which matures to the formation of guiding ideals and admiration of idealizable figures. Thus, for me, the true or nuclear or real self is an amalgam of the expression of innate capacity, the fine-tuning and maturation of identification, the neutralization of grandiosity to the expression of ambition, and the maturation over an entire life span of values that are arrived at by a functioning self within a social context.

The reader familiar with Kohut will see the profound influence of his thought in this conceptualization, though there are some subtle differences of language and model. There is in this conceptualization a treatment of both the lower and higher selves, although it is often difficult to know exactly where one leaves off and the other begins. The "self" is a complex construct on the one hand and a simple experience on the other. It is the experience of self that is ultimately most important to the individual, but it is the integration of lower and higher elements that makes that experience whole. At the "lower" level, it is an experience of wholeness in the body, groundedness in one's reality, continuity over time, and cohesiveness. At the "higher" level, it is the experience of integrity, meaningfulness, and purpose in the context of a lifetime. Thus, in a sense, the experience of a whole self integrates the body-mind duality and, though we can have words for that duality, the *experience* of self in its most complete form is not dualistic, but unitary.

As Kohut has so poignantly pointed out, we live in a time in which that unity or wholeness is rare and difficult to achieve. The tragedy of Kohut's "tragic man" is the conscious experience of the lack of wholeness and unity, indeed the experience of fragmentation, enfeeblement, and unrealized potential. The depression of tragic man is the awareness of *what could have been* with the achievement of wholeness compared with *what is* in the reality of his experience of fragmentation and enfeeblement. The compensation for this tragedy, which is tragic itself, is narcissism.

Defensive Functions

A useful paradigm for understanding the narcissistic character was offered by Werner Erhard in his *est* training. I paraphrase this presentation to be more consistent with the present object relations metaphor for understanding narcissistic behavior. The essential proposition is that, for the narcissist, the ego creates the false self to meet the needs of the real being as well as they possibly can be met under the circumstances. In this creation, however, the ego begins to mistake the false self for the real self. Thus, any threat to the false self is responded to as if it were a threat to the real self—a threat to the integrity of the being. A threat to the false self threatens annihilation-abandonment and the associated anxieties of any prior developmental phase in which there was trauma. This state of extreme alarm automatically calls up defensive maneuvers available to the individual. In the case of the "pure narcissist," all psychological defenses are available from the earliest developmental periods (e.g., denial, introjection, projection, reversal), as well as the more developed defenses of the rapprochement period (e.g., splitting, coercion, and other forms of acting-out). In its often frantic attempts to save the false self, the ego will marshall all defenses, even to the point of destroying the *life* of the real human being. So, for the narcissist, if you threaten his self-image or self-concept, it is as if you are threatening his very being. This, in part, explains the intensity of the annihilation-abandonment crisis and the extremity of the defensive maneuvers to which the narcissistic individual may resort for self-protection.

It is very easy to conceptualize the defensive functioning of the false self because its reliance on achievement, perfectionism, grandiosity, pride, and manipulation all obviously serve to protect the individual from the confrontation of the basic injury and continuing reality of archaic demands and their disappointments. The functions of the symptomatic self are less obvious and therefore deserve further elaboration. I view the characteristics of the symptomatic self as being both symptomatic of the underlying characteristics of the real self *and* symptomatic of the breakdown of the false self compromise. The symptoms are really the battleground for the struggle between the demands of the real self with its painful emotional reality and the valiant attempts of the compromised false self to avoid that pain and maintain functioning.

The propensity to shame and humiliation, for example, at once signals the "press from below" of the basic narcissistic injury, the enfeeblement of the real self, and the associated archaic demand for mirroring. Concomitantly, it signals the unrealistic, grandiose demands imposed by the infantile false self with its arrest in grandiosity. The extremity of the feelings of worthlessness, humiliation, and shame associated with any failure or embarrassment is symptomatic of the refusal to relinquish the grandiose self-concept, which allows no human fallibility.

To the extent that the blows of failure or disappointment can be cushioned, the frustration can be made "optimal" and result in a gradual accommodation of the false grandiosity. Otherwise, the propensity to shame or humiliation persists as a casualty of the battle between the demands of the real self and the equally archaic and arrested demands of the false self. This same dynamic explains the feelings of worthlessness and the propensity to self-depreciation whenever there is a failure or embarrassment.

Psychosomatic illness and hypochondriacal preoccupation are similarly casualties of the battleground. The psychosomatic illness can often be a symptom of the tension created by this epic conflict. Further, the illness may be maintained by the function it serves in releasing the patient from the unrealistic and grandiose demands of the false self. The hypochondriacal overinvolvement with the body may usefully be conceptualized as an example of isolation of concern with the self. Since the body is the concrete manifestation of the self, a preoccupation with its enfeeblement may be defensively isolated in a body part or specific illness (Kohut, 1971). This maneuver defends against the real affective experience of such enfeeblement at a more psychological level.

Depression may represent a real deadening of the organism so as to avoid the underlying feelings of void, panic, and fragmentation when the false self compromise has failed and the underlying emotional reality of the real self threatens to become overwhelming. I view true depression as a deadening rather than experiencing of affect and, as such, a defensive maneuver. Like illness, depression also serves to protect the grandiose-omnipotent expectations of the false self ("I could do it if I weren't so depressed/ill."). The inertia and work inhibition frequently seen in narcissistic individuals relate to this defensive posture. In the full flower of his grandiosity, the narcissist believes that he should be able to achieve great things with little or no effort. Thus, even outstanding achievement may not be very rewarding if it has to be earned by hard work.

Finally, the isolation to which the narcissist usually subjects himself is in part the result of his grandiosity and associated perfectionism for others. No one is really good enough when known well—the narcissist's social distance defends the breakdown of idealization. In addition, the isolation really protects the individual from intimacy, which would trigger the threatening archaic demands of the real self, as well as challenge the perfectionism that the narcissist retains about his potential interpersonal relations. The loneliness that can result from this isolation is primarily symptomatic of the push from below—the needs of the real self. Such demands are very threatening to the false self; this, in part, explains why many a narcissistic individual will suffer loneliness rather than use it as a signal to reach out.

Thus, the qualities of the symptomatic self are the result of the intense pressure and resulting conflict between the false and real self. The symptoms are, in part, compromises in this struggle, which protect from awareness the grandiose elements of the false self as well as the affective demands of the real self. The symptoms are at once signals of the underlying demands and defensive compromises, which protect from awareness what they are signaling. The crucial therapeutic task is to help the individual discover and identify with what the symptoms are signaling, while simultaneously defusing the defensive use of those symptoms. Psychotherapy is a tricky business.

ENERGETIC EXPRESSION

In understanding and utilizing the present character typology, it is important to remember that the narcissistic character will show greater diversity in all forms of expression than those structures outlined earlier in the developmental sequence. This fact follows the developmental theoretical model in that the etiology of narcissism, in the narrow sense, is later in the developmental sequence. At this time, the child possesses a relatively larger number of resources and defensive capabilities. In addition, and perhaps more importantly, there is greater variability concerning which parts of the real self are unwelcome in the environment. Because of the variability in the type of frustration experienced, there will be greater variability in the characterological expression at all levels. To complicate things even further in the actual clinical situation, narrow narcissism per se probably never occurs singularly, without any other forms of earlier character pathology. In other words, every narcissist I have seen has demonstrated aspects of schizoid, oral, or symbiotic characteristics. In spite of all this complexity, however, I still find the archetypal guidelines useful.

In orienting to the understanding of the energetic expression of the narcissistic character, it is useful to remember that energetic distortions are primarily the result of the self-negation process in character formation. In other words, we develop energetic blocks in the body to restrain or render unconscious those impulses and reactions that are unacceptable or punished. To a lesser extent, the bodily expressions of character can reflect the ideal or false self presented to the world in compensation for the original injury. In the narcissistic character, both etiological factors are operative on the body level.

In their discussion of the "psychopathic" character (which I believe is better named narcissistic), the bioenergetic analysts have distinguished two types of bodily expression, emphasizing one or the other of these basic processes. The "upward displaced psychopath" is characterized by underdevelopment or weakness in the lower half of the body with accompanying overdevelopment—a sort of a "puffed up" appearance—in the upper half of the body. This body type is thought to reflect that narcissistic development in which there is an ungrounded and weak base supporting exaggerated power, willfulness, and achievement. The "chameleon psychopath," on the other hand, shows no obvious distortions in the body; rather, a false self mask is presented to the world.

In either case, however, there are blocks in the body that prohibit a full feeling awareness of all or part of the real self. Because the body is the real self and the feelings that it signals, both types can share rigidity and constriction in those areas that block that natural flow. Since the parental using or restriction of the narcissistic patient often involves the sexual realm, the narcissistic client often shows a pelvis that is rigidly held, the tension therein blocking the awareness and release in the sexual charge. Together with this, there is often a block or constriction at the waistline that further inhibits the awareness of sexual impulse. In the upwardly displaced narcissist, this break also inhibits the awareness of the ungroundedness or weakness in the lower half of the body.

Moving up the body, the narcissistic character often also shows a tightness and constriction in the diaphragm, inhibiting full body breathing and often yielding shallow chest breathing that inhibits full awareness of the body and its feeling. Symbolic of the narcissistic "rising to the occasion" of parental manipulation and expectation, the narcissist often shows raised shoulders with a good deal of tightness across the shoulders. There is often tightness in the narrows of the neck region, inhibiting the flow of feelings between body and head, a constriction that is also seen in schizoid and oral structures.

Similarly, and in common with the schizoid structure, the narcissist often has a severe block in the muscles at the base of the skull or the "ocular segment." This block is, among other things, the "one-yard line" through which bodily feelings might break through to awareness. In addition, that block is often associated by the bioenergetic therapists with the narcissist's unwillingness to see the reality of his family situation. In a more contemporary sense, the eye block also prevents him from really seeing others as real human beings and allows him to dissociate, seeing others as objects for his gratification and manipulation.

Not surprisingly, many bioenergetic analysts have reported noticing the eyes of the narcissistic character to display suspicion and/or charm and beguiling qualities. Both are consistent with the narcissist's concern about being used and his adaptation of using others to prevent this dreaded result.

Though the upwardly displaced narcissistic character with all of these energy blocks is the easiest to spot in clinical practice, many truly narcissistic characters will share an energetic block in at least some of these areas. The chameleon character is often harder to spot from the energetic point of view. In this case, there can sometimes be a more truly psychopathic character disorder that represents injury at a far earlier etiological base. The slipperiness and smooth manipulativeness of this person may warn of a more truly dangerous character pathology.

THERAPEUTIC OBJECTIVES

At all levels, the therapy for the narcissistic person must be consistently devoted to the discovery and enhancement of natural self-expression. The narcissist, for good reason, has martyred himself and reinvested depleted energy in egocentric pursuits. To regain his life, he must become aware of this martyrdom, feel how he has sacrificed and is continuing to sacrifice himself, and mourn the irretrievable losses in that historical and continuing death. Eventually, he must rediscover his own deeply buried needs and, however clumsily and tentatively at first, meet them. This is a person who, however glamorous and successful he may appear, is *bereft in his internal experience.* Often obsessed with success, he is a failure by the criterion of the very experience of life itself. The effective and cognitive awareness of this fact is necessary to initiate any change.

Cognitive Objectives

An organizing therapeutic objective with the narcissistic person is to enhance self-awareness—awareness of the grandiose false self, the dystonic symptomatic self, and the underlying, if enfeebled, real self. I will begin this discourse with cognitive objectives because it is often easier for a person to discover who he is trying to be, who he hates being, and ultimately who he really is at a more cognitive level. Of course, a cognitive understanding of this alone is totally insufficient, but it is a beginning and one that often triggers the more central underlying feelings. In a very real sense, the narcissist may need to fill in his own "three faces of narcissism" as listed in Table 12 to fully understand himself.

The overall therapeutic objectives with the narcissistic patient are (1) to erode the compensations to the experience of reality whether they are ego-syntonic or -dystonic, (2) to assist and pace the patient in experiencing the painful but real underlying realities of the self, and (3) to support and nurture the discovery and development of the real self. Successful therapy with the narcissist must set the wheels in motion toward what Kohut has called the "transformation of narcissism," which involves a deep maturation of the human being and results in the development of creativity, acceptance of transience, the capacity for empathy, a sense of humor, and wisdom. To cure the narcissist is to effect at least the beginnings of a real "growing up" of the individual—often from a quite immature little boy or girl to a very wise man or woman capable of living at once in the body and in the expression of ideals. This, of course, is an ideal, but not a bad one by which to be pulled.

Because most narcissists will begin psychotherapy with symptomatic expression, it is often possible to begin movement in treatment with the therapist's empathic experiencing of the client's pain. This gives the patient an experience of empathic regard, provides an appropriately utilizable model of this natural human capacity, and begins the creation of a safe place in which many painful experiences will be confronted.

A very therapeutic interpretation or reframe of the symptomatic self is this: The pain of the symptoms is a signal from the denied real self that its needs are not being met. The worthlessness and self-depreciation are signs of the underlying injury; depression or inertia a signal of unwillingness to martyr the real person for the nonsustaining nutriment that the false compensation provides; the loneliness a signal of the deprivation that occurred earlier and that persists now as a result of the narcissist's objectification, manipulation, and rejection of others. Physical pain is a direct signal of psychic pain—a result of the chronic holding back of impulses in defensive preoccupations, which prevents the experience of that self and real underlying emptiness, injury, and rage. The pain of the symptomatic self is at once real and bogus. The patient hurts, but the hurt is only an approximation, a signal, a defense against a deeper level of pain and an acquired inability to deal with it.

A detailed analysis of how each symptom may be defensive to the underlying pathology will, especially at first, be experienced as a narcissistic reinjury. Such premature analyses can usually be experienced only cognitively, yet have the unwanted affective result of causing people to feel guilty and overwhelmed. They encourage a migration of conscious awareness to the head, resulting in fruitless obsession. The overall reframe, *pain is a signal*, however, can be very empathically delivered and facilitate turning attention to where it belongs. The reframe also provides the rationale for techniques that open the person to greater awareness of the psychic reality of the real self. There can then be the self-exploration of the psychic and historical meaning of those peculiar vulnerabilities to criticism and shame and those persistent feelings of worthlessness. Similarly, the reframe can pave the way for an internal search, using numerous therapeutic methods, for the meanings of the signaling function of depression, inertia, loneliness, and physical symptoms. In that process, it will then be useful to access in some detail the self-statements that accompany dysphoria.

It will be very therapeutic for the narcissistic client to fully access, explore, expand upon, and find the exact language for the uncomfortable states that she experiences. Perhaps even more important, it will be therapeutic for her to have this understood and fed back to her in an empathic and caring way. A narcissistic individual will often express surprise that another person is genuinely interested and caring and, after that surprise, will begin to experience the extraordinary longing that she has always had for such concern. In this process, the focus on cognitive content will naturally lead to the important affective experiences surrounding these issues and ultimately lead to the deeper affective experiences of the real self.

Once some of this affective experience has been accomplished and trust has been built, it will be more possible to move on to at least a cognitive understanding of the compensatory grandiosity of the false self. Here it is important for the person to realize the very real and infantile extent of his grandiosity, reliance on achievement, pride, and his attitudes of entitlement, manipulation, and objectification. At the lower or borderline end of the continuum, the individual will, at least initially, be more likely to experience these tendencies as ego-syntonic. He may, for example, be angry with others for not recognizing his special status, which entitles him to be the center of other people's universe. Even here, however, the repeated verbalization of these attitudes to a therapist who is empathic, yet not fully indulgent of these beliefs, will begin the growth and the healing process. Fortunately, this extremely low level of functioning is relatively rare and most patients who present themselves for outpatient care will have less conscious access to these more infantile attitudes and will experience some surprise, embarrassment, and even disbelief at uncovering them in a safe therapeutic context. In these more common cases, their repeated accessing and verbalization will more quickly establish greater ego control over these tendencies and thereby pave the way for the emerging awareness of the underlying real self with its painful but real emotional experiences.

When one gets to this point in the therapeutic process, a cognitive exploration of the defensive functions of the compensatory false self is usually possible without serious narcissistic reinjury. When such explanations or interpretations are provided or when they are elicited from the client herself, they give a very real hope for significant change. Even though there is a good deal of negativity as these disagreeable qualities are brought to awareness, the insights regarding them have the same results as other insights—they provide a kind of cohesion to the self in their offering self-understanding and providing historical comprehension. In addition, this kind of self-understanding is self-supportive because of the very significant use of the self's intellectual and rational functions in achieving it.

As the compensatory qualities are revealed, understood, and dissolved, more and more of the underlying emotional reality—the real self—is brought up for examination. Though much of the initial work at that level will be of an affective nature, the organization I have imposed on this presentation calls for elucidating the work at a cognitive level. Here the primary work is one of explanation, reconstruction, and interpretation, which relates the current disappointments, injuries, and rage to the earlier failures of the environment to meet legitimate child demands. Further, the resulting emptiness, void, panic, and fragmentation are the result of a self that has been undernourished, unsupported, and undeveloped in certain crucial areas of functioning.

Although it is important in this discourse to emphasize that not all of the work at this level will be of a cognitive nature, the cognitive work has largely to do with the person's understanding of who he is currently and achieving a cognitive history of the self so that he understands how he got here. Furthermore, this cognitive work will then lead to presentation of a road map for the client in his work of self-discovery and self-development. The therapeutic work will involve a good deal of support for his innate capacities, his right to live out his mature ambitions, and his need to identify his values and live consistently with them.

Through all of this, the therapist will repeatedly encourage and support a realistic assessment of the client's abilities, resources, and achievements, while at the same time encouraging a realistic assessment of his limitations, weaknesses, and vulnerabilities. This work, then, is really a rapprochement between the three selves heretofore isolated. Cure is a rapprochement and acceptance of one's abilities, achievements, and ambitions with one's vulnerabilities and weaknesses in the context of achieving an expression of one's innate true self within the larger context of an imperfect world.

Affective Objectives

The essential affective objectives with the narcissistic person are to mourn the injury and the loss of self and to then build a true sense of self. Additionally, in the course of the therapeutic process, the person will need to expose the disavowed parts of his grandiose false self, including the feelings of superiority, entitlement, pride, disgust with others, etc. Then, as the grandiose elements of the false self are exposed, the patient will need to be assisted in dealing with the terror that arises when the compromises of the false self are seen for the failures they are and relinquished. If I am not my accomplishments, my beauty, or the other false, grandiose symbols that have heretofore defined me, then who am I? As that question is posed, the terror of the void arises. To face this, or course, requires courage and a therapeutic relationship of considerable trust.

The building of such trust will be necessary in implementing all objectives, but particularly the affective ones. The narcissist needs above all else to be understood. There is a great propensity to shame in revealing the exaggerated claims of the grandiose false self, the human failings of the symptomatic self, and the intense archaic demands and feelings of the real self. It is very therapeutic for the narcissistic client simply to show his vulnerability and confess his grandiosity in a setting where he can be empathically understood. Whichever side of the polarity he begins with (false or symptomatic self), he will typically oscillate between the two throughout much of the initial phases of the therapeutic work. The therapist's deep understanding of the "phase appropriateness" of his grandiosity on the one hand and his vulnerability on the other will assist the therapist in giving the kind of empathic response required. Often, little more than this ever needs to be done.

I have found that the more purely narcissistic the individual, the less I have to rely on any "technique" to bring up the affective realities. If you provide empathic understanding, you will, often without any further probing, go deeper into the levels of the false self and eventually to the archaic demands and affects of the real self. Techniques are differentially more useful, in my experience, as the client is less obviously narcissistic, better defended, and thereby more functional—the narcissistic character neurosis or style. Whether more obvious techniques are used or not, it will be the client's life and current level of awareness that will dictate the order in which his affective realities—either in the grandiose false self or in the repressed real self—will be brought to awareness. In many cases, to simply own the disavowed grandiose aspects of the false self is adequate to begin their frustration and maturation.

In working with the affects of the real self, it is often the feeling of injury at the empathic failures that most needs to be accessed.

That accessing of injury will also lead to the fears of reinjury that underlie the suspicions, distrust, and even paranoia of the narcissistic person. Further, this distrust is a very close cousin to that disappointment experienced around the failures of idealized others in the past. In all of this, underneath the feeling of injury are the repressed needs for merger, twinship, and/or mirroring. And, underneath the feelings of disappointment are the repressed needs for idealization.

Mixed in among all of this, of course, is the well-known narcissistic rage, which can be of overwhelming proportions. Particularly in the more borderline narcissist, it is wise to be careful in accessing this rage and to manage its resurrection at tolerable levels throughout the treatment course. As these more negative affects are handled, it begins to become more and more possible to transform them into their more mature counterparts and to nurture the narcissist's abilities toward empathy and love. As structure is formed and made more solid, the narcissistic person is in an ever-better position to open himself to these softer feelings with the knowledge that he can protect himself and survive any future disappointments.

Behavioral-Social Objectives

In a general way, the behavioral-social objectives for the narcissistic client are the same as for all other pre-oedipal characters. It is important to support those behavioral strategies and social support resources that will sustain the client through the hard work of a very basic and therefore very threatening change in his way of being. Anything that supports the viability of existing resources will be important. A number of techniques can be employed to enhance the value of already existing resources. Where strategies exist to combat work inhibitions, for example, they can be acknowledged and supported. Where such strategies do not exist, they may be taught and then supported. In a very meaningful way, psychotherapy for the narcissist is disorganizing. Yet, compensatory and consciously applied strategies for organization may be very therapeutic in preventing very real structural breakdowns, which can reach dangerous proportions when the affects of the underlying real self become overwhelming.

Most narcissistic individuals are in some very meaningful way isolated. However active their social life, there is an isolation from real contact with a real human community. A great deal of the narcissist's treatment will involve accessing his real need for others and assisting him in getting his needs met. Both directly and indirectly, this will involve training in becoming a more social being—one who is able to initiate and sustain empathy, regard, and understanding of others. This behavioral-social work is so interwoven with the affective and cognitive work that it is difficult to separate. Still, it is possible, in some very meaningful ways, to directly retrain the narcissist in open communication through the use of modeling, practice, and reinforcement. He may be taught active listening skills or empathic responding and asked to participate in exercises that directly teach him how to receive the caring responses of others.

Perhaps the most important work with the narcissist on the behavioral-social level is to assist him in finding and then sustaining a support system that really helps him find himself, rather than one that merely mirrors his grandiose, false self with its associated achievements and symbols. If he can find, and then sustain, a social system that gives him the support and understanding he needs to really find and develop himself, he is on the road to that outcome. If he can find people who really like *him*, who can accurately see and accept his virtues and vulnerabilities, who can lend him the support he needs, give him the acceptance and understanding he needs, and provide for him the role models and realistically utilizable figures he needs, he will get better. To do this, of course, he will have to accept his need for others and accept a level of humanity and fallibility in others that he probably has heretofore rejected. To a very great extent, it will be his confrontation with the void and its associated panic that will motivate him in this direction.

A significant amount of failure and frustration appears to be necessary for the narcissist to get on the right track in terms of his own maturation and healing. Once he does, however, the system may provide the increasingly mature levels of acceptance and frustration he requires to effect the internalization of resources, resulting in real autonomy in the context of greater real support. While a good deal of understanding, release, forgiveness, and growth can occur in psychotherapy, the narcissist really requires a functioning social system in which to mature and transform his narcissism. Without that functioning social system, the therapeutic gains of the narcissistic client will be severely limited.

The healing of narcissism, like all characterological healing, involves, at core, the *decision to grow up* — a decision to mature with respect to those infantile issues at which one is quite literally *arrested*. The decision to grow up is a decision to finally give up the infantile hopes of magical fulfillment — fulfillment without effort, without compromise, without limitations — without a rapprochement with reality. My way, right or wrong, is the infantile demand. It is hard to give up, and the elaborate unconscious maneuvers reflective of this refusal are truly impressive. The objective of therapy is to defeat those maneuvers but, particularly in the narcissist's case, that defeat must be gentle — neither humiliating nor destructive of the human spirit. The narcissistic person, no matter how disagreeable he may be initially or from time to time, deserves love like all other human beings. The task of growing up that he faces is formidable and other human beings who can love will be willing to help. In accepting such help, the narcissist accepts his essential humanity, begins his rapprochement, and finally lets in what he has always wanted, the love and acceptance that only other people can provide.

CHAPTER 9

The Defeated Child: Social Masochism
and the Patterns of Self-Defeat

If you bring forth what is within you, what you bring forth will save you.
If you do not bring forth what is within you, what you do not bring forth
will destroy you.

—Jesus

One does not become enlightened by imagining figures of light but by
making the darkness conscious.

—C. G. Jung

The great epics of our lives are at the points when we gain courage to
rebaptize our badness as the best in us.

—Friedrich Nietzsche

HISTORICALLY, MASOCHISM HAS REFERRED to two conditions.
First, sexual masochism is an apparent perversion of sexuality such
that pain, humiliation, and degradation are sought out in the sexual
context either because they are pleasurable in themselves or because
they make possible or heighten sexual release. Second, masochism
can refer to a more pervasive tendency to engage in a wide range of
self-defeating behavior in one's social, emotional, and work life.

Freud (1924) termed this "moral" masochism and Reik (1941) called it "social" masochism. This chapter is devoted to the second, "life style" form in that it is viewed as reflective of a basic existential life issue having to do with self-determination and self-control. Sexual masochism may or may not coexist with general social masochism.

ETIOLOGY

The essence of the theory of character development espoused here involves the interaction of three variables. The first is the developmental emergence of innate needs specific to human beings. The second is the environment's capacity to be attuned and responsive to these needs. The third involves the natural evolution of affective, behavioral, and cognitive abilities to cope with and process environmental failures in attunement to these innate needs.

Employing this model, the problem of masochism derives from the operation of these three variables as they affect the issue of independent self-determination or, in a word, *will*. While examples of a child's willfulness can be seen in the first year of life, it is not really until upright locomotion is secure and simple language skills are emerging that one typically sees a *sustained* expression of the child's need to determine his own self-expression and resist the will of others. Prior to this time, even where willfulness is shown, babies can be easily distracted to an alternative activity and protracted contests of will can be more easily avoided. With greater development of locomotion, manipulation, memory, and language, the child has more and more opportunities for independent actions and greater ability to sustain them, thereby increasing the potential for conflict between his desires and those of his caretakers. As this progresses, so does the need for socialization in such things as feeding, social interaction, and control of elimination. All of this steadily increases the possibilities for a conflict of wills. Where social masochistic behavior and self-defeat are most obvious and dysfunctional there has, in my experience, been a history of crushing defeat in battles such as these where the child's will has been persistently, intrusively, and often sadistically beaten into submission. Similarly, it is in these cases that the pattern of self-defeat has become persistently defeating and abusive to others and extraordinarily resistant to attempts to change it.

What is most fascinating to me about each characterological expression is the particular collection of psychological mechanisms that define the character type and the particular developmental stamp these mechanisms carry, which define the probable age range when such mechanisms could first come into play. This information gives the likely period of developmental arrest for any characterological expression. This information is, among other things, useful clinically because it informs us of the kind of psychological development reflected in the adaptation to the particular character issue in question. It informs us of the nature of the human needs that were frustrated, the nature of the consequent injury and pain, and the quality of the defenses that were used to cope with that pain.

As children get older, psychological mechanisms and defenses get evermore sophisticated, complex, and intricate. In the case of masochism, some of these more advanced mechanisms are operative and their emergence at a time when the child had awareness of a will to express and protect accounts in part for the persistence of these patterns. There is a remembrance, albeit often unconscious, of the will being broken yet surviving and an undying commitment to resist the defeat and preserve the will, even if that is done secretly, spitefully, and with much suffering.

To identify with the masochist, it is often useful to remember any time when you have been unfairly beaten and there was no means of retaliation. The persistent and impotent rage you may have experienced at that time corresponds to the unconscious, and sometimes semi-conscious rage the masochistic person harbors. "I don't get angry, I get even," is a phrase that captures the underlying phenomenology of the masochistic person. The problem for this person, however, was that the power differential was so great that there was no way to get even save one—self-defeat, which by displaying itself, perversely preserves pride. The only way to defeat the other was by learning to enjoy one's own defeat, displaying it to the world, and defying any attempts to alter it. The patterns of the masochist may be instructively compared with the kind of passive resistance that exists in response to the most totalitarian and sadistic political regimes. During the Nazi's domination of Europe, for example, any obvious acts of resistance could be punished by retribution against the civilian population, including mass executions. Thus, any acts of sabotage had to appear absolutely accidental and deniable. Similarly, self-sabotage, which is unconsciously driven, becomes the most deniable act of aggression. The pleasure in such degradation of the self is securely hidden.

The research in child development confirms that, by the age of two, children have developed a fairly complex set of cognitive abilities at the same time that they are facing conflicts between compliance to the requests of others and the drive to operate more independently. To set the stage, it is between one and two years that children show they can recall past experience (Ashmead & Perlmutter, 1980; Daehler & Greco, 1985) and that they can repeat and recall sequences of common events (Mandler, 1983; O'Connell & Gerard, 1985). These findings are important because they indicate that the child, by two years of age, has clearly developed the ability to anticipate consequences of his behavior. Gopnik and Meltzoff's (1987) research place the beginning of the use of insight and problem-solving at or about 18 months of age. A number of investigators have found that it is at two years of age that children begin to display a tendency to meet the compliance requests of others (Golden, Montare, & Bridger, 1977; Kopp, 1982; Vaughan, Kopp, & Krakow, 1984). At exactly the same time, Wenar (1982) finds that children begin to display a noticeable resistance to compliance. Geppert and Küster (1983) find that it is again at about the two-year point when children begin to make a noticeable demand to perform activities independently. Furthermore, it is exactly at this two-year point (varying, of course, with individual differences in development) when a whole host of cognitive abilities are beginning to appear, which permit a far more sophisticated, intricate, or complex set of social maneuvers and internal processes, which were unavailable up to this point. Stern (1985), for instance, sets the two-year mark as the time when children develop the ability to think and play symbolically and truly begin language development as opposed to simply using a few words. At this very same second birthday, Bretherton and Beeghly (1982) and Fischer (1980) find children begin to give their first representations of self, and they give evidence that they can think of themselves as objective entities. Aligned with this are the findings of Bertenthal and Fischer (1978) and Brooks-Gunn and Lewis (1984) that children at two years demonstrate self-recognition. Hetzer

(1931) observed that it is at about two years when children's play is directed far more by the pleasures they get from producing outcomes than by the more simple attraction to and manipulation of objects.

While it is possible for masochism to be produced by inappropriate dominance and intrusion in any life issue, I think one must have a sufficiently well-developed self-identity and the pride that accompanies it to produce the masochistic response. In other words, there needs to be a conscious sense of self-integrity to defend in the manner that is masochistic. Thus, while there can be increasing conflicts between child and caretaker between one and two, the full masochistic adjustment probably cannot be in place until after two years of age. There also appears to be a need for an extended conflict of wills before the child will settle for the painful compromise of the self-defeating pattern that is masochism.

In this context, then, let us consider the issue of toilet training, not as the sine qua non of the masochistic issue, but rather as a universal issue of socialization, which presents itself at about this time. This is an example in which the needs, ambitions, and proclivities of the child can be nicely meshed with the needs of the parents and society, or can be the occasion for nasty clashes of will, anxiety, shame, and overpowering. The timing of the optimal toilet training is not only dependent on the obvious readiness of the child in sphincter and bowel control. Optimal timing also relies on the child's ability to learn a sensitivity to his own internal cues, his evolving ability to use language to signal a readiness to go, his increasing desire for imitation of parents, siblings, and peers, and his natural evolving pleasure both at pleasing others and appreciating his own accomplishments. When a child is sensitively mirrored with respect to all these tendencies, toilet training and other tasks of socialization may be accomplished with relative smoothness and lack of trauma. Such effective mirroring also must include tolerance for times when the tendency to resist demands or to act independently is stronger than the tendency to comply and please. The acquisition of skills in such an optimally mirroring home is typically not fast nor error-free but is relatively free of anxiety, contests of will, and shaming.

As is obvious from the number of abilities and proclivities that must be sensitively tracked, however, the possibilities for mistakes by caregivers are numerous. Additionally, the results of such mistakes may be hard to detect because they may not appear in toilet training per se but in other areas of behavior or affect, such as difficulties with going to bed or sleeping, excessive tidiness and cleanliness, or in other fears or anxieties. Additionally, toilet training is an interesting example for this discussion because it involves establishing voluntary control over what has been involuntary. Such a delicate process can be easily interfered with by feelings of anxiety or rage, which may be the natural concomitant of a training process that is badly timed, forced, or that involves shaming or caregiver anxiety. Additionally, control battles in these areas can be even more difficult because the child's production may be totally out of his control or he may be able to consciously or unconsciously refuse to produce.

Now, in case anyone may have missed it, I am not saying that masochism is the result of poor toilet training. I am merely saying that this universal problem is a uniquely illustrative prototype for socialization training that *can* elicit the kind of parental treatment and subsequent parent-child interaction that can produce masochistic adjustment. Toilet training is particularly prone for all this due to the time at which it typically occurs, the nature of change from involuntary to voluntary control, and the inherent difficulties in the process, which produce particularly good material for the experience of anxiety, shame, and a contest of wills.

All character structures, as outlined in this book, are formed by environmental (usually parental) failure, which is at best imperfectly attuned to the developmental needs, limitations, and emerging abilities of the child and, at worst, represents the most disturbing and heinous examples of child neglect and abuse. It is in the area of child control that there is a clearly documented history of sanctioned support for poor treatment of children. Alice Miller (1983, pp. 8–91) has provided a real service in abstracting from the laborious works of historians who have documented essays and manuals on child-rearing, which self-righteously instruct parents in singularly abusive methods for establishing iron-clad parental control and breaking the child's will. These methods include extreme and unremitting force, trickery, deception, manipulation, humiliation, and obviously cruel degradation. All of this, of course, is beautifully rationalized to be "for the child's own good."

These recommended methods for establishing absolute control begin in the very first months of life and there is developmental sophistication in the choice of techniques for overpowering children. For example, Jay Sulzer (1748, cited in Miller, 1983) wrote in *An Essay on Education and Instruction of Children*:

One of the advantages of these early years is that then force and compulsion can be used. Over the years, children forget everything that happened to them in early childhood. If their wills can be broken at this time, they will never remember afterwards that they had a will . . .

This same author provides excellent examples of the self-righteous rationalization for such procedures:

I advise all those whose concern is the education of children to make it their main occupation to drive out willfulness and wickedness and to persist until they have reached their goal. As I have remarked above, it is impossible to reason with young children; thus, willfulness must be driven out in a methodical manner, and there is no other recourse for this purpose than to show children that one is serious. If one gives in to their willfulness once, the second time it will be more pronounced and more difficult to drive out. . . . If parents are fortunate enough to drive out willfulness from the very beginning by means of scolding and the rod, they will have obedient, docile and good children whom they can later provide with a good education. If a good basis for education is to be established, then one must not cease toiling until one sees that all willfulness is gone, for there is absolutely no place for it. Let no one make the mistake of thinking he will be able to obtain good results before he has eliminated these two major faults . . . these, then, are the two most important matters one must attend to in the child's first year . . .

The author then goes on to instruct parents on the two most important matters to be taken up in the second year of life—orderliness and obedience.

Everything must follow the rules of orderliness. Food and drink, clothing, sleep, and indeed the child's entire little household must be orderly and must never be altered in the least to accommodate their willfulness or whims so that they may learn in earliest childhood to submit strictly to the rules of orderliness. The order one insists upon has an indisputable influence on their minds, and if children become accustomed to orderliness at a very early age, they will suppose thereafter that this is completely natural because they no longer realize that it has been artfully instilled in them. . . .

The second major matter to which one must dedicate oneself beginning with the second and third year is a strict obedience to parents and superiors and a trusting acceptance of all they do. These qualities are not only absolutely necessary for the success of the child's education, but they have a very strong influence on education in general. They are so essential because they impart to the mind orderliness per se and a spirit of submission to the laws. A child who is used to obeying his parents will also willingly submit to the laws and rules of reason once he is on his own and his own master, since he is already accustomed not to act in accordance with this own will. Obedience is so important that all education is actually nothing other than learning how to obey.

Unfortunately, the historical research indicates that this is not an isolated exception, particularly where it comes to the issue of contest of wills.

The only vice deserving of blows is obstinancy. . . . If your son does not want to learn because it is your will, if he cries with the intent of defying you, if he does harm in order to offend you, in short, if he insists on having his own way: *then whip him well till he cires so: Oh no, Pappa, oh no.* Such disobedience amounts to a declaration of war against you. Your son is trying to usurp your authority and you are justified in answering force with force in order to insure his respect, without which you will be unable to train him. The blows you administer should not be merely playful ones but should convince him that you are his master. . . . If he has seen that he is vanquished the first time and has been obliged to humble himself before you, this will rob him of his courage to rebel anew. (Kruger, J.G., 1752, quoted in Miller, 1983)

Or, note the advice of J. B. Basedow in his *Handbook for Fathers and Mothers of Families and Nations* (1773, quoted in Miller, 1983):

If after the chastisement the pain lasts for a time it is unnatural to forbid weeping and groaning at once. But if the chastised uses these annoying sounds as a means of revenge, then the first step is to distract them by assigning little tasks or activities. If this does not help, it is permissible to forbid the weeping and to punish them if it persists until it finally ceases after the new chastisement.

This quote particularly reminded me of the client I had once whose father repeatedly would threaten the following and then make good on his threat:

I will beat you till you cry and then I will beat you for crying.

In addition to their advocacy of orderliness, obedience, and the suppression of willfulness in children, these manuals on child rearing are also noteworthy for advocating the suppression of liveliness and emotion. For example, S. Landemann (1896, quoted in Miller, 1983) wrote a piece entitled *On Character Fault of Exuberance in Children*.

As is the case of all illnesses that are difficult to cure, so too, in the case of the psychic fault of exuberance, the greatest care must be devoted to prophylaxis, to prevention of the disorder. The best way for an education to reach this goal is by adhering unswervingly to the principle of shielding the child as much as possible from all influences that might stimulate feelings, be they pleasant or painful.

Or, consider this view of discipline:

Discipline, as the Old Testament word indicates, is basically chastisement (*Musar*). The perverse will, which to its own and other's detriment is not in command of itself, must be broken. . . . A consideration of the idea of punishment reveals that, in the task of education, healthy discipline must always include corporal punishment. It's early and firm but sparing application is the very basis of all genuine discipline because it is the power of the flesh that needs most to be broken . . . (Enzy Klopädic, quoted in Miller, 1983)

Granted, these child rearing manuals are a bit out of date, but as Miller cogently points out, the control of children has always been a problem in all cultures at all times, and these culturally ingrained notions have not died but have gone increasingly underground. This is particularly true when parents unconsciously act out the desire to have power over another and compulsively repeat the overpowering that they experienced. This form of repetition is particularly insidious in that almost nowhere else is it possible to engage in overpowering abuse that is so unavailable for detection. As Sulzer so accurately pointed out in 1748, little children "forget everything that happened to them . . . they will never remember afterwards that they had a will."

As with every other issue, I believe there is a continuum. In the severest cases, we hear of histories in which the caregivers are sadistic, intrusive, humiliating, and overpowering in the extreme. In these cases, the bad objects who themselves are often psychotic, brain-damaged, borderline, sociopathic, or otherwise severely disturbed, produce children who are damaged in several essential areas and may often be diagnosed as borderline personality disorders. These children are often physically, sexually, and psychologically abused with such intrusions as ritual abuse, frequent enemas, forced feeding, parental rages, and extraordinarily humiliating and depreciating experiences, which sadistically display their weakness and vulnerability. These individuals cannot help but internalize such bad objects and live a life characterized by intrapsychic relationships with them. Problems in negotiating all or most of the essential existential issues presented in this volume are common. With these individuals, the insights given here about masochism can be particularly helpful when we witness that aspect of their adjustment to abuse that represents self-defeat and simultaneously reproduces and preserves the bad object ties while expressing resistance, rebellion, and retaliation against that object.

At the other end of the continuum are individuals who come from parental or caretaking environments that, while they may be adequate in other ways, take a very dim view of child opposition. From the first "no" in the second year to the last minor violation of a teenager's curfew, punishment for any violation is sure, swift, and uncompromising. This kind of control is typically exerted with a great deal of self-confidence, even self-righteousness, being seen in the best interests of its recipient. In these families, there may be love, accurate mirroring and appreciation, and allowance and acceptance of self-expression, but there is no tolerance for opposition or any signs of disrespect. An individual child who is particularly willful or oppositional may create more of this kind of parental response than one who is more easily controlled. These individuals also internalize this saner but nevertheless stifling and controlling object and are more plagued by a kind of chronic stasis and diminished energy, while carrying out a life of socially sanctioned roles and obligations. While these more highly functioning individuals really provide the solid backbone of any number of social organizations, including, of course, their own families, they typically show relatively little spontaneity, creativity, originality, or spark. Their false self is one of compliance, service, and forbearance with the ability to sustain a great deal of frustration and self-sacrifice. These are often the people who take on the dull and dirty jobs because "somebody has to do it." And, they are truly better at playing this role than the rest of us. Those displaying the masochistic style are relatively perfect servants for hierarchical bureaucracies wherever they may be found.

SYMPTOMS MODELED AS INTERNAL OBJECT RELATIONS

In an earlier book (Johnson, 1991), I outlined a model for understanding symptomatic behavior as the expression of internal object relations. Using Fairbairn's (1974) model of intrapsychic structure, I provided four prototypes of internal object relations, which can account for all symptomatic behaviors. I offer that model again here as a way of mapping the internal dynamics of the masochistic person all along the continuum from character style to personality disorder. First, it will be necessary to briefly outline Fairbairn's model, which derived from his clinical work. In his work with abused children, Fairbairn noticed what so many others have noticed since—abused children want to return to their abusive parents. Furthermore, they often forget the abuse and it often takes considerable clinical skill to release these memories from repression. Finally, children will often make extraordinary efforts to maintain the perceived goodness of their parents when they do recall the abuse, through explaining away, justifying, or altering the parent's motivation (e.g., "He didn't mean to. It was an accident." etc.). Fairbairn later worked with schizoid individuals and later still with individuals experiencing "war neuroses." In these latter groups, Fairbairn was struck by the extent to which these people were haunted by internal self-destructive forces. Fairbairn posited that this resulted from an internalization of the bad object forces to which they had been exposed. His theory concerning the *internalization* of bad objects became the most essential aspect of his theory explaining psychopathology and relied on the concepts of *repression* and *splitting*. In his later work, Fairbairn believed that this internalization was simply a natural human process needing no explanation. Earlier on, he had hypothesized that we internalize bad objects to gain control over them and to remove the badness from the external object on whom we are dependent.

The key concept of repression is evidenced by the abused children forgetting their abuse and by the schizoid and war neuroses patients' ownership of the mysterious self-destructive forces of which they had been the targets. Splitting, the second key concept, is a primitive defense mechanism, which is used to separate the bad qualities of an object from the good. Splitting is used when the individual is unable to integrate in a whole conceptualization the good and bad object qualities.

Fairbairn posits that it is the bad object that is internalized and repressed and this is evidenced when an individual attacks himself in the way he was attacked. Thus, for example, an unwanted, schizoid person may have a mysterious destructive force that literally or metaphorically calls for his own destruction. So far this theory is relatively straightforward, but it gets more complicated and interesting. Fairbairn suggests that we *split the bad object into good and bad parts*. How can this be? Where's the good? *The good in the bad object exists in those entitled hopes and innate expectations for gratification with which the human being is instilled at birth.* Thus, a new baby deserves to be welcomed into the world and held; a young child deserves to be mirrored in his marvelous accomplishments of locomotion, language, and emerging independence; a school-aged child deserves to be taught by methods attuned to his emerging abilities and encouraged for his achievements. What is repressed and split off are, then, these developmentally arrested entitled expectations. In a very real way, the schizoid is still looking for acceptance in the world, the oral for complete and nonreciprocal need gratification, the symbiotic for an attuned mixture of connection and freedom, the narcissist for perfect mirroring and a completely idealizable other, etc. In Fairbairn's model, this is the good split-object, which has been internalized and repressed. Another way of saying it is that this is not the good object as experienced, but the good object as innately expected. Since this expectation is disappointed, it remains in its developmentally arrested and infantile form, unconscious and thereby unavailable for the optimal indulgence and optimal frustration that would mature it. So, what is now unconsciously hoped for is realistically impossible. Every inevitable disappointment is then followed by maneuvers that defend against the resulting pain.

We may use Fairbairn's model to depict any behavior as a representation of these internal object relations. Figure 1 is essentially four separate reproductions of that part of Fairbairn's model necessary for this discussion of symptomatic behavior modelled as internal

Figure 1
SYMPTOMS MODELED AS INTERNAL SELF-OBJECT RELATIONS

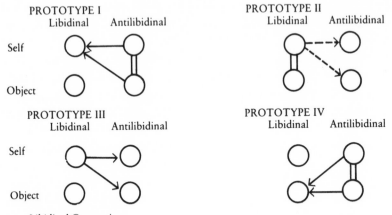

	Libidinal Connection
——>	Aggression
- - - ->	Aggression Possible

I. Antilibidinal self coalesced with antilibidinal object wherein aggression is directed at the libidinal self. Resulting symptoms are maintained by the bond of antilibidinal structures.

II. Libidinal self to libidinal object with concomitant *possibility* of aggression directed at antilibidinal structures.

III. Aggression from libidinal self to antilibidinal self and object. The pattern is maintained by the irrepressible nature of the libidinal impulses, as well as by the bond of the libidinal structures (not pictured here so as to distinguish this analysis from prototype II).

IV. Antilibidinal self and object to libidinal object wherein the aggression is directed at the libidinal object. The pattern is maintained by the bond of the antilibidinal structures.

self-object relations. In these four prototypes, *internal* self and object *perceptions* are represented as *split* into libidinal and antilibidinal parts. The circles represent these self and object structures.

Fairbairn's model uses two elemental forces. The first is aggression, symbolized by arrows, and the second is libidinal connection between self and object symbolized by two parallel vertical lines. I believe that Fairbairn's most essential contribution is the critical understanding that it is the desire for this maintenance of "libidinal" contact with even the bad object that keeps the dysfunctional patterns going and makes them so extraordinarily resistant to change.

In the present context of masochism, much of what the masochist does that is self-defeating, self-restraining, or self-torturing can be usefully understood as the individual doing to himself now what was done to him earlier. When he does this it can be usefully conceptualized as his own "internal saboteur" (Fairbairn, 1974) reacting against his natural, real, or "libidinal" self. This represents symptom Prototype I, depicted in Figure 1, wherein the antilibidinal self *and* object aggress against the libidinal self and thereby preserve their libidinal connection.

In the masochistic character, when self-defeat, humiliation, intrusion, restraint, and abuse are *perceived* to come from the object, this can usefully be conceptualized as aggression from the object end of the internal relationship as depicted in Prototype I, Figure 1. This can occur in at least three ways. First, there is projection of the internalized object onto the environment. Or, there is "projective identification" behavior, which elicits these kinds of negativity from the object. Or, third, masochistic individuals will tend to select individuals and environments that are consistently restraining and abusive in these ways. There is, of course, real abuse in the world, but the masochistic may have continuous involvement in these kinds of relationships and extraordinary difficulty in extricating herself from them.

Stopping behavior associated with the Prototype I dynamic involves the loss of the internalized object and those aspects of self-identification that have developed from that connection. In a very real sense, changing these dysfunctional patterns requires one to give up the ties to the family and to the identity that arises from this primal connection. Particularly when other significant ties are unavailable, as they often are in dysfunctional childhoods and later adult adjustments, relinquishing the bad object leaves the individual identity-less and eternally alone in the world. A bad object is better than none.

The model presented here is a motivational one, emphasizing why people do what they do. It yields interpretations and interventions based on the understanding of these motivations, which attempt, for example, to facilitate ecologically sound separation from bad object ties and the provision of external "good enough" object ties. For Prototype I behavior, for example, a number of therapists recommend the labelling and challenging of "separation guilt and survivor guilt" and provision of "corrective emotional experiences" in the therapeutic context in which the client learns that his expression of difference, opposition, or success does not threaten, destroy, or provoke retaliation in the therapist (e.g., Friedman, 1985; Horowitz, 1986; Modell, 1965, 1971; Weiss & Sampson, 1986).

I have labeled Prototype I symptomatology "Fear, Guilt, and Shame." While the label is not comprehensive, it does begin to list the kinds of behaviors that are very often the expression of this kind of antilibidinal aggression toward the libidinal self.

Prototype II is labeled "Entitlement/Addiction." Behaviors explained here are those that express the individual's entitlement to the originally and innately expected good object. We have a very hard time giving up that to which we are innately entitled. Because we can't live with the extreme pain of such a disappointment, we repress and otherwise defend against it. But until this grave disappointment is acknowledged, worked through, and ultimately accepted, we are inevitably driven by the force of this pain and our reaction to it.

While not all addictions may most usefully be modeled in this way, it is nevertheless true that many are at least partially explained by this dynamic. Food, alcohol, tranquilizers, analgesics, and narcotics can provide the kind of reliable and nonreciprocal immediate soothing that many an addict has missed from more natural, interpersonal sources. Amphetamine, cocaine, work, sex, and love addictions can all support the grandiose false self, which has been mobilized to cope with the narcissistic injury and loss of the undernourished real self. Gambling, spending, food, and love addictions can fill the emptiness of the borderline and other self-disordered pathologies. What keeps these patterns going and so resistant to change is the arrested, libidinal hope for contact with that "libidinal other" who was vitally needed for optimal human development. To move forward in the absence of that requires mourning this critical loss and, once and for all, giving up hope that the loss will ever be undone. To really change the behaviors associated with the Prototype II dynamic, one must accept one's life on its own terms and relinquish the undoing of lost entitlement.

The masochist is unique in that his self-defeating behavior is an expression of his determination to maintain integrity. In encountering a truly masochistic patient, one is struck by the extent to which he seems "addicted" to humiliation, degradation, defeat, and pain. This fact becomes less mysterious, however, when we find a history of abuse and a phenomenological history in which the only way of maintaining pride in the self was by deriving satisfaction from being able to "take it." To hold out, to refuse to cry, to endure the pain was the only way to show that one possessed an independent self. Thus, in many cases of masochistic self-defeat, what appears as symptomatic is really the individual's fixed strategy for coping with the internalized abusive object and maintaining the entitlement to a will of one's own. Giving up such well-endured defeat and pain, then, can represent the final surrender of this hard-won integrity of the self. In some of these cases, indeed, the intrusive, abusive object has acknowledged that ability to "take it" and this is as close as the victim ever got to having his independent, integrous self recognized. The entitlement represented here is to the recognition, acknowledgment, and encouragement of this innate right to autonomy and integrity. In the masochist's case, self-defeat paradoxically keeps this entitlement alive.

Prototype III is labeled "Resistance-Rebellion," and refers to behavior that can be explained most accurately by the aggression of the libidinal self and object against the antilibidinal object. Here, the child is fighting back against the restraint, intrusion, degradation, and abuse. The resistance and rebellion can, of course, be active and obvious or passive and intricately hidden. In the masochistic character, the self-torture, defeat, and abuse maintain contact with the original object (Prototype I), represent the integrity of the self that has been developed (Prototype II), and, at the same time, express the resistance and rebellion against the forces that produce this torture (Prototype III). Once again, in the masochist's case, all other avenues of resistance and rebellion have typically been disallowed. It is only through the exaggeration and display of self-defeat that there was any possibility for libidinal self-expression. I believe it is this sad state of affairs that accounts for the oft-noted extreme resistance to change of the masochistic character.

If he gives up self-defeat, there is no other means of libidinal self-expression. The well-known, underlying insidious spite of the masochist is all that is often left of the suppressed life force. Paradoxically, to give up self-defeat means total surrender to defeat. Again, what maintains Prototype III resistance and rebellion is the organism's commitment to his own libidinal self-expression in relation to an object—an object who can receive, appreciate, mirror, and delight in it. When all hope for that is lost, the organism will settle for having an impact in the only way that is left to him, through self-defeat, which is defeating to the object. This is an insidious and self-perpetuating trap, but the subjective, now unconscious, alternative was experienced as death.

Prototype IV is labeled "Abuse." In this paradigm, behavior is most accurately described and explained as the individual abusing others in the way he was abused. The antilibidinal self and object aggress on the libidinal object. The clearest examples of this are the child abusers who were themselves abused as children. The "role relationship model" is one of abuser and abused and, particularly in situations of low security or threat, the individual is prone to act out the abuser role. Weiss and Sampson (1986) have labeled this "turning passive into active." The masochist's servitude, passivity, and intractability very often have a martyred and guilt-inducing quality, which lead others to feel responsible, incompetent, ineffectual, and defeated. The malignant indirectness of masochistic hostility is often palpable but very difficult to identify and even more difficult to address in its eminent deniability.

The masochistic dynamic is particularly unique in that self-defeating behaviors can simultaneously represent all four prototypes. First, they do the individual in, in the way he was done in eliciting some of the assistance, sympathy and support that was originally required. Self-defeat maintains connection with the original bad object and related aspects of one's identity. Second, bearing pain and defeat expresses the integrity of self and the self-possession of will that is the human entitlement. Third, displayed defeat and tolerance of pain express the only form of resistance, rebellion, and libidinal expression not already crushed. And fourth, well-engineered, self-inflicted pain can return to sender the experienced abuse. Such a solution, though painful, is very difficult to give up.

AFFECT, BEHAVIOR, COGNITION

Affect

The essence of the masochist's subjectivity is the hopeless sense of being trapped in an endless circle of maximum effort leading to defeat. This chronic, effortful stalemate of life breeds hopelessness, pessimism, despair, deep distrust, and hopelessness for the future. This chronic suffering of sameness is usually dealt with only by bearing it and sharing it with whomever will listen. Friends, family, associates, and therapists typically hold out hope for these burdened ones only to be eventually defeated themselves. Those who have worked with masochistic clients consistently report of this defeat and discouragement, mirroring the masochist's own:

The problem of masochism has been, and still is, one of the most difficult therapeutic problems that faces the analytic psychiatrist. . . . After a superficial improvement there generally is a relapse of the old symptoms and complaints, and this pattern tends to repeat itself throughout the course of the analysis. . . . Freud's failure to overcome this "negative therapeutic reaction" in the case of masochism led him to formulate the concept of the death instinct. (Lowen, 1958, p. 194)

In short, something very active in the patient attempts to destroy time, love and concern and cognitive understanding. I think that the therapist is here facing the activation of the deepest levels of aggression. Sometimes it is hopeless to resolve these severe treatment stalemates; however, it is sometimes possible to do so with an essentially analytic approach. (Kernberg, 1984, p. 244)

If he puts himself with the patient in the actual world that fails her, she will tell him nothing but problems, and the morale of both will sink into the morass. The only force forceful enough to take a person out of the morass is desire. Duty is too weak. But desire that delights this particular person may be hard to find. (Gustafson, 1992)

The thoroughness of this discouragement can be readily understood from the etiology and model of object relations already presented. When every expression of the libidinal self has been blocked to the point of defeating one's will, it makes sense to give up hope at all but the most subterranean level so as not to be beaten, humiliated, or fooled again. Similarly, one's aggression, resistance, and rebellion can only be expressed in the subterranean closed system in which the internalized bad object is the target of that rebellion and aggression. So, whenever there is rebellion, it is self-defeating. The only outward aggression exists in self-defeat, which simultaneously defeats the other.

To review this most essential understanding of masochism again, the peculiar stuckness of the masochistic character revolves around the fact that self-defeating behavior is about all that's available. The self-defeat maintains contact with the original controlling or sadistic object (Prototype I). It expresses rebellion in the only way available (Prototype III). It controls and sadistically abuses without the admission of responsibility for doing so (Prototype IV), and it achieves the status of an addiction, which secretly keeps alive hope and pride by perversely demonstrating the individual's ability to take punishment (Prototype II). For this character structure, all roads lead to the same end — self-defeat. The masochist is a kind of "one trick pony" but with incredible diversity within this one trick, and with variations of the motivational determinants for any given trick within this single class. In other words, sometimes the trick represents an attempt to reconnect with the bad object, at other times it serves to rebel against that object, and at still other times it seems to defeat others or to maintain integrity through demonstrating one's ability to hold out in suffering. Many times, more than one of these motives are served by the same actions.

The masochist is also marked by a distinct lack of pleasurable experiences. The masochistic character exists on a continuum from very oversocialized to sadistically controlled. Much of this socialization has to do with inhibition of those natural human responses that bring pleasure. Pleasure is a threat and its experience will lead to anxiety and guilt. So, it is avoided automatically, and, even when he tries, the masochistic individual finds it extremely difficult to experience any real or deep pleasure. Pleasure invites control or punishment from the internalized bad object, and pleasure invites the hope for freely given love, which the masochist has long ago foregone.

Not surprisingly, it is the spiteful hatred and resentment of this character that has been most often noted as the primary identifying characteristic. The awareness of this deep negativity varies among individuals of this character type, with generally more awareness at the lower levels of structural functioning. As we move to the character style end of the continuum, individuals tend to be more compliant, anxious, and guilt-ridden with little awareness of the ways in which their self-defeat is defeating. Their deep hatred and attempts at rebellion are typically unconscious to them. Others, however, often see and feel the hateful consequences of their underlying aggression.

Though often characterized by her hopelessness, the masochistic character retains hope, however secretly. Theodore Reik's (1941) treatise on masochism is among the best in reflecting this characteristic. Reik posits that the attainment of release in pleasure of whatever kind is anxiety-provoking because of the punishment it heralds. To control this anxiety, the masochistic individual produces a "flight forward" of the punishment so that the punishment is experienced first (Prototype I), thereby reducing the anxiety and justifying or licensing the pleasure or release. In Reik's view, sexual masochism involves this process in the sexual sphere and social masochism involves this process with respect to aggression and self-expression in the social sphere. The difference, according to Reik, is that the primary sexual pleasure and the pleasure in suffering are often conscious in sexual masochism but rarely conscious in social masochism.

Masochism in its social form often relies on the very hidden and often unconscious hope of vindication or satisfaction in some very distant future (modelled here as Prototype II). Reaping one's rewards in heaven or in the future exemplifies this deeply held, often secret, and/or unconscious form of hope. Herein also lies the masochist's egotism, superiority, and eventual vindication. As Gustafson (1992, p. 34) writes, "We dwell delighted, all of us, however demeaned, somewhere secret."

The continuing tragedy for the masochist, however, is that even when release is earned by suffering it can lead to guilt. In the social sphere, a masochistic individual will sometimes cash in on a well-earned aggressive outburst or other assertive self-expression. This will in turn activate the internalized bad or antilibidinal object who will activate guilt and anxiety no matter how justified the outburst. Frequently, the environment also reacts punitively, putting the individual back in his masochistic place. This is, of course, the familiar place in which aggression, and particularly resistance to the will of others, was crushed. Thus, conscious hope and trust of a positive or immediate kind is driven further into secrecy or unconsciousness. One so consistently defeated becomes entrenched in distrust of the world and particularly of anyone who could be so naive and foolish as to offer hope. The spiteful desire to drag anyone down who tries this is endemic.

Behavior

Before describing the behavior that is characteristic of masochism, I want to emphasize again that I am presenting a theoretical model in this book, not an actuarial one. In other words, practically any behavior can be found in any character structure, and it is really the dynamic motivational structure underlying the behavior that determines the characterological issues represented by its expression. Nevertheless, a collection or pattern of behaviors expressed in a certain characteristic attitude certainly does signal the high probability of a given characterological issue. In the case of masochism, the persistent demonstration of a whole plethora of behaviors that could be broadly called self-defeating is often definitional. This is particularly true when self-defeating behavior is permeated with a good deal of negativity not only toward the self but toward others. Even if the behaviors in question are quite self-effacing and apparently passive, they do tend to elicit annoyance, irritation, and even abuse from others, thereby provoking further self-defeat.

All behavior that could be characterized as psychopathological or dysfunctional in any of us is in some way or another self-defeating. What distinguishes the masochist from others is that there is, at some level of consciousness, a perverse pleasure or satisfaction in self-inflicted punishment. This pleasure comes from the fact that libidinal pleasure can only come from self-defeat or resistance. What distinguishes the masochistic patients from all others is that such self-defeat is the only form of self-integrity, resistance, and rebellion left in the repertoire. This perverse pleasure in pain that is self-inflicted or otherwise self-initiated is masochism's distinguishing feature. And, it is this feature that makes masochistic self-defeat even more resistant to change than it is in other character structures.

The knowledge of these dynamics, however, provides the singularly most important direction for those who wish to change this adjustment. Here, recall Gustafson's (1986, p. 201) cogent statement of an element of Bateson's work: "All the moves *seen* are but members of a class which is *unseen*." With this character structure, the moves that are seen are all forms of self-defeat, but the classes that are unseen are loyalty, resistance, rebellion, and integrous, autonomous expressions of will. The other forms of libidinal self-expression can be liberated in such a way that the person's will is not crushed again. The masochist can then relinquish "cutting off his nose to spite his face."

Sometimes, the masochist will release his spite in such a vitriolic manner that he will provoke the kind of retaliation that will only further the masochistic process and reinforce the script decisions or pathogenic beliefs of this structure. This may even be part of some masochists' standard operating procedure in displaying the provocation that occurs in this personality. An effective psychotherapy will have to release the spite from unconsciousness, encourage its expression, and help the client to direct and modulate that expression.

Having said all this, let us now return to cataloguing the *seen* members of these *unseen* classes, always remembering that these behaviors are not, for our purposes, masochistic unless they are members of these unseen classes of libidinal expression and thereby pleasurable.

Subservience. "The meek shall inherit the earth," said Jesus. Fictional literature on sexual masochism is perhaps the best place to acquire an understanding of the possibility of learning the satisfactions of painful, demeaning, and relentless servitude (e.g., see Rice, 1985). Both Reik and Reich emphasized in their treatments of masochism that the pain was not endured for itself but rather for the release and pleasure of sexuality, which would otherwise be prohibited. With social masochism, the consciousness of pleasure or satisfaction is most rare and less obvious. In general, however, the secret satisfaction of servitude is moral superiority. Masochistic individuals are often at least dimly aware of the guilt redemption associated with good works. Because of the kind of parenting the masochist has had and the natural reactions to it, she has a great deal of guilt to work off. The development of healthy, normal narcissism was typically not allowed in these families so it is consciously disavowed yet unconsciously maintained in a kind of martyrdom, the rewards of which come later. Reik (1941) is particularly prolific in his reports of the fantasies of masochistic patients, which ultimately prove their superiority, even including the tormenting of those who have tormented them. These fantasies particularly illustrate the payoff of earning narcissistic superiority and aggressive expression just as the sexual masochist earns sexual gratification.

Delay. Here is an excellent strategy for being chronically miserable and maddening to others: Be chronically dissatisfied with everything in your life, complain constantly, but do nothing effective to change your situation. If you are in a particularly bad marriage or work situation, be sure to stay there, in that it provides a never-ending supply of material to complain about and to justify why you feel so badly.

If someone suggests an alternative, reject it as something that wouldn't work or that you've already tried. Or, try it out, but make sure it doesn't work. If anyone ever criticizes you for any of this, either agree profusely with their criticism and extend it even further, or, if you feel you have enough credits to do so, finally let out your frustration and spite on them for their insensitivity, ineptitude in trying to assist you, or their stupidity in not seeing the hopelessness of your situation. Whether you continue with your habitual passive-aggressive behavior or show a rare indulgence of aggression, remember to always hold to the morally superior position. By adopting this strategy, you will remain defeated but you won't be alone. By dragging the other down with you, you can further justify your position and enjoy a certain amount of triumph. After all, you are used to this and have never expected anything different. This will be a particularly effective strategy with your children who will find it more than usually difficult to reject you. With any luck at all, they will never give up on you, and you can sustain this solution to life's problems for a life time.

Victimization of Self. Masochistic individuals have a high propensity for getting themselves into and great difficulty getting themselves out of bad situations. Marrying an alcoholic or otherwise seriously addicted person or one who is physically or verbally abusive is common. Alternatively, getting stuck in a dead end or unsuitable job, working for an abusive or exploitive boss or company or pursuing a career for which one has little talent, are similarly common. These choices have both the internal and external psychological advantage of not appearing self-inflicted. In this way, the masochistic person can avoid taking responsibility for what really is a pattern of self-defeat. In this connection, it is interesting to note that the American Psychiatric Association's decision not to include the self-defeating personality disorder in their *Diagnostic and Statistical Manual* has been more political than objective. The understandable yet misguided reason for this is to avoid "blaming the victim." It is unfortunate if this charitable decision works to blur our understanding of bringing responsibility to consciousness, which is a necessary step in altering these unnecessarily painful patterns. For a data-based discussion of the self-defeating personality disorder, see Fiester (1991), who concluded that "data from existing studies show a relatively high prevalence, slightly higher female:male sex ratio, good internal consistency, significant overlap with several other personality disorders . . . " and other less critical findings concerning this diagnosis.

Negative Success Reactions. As early as 1923, Sigmund Freud noticed a phenomenon he labeled negative therapeutic reaction. Therapeutic interventions that should be beneficial or that were initially effective led to just the opposite result: Patients got worse. Freud associated this phenomenon with masochism and eventually with his posited death instinct. Such reactions certainly are common in the psychotherapy of individuals with this issue, but similar reactions extend to other experiences in life that should be positive, encouraging, or cause for celebration. These reactions certainly do suggest to anyone who witnesses them that here must be an individual who truly enjoys suffering and who wouldn't be caught dead experiencing any pleasure. It's almost as if they won't give themselves or anyone else the satisfaction of having any satisfaction. These reactions are particularly fascinating and diabolical when they involve an apparently unconscious provocation of others so that others, and not the self, are responsible for this resulting negativity.

Any of the following categories of self-defeating behavior may fit into one or more of the first four categories: subservience, delay, self-victimization, and negative success reaction. I list the following merely for their heuristic value in helping you identify these kinds of masochistic tendencies.

Problem Flooding*. An excellent means of staying the same and delaying any effective problem solving is to overwhelm oneself with the most negative construal of all the problems that one faces, simultaneously. By never staying on one problem long enough to formulate and implement action, one can keep a flood of such complaints going indefinitely. With experience, you can easily involve others in this process and induce the same kind of trance of helplessness and confusion you originally experienced. As you get better at doing it and tolerating it, you can induce more uncomfortable helplessness and confusion in others than you yourself experience. Berne (1964) was particularly astute in cataloguing the internal and external psy-

---

*I would like to acknowledge Gustafson (1986) for delineating this characteristic, which he labelled "problem saturation."

chological gains of these kinds of maneuvers in such games as "Why don't you, yes but."

Provocation. As Reik (1941) has noted, provocation of punishment is far more operative in social masochism than in sexual masochism. I think it's obvious by the foregoing examples how the masochistic character can be maddeningly provocative. The provocation is further accentuated by the usual deniability of the provocation itself. After all, this downtrodden person is only telling us how badly he feels, how insoluble are his problems, and how no one can help.

In addition to the kinds of provocations listed already, masochistic individuals are noted for their innocent, "Who me?" passive aggression in such forms as forgetfulness, missing critical details in the midst of overly conscientious and sacrificial work, or "accidents," which damage others but which are deniable and suitably humiliating to the perpetrator. Such "accidents" are a good example of masochistic behavior, which is at once punishing yet unconsciously gratifying of the masochist's spite and hostility.

The masochistic individual is often particularly good at what may be called "water torture provocation." Every single act may be relatively inconsequential so that when the last act finally succeeds in provoking an enraged response, that response is not justified by what has just happened. This enables the masochist to simultaneously be beaten and yet retain the moral high ground. Again, when practiced on one's children, this masochistic strategy can be particularly effective.

Generalized Anhedonia. The social masochist is sometimes most easily recognized by the singular absence of any pleasure in life. Masochistic individuals often present as chronically burdened, self-effacing persons who typically are making maximum efforts, continually struggling, but getting nowhere. Watching and listening to them typically calls to mind the myth of Sysiphus, the result always the same, salvation permanently out of reach. Theirs is a chronic depression. As with all depressions, there is some fluctuation, but the masochistic depression typically has less variation than most and has the feeling that Reich labelled "the masochistic bog or morass." There is no exit. And yet, masochistic individuals are often remarkable in their ability to keep going in spite of massive burden and hopelessness. They are chronically discouraged yet keep going. And that, I believe, is the key to the masochistic adjustment. They have found a perverse way of winning through losing.

Masochists' Behavior in Therapy. In psychotherapy, the masochist is often compliant to all the ground rules and procedures. These clients are usually chronically unsatisfied or describe themselves as "stuck" in one or more areas of their life. They may very well have a history of prior psychotherapy, which, though it may have gone on for years, was essentially ineffective. These clients will rarely show any resentment or direct aggression in their daily lives or in the therapy process itself. Their former therapist or therapists may provide the only exception to this in that these clients may be very derogatory or mean-spirited toward them. If you're the therapist, you're next. These clients are typically initially appreciative and responsive to whatever therapeutic interventions are chosen, but in their external life, nothing ever changes. Their unsatisfactory job, marriage, or personal difficulties, such as persistent depression, procrastination, or other self-defeating behaviors are characterized most by stasis. They may become quite discouraged with this, self-recriminating, or withdraw somewhat from the process, but they almost never get actively angry with the therapist. Yet therapist responsibility for failure is implied, and it is a rare therapist who doesn't feel somehow responsible and not quite capable. The therapist's natural reaction to this kind of passive-aggressive defeat is, of course, anger and frustration. The two most common countertransference errors with this kind of client are (1) acting out this frustration and anger so that the client is shamed once again, or (2) denial of the frustration and anger leading to a prolonged therapy characterized by deadness and lack of meaningful change or relationship. Very often, therapists will choose the second course until they can't take it anymore, and then they will resort to the first.

The treatment of choice, which is much easier said than done, is to utilize these natural human reactions to begin the liberation of the client's aggressive, spiteful, shadow side, which may be all that is even potentially available of this person's suppressed life force, exuberance, willfulness, and all other authentic feelings. Such a client has a long history of passive-aggressive defeat of others, and it is sometimes possible to catch the current self-other defeat in progress and use this to lead the client back through this history. Particularly when the client's delight in his frustration and defeat of others can be engaged, the embers of his suppressed true self may be reignited. Indeed, in this character, resistance is all that is left of the real self. So, resistance needs to be welcomed and acknowledged for its survival value and underlying intents. Attempting to suppress such resistance is the most deadly mistake a therapist can make. The masochistic person is far better at maintaining his own resistance than any therapist can be in holding out against it. This was the only revenge he could exact for being suppressed and he has spent nearly all of his life perfecting it. In a struggle, the therapist doesn't have a chance.

Cognition

Before beginning the outline of the cognitive characteristics of the masochist, it might be useful to remember once again that this, like all other characterological issues, exists on a continuum from most to least severe (i.e., from personality disorder to character style). At the lower end of the continuum, the force applied for socialization or any other domination is truly abusive and comes out of the parent's own pathology, which is extreme. Here, abuses will always be more generalized and not exclusively directed at strictly controlling the child's socialization. In these cases, other characterological issues will be present and often more dominant than the masochistic one. At the other end of the continuum, you will more likely find more loving, compassionate, and healthy parents who have themselves been indoctrinated to accept an overly rigid and dominating approach to socialization. In this, they themselves have a definite masochistic predisposition. The discipline they mete out and the extinction of exuberance they effect may indeed hurt them as they hurt their children. Nevertheless, they comply and produce compliance in their children. These children may well feel that their parents loved them but, like their parents, believe that there are powerful negative forces in themselves, which must be tamed. In the more common middle ground, parental psychopathology is less severe than that which produces personality disorder and is coupled with societal sanctions for training, controlling, and disciplining children. Where parental psychopathology and societal sanctions combine to emphasize the control issue, you see a more singularly masochistic personality.

When you get to know a masochistic person, you are most commonly impressed by their singularly burdened attitude. Life is hard, things often don't work out, it's important to be careful about what you do, say, or feel. If these people are not always unhappy, they are almost never truly happy. And if they express positive feelings or attitudes at all, this is not done with any real enthusiasm or optimism. These people are burdened, inhibited, and always a bit wary of the world. They don't feel deeply, fall desperately in love, get uncontrollably angry, or ungroundedly excited. Even their depression, which can be quite profound, is never really desperately felt as say, that of the oral or narcissistic character might be. Over a period of time, one may wonder how they can bear so much chronic pain without being more devastated by it. More than any other character structure, they can truly "take a licking and keep on ticking." They can hold out remarkably well and for remarkably long periods of time without collapsing or breaking down. They don't like it, but they've accepted long ago that this is how life is. Any real hope for things being substantially different has long ago been extinguished and any revivification of that hope is profoundly upsetting to their psychological equilibrium. This is a truly conservative person who is quite distrustful of change or hope. Things are bad all right, but they could get worse. The almost reflexive response to any suggestions for change is—it won't work, there's something wrong with it, I've tried it before, or it's dangerous.

A second characteristic attitude of the masochistic character all along the continuum is that he tries to be good. That was his essential script decision when he gave up the fight for independence. There is, of course, the fear of doing wrong and being punished as before. These attitudes underlie the oft noted tendencies toward compliance, self-effacement, subservience, and appeasement. Consciously, this person sees herself as innocent, well-intentioned, but misused, unappreciated, unfortunate, victimized, or unlucky. The innocence of "Who me?" and the victimization of "Why me?" pervade the masochist's consciousness and conscious self-presentation. The masochist will come to therapy or ask for help but she doesn't really believe that help will be forthcoming or that anything will ever really work. But, what else can she do?

In the masochist there is also the attitude, not always conscious nor always unconscious, that pleasure is wrong, sinful, and to be distrusted. This can be expressed in conscious morality or religiosity or it may simply be represented in the body by a now very "hard-wired" restraint and inhibition of any pleasurable experience.

The masochist's essential, repressed cognition with the appropriately associated affect can be summarized in two words: "fuck you." More explicitly: "You will never conquer me. I am indomitable. I have fooled you. You think you have suppressed me, but just you wait. You think you have beaten me, but just you wait. I will get even. And you won't even see it coming. Vengeance will be mine if it takes forever. You will pay for this. My spirit will be avenged. I can wait as long as it takes. You have taught me forbearance; some day you will regret it. I will never give in, I will never trust you or love you again. I will defeat you if it kills me."

The human spirit is indomitable. Attempts to completely extinguish it will merely drive it very deeply underground to the psychic bomb shelter where it can wait indefinitely and from which it can strike vengefully and unexpectedly. Totalitarian regimes are ultimately overthrown and the rage finally unleashed in those rebellions is usually violent, swift, and satisfying (cf. the French, Russian, and Romanian Revolutions).

The therapist's job in this situation is to help the person see that, externally, the war is over, the danger is past. The person can emerge from the deeply subterranean bomb shelter. But to do so, he has to give up revenge and that is very difficult to do. When you have been this injured, it is very difficult to forgive and go on. The therapist's job is somehow to help this defeated child to give up revenge except insofar as "living well is the best revenge."

The internalized bad object must also be released from the unconscious and eventually expunged. For, as long as the antilibidinal self and object resulting from the internalization process is present in the self, the war continues and is ultimately passed on to one's children who really become the innocent objects of the masochist's vengefulness. Children are the only ones helpless enough to truly get even on and this, of course, is the ultimate defeat for any parent.

Prior to the exorcism of the bad object, the content of the masochist's cognition includes the shoulds, prohibitions, beliefs, and restraints of the controlling, intrusive parent. The exorcism will also uncover the developmentally arrested attitudes of the libidinal self, and these attitudes will, at times, be self-centered, absolute, and in need of maturation. As therapy progresses, this may initially frighten and embarrass the patient and lead to these attitudes being driven underground again. Here is a situation where the therapy does indeed require a "corrective emotional experience." The client cannot really provide himself with what has never been provided. Asserting otherwise and expecting the client to do this for himself is where the traditional psychoanalysts have simply been wrong and have failed their patients. The therapist, both in his own self-management and in the exercise of his authority role with the client, can provide, over time, a good enough object and model for a reinternalization of both appropriate standards and self-treatment in the area of social rules, discipline, responsibility, and ethical-moral behavior. The masochist has truly internalized someone not entirely unlike Messrs. Sulzer and Basedow, quoted earlier from the eighteenth and nineteenth centuries. The patient can really do a lot better and most therapists can provide substantive help as the "good enough" object for internalization.

This then is not the place for therapist abstinence and neutrality. While that therapeutic stance may be initially useful to promote the necessary negative transference for a reconstruction and analysis, it does not help at all in the process of the eventual maturation of the libidinal self. Metaphorically, it leaves the young child alone when he really needs a good enough model and mediator for negotiating optimal freedom and social responsibility. While the therapist is certainly not the only person who can be constructively used in this manner, she is usually a very critical figure for this process. To leave the client alone at this point justifies the very hopelessness and distrust with which the person began the therapeutic process.

THERAPEUTIC OBJECTIVES

The therapist with a need-to-cure and the patient with a need-to-fail establish one of the most stable and enduring and unchanging pairs in the civilized world.
—Herbert Gross, 1981

The primary objective of psychotherapy with the masochistic character is to assist the client in giving up a lifestyle characterized by *depressive affect*, *self-defeating behavior*, and *cognition charac-*

terized by pessimism and distrust. As I hope has already been made clear, however, this entire constellation serves the dual purpose of defining and maintaining the self while defending against the emergence of very threatening affects. As one descends on the continuum of structural functioning, the self-defining and sustaining role of masochistic behavior will increase in importance and the difficulties encountered in giving it all up will be correspondingly greater. It will not be possible for the masochistic person to give up this way of life until she begins to develop other avenues for defining and sustaining the self. Similarly, the compromise solutions of masochism will not be relinquished until she works through the feelings that will be emerging and until she experiences the strength of self required to endure them. Thus, the treatment of this and all other personality issues outlined in this volume needs to be approached with a cognizance of both the conflict model and deficit model of human problems.

As the individual relinquishes this lifestyle, he will begin to revivify hope and trust. His expectations for the results of his own actions, his relationships, and the quality of his internal experience will change. He will look forward to things, have faith in others, risk to dream, express ambition, and experience pleasure in his senses, ideas, and accomplishments. Finally, he will be able to do things that meet his needs and further his dreams.

If you know someone who is very profoundly masochistic, the foregoing description must seem almost impossible. And, it may well be, because any true change in a masochistic personality is truly transformational in nature. It means an almost complete relinquishing of identity, lifestyle, and basic orientation to one's self, others, and the world. Though the therapeutic process with this personality will be characterized by fits and starts, it ultimately cannot be of any real use if it is at half-measure. To be helped, the masochistic character must truly experience a major shift in identity and orientation. Yet, he will make it very difficult for you to do anything for him. Any therapeutic endeavor will be defeated, one way or another. It is this pattern of defeat, with its concomitant affects, behaviors and cognitions, which will provide some of the most useful content for psychotherapy. It almost doesn't matter what you do or where you start. This is where you will end up.

The masochistic character is particularly skilled in getting others to collaborate with his lifestyle in one of two ways. First, if people respond with sympathy and similarity in affective state, he has created a mirror and confirmation of himself, particularly if the sympathetic person tries to help. The helper can then be defeated and thereby experience even more of the masochist's internal reality and collude with it. Second, individuals will respond in a complementary fashion by initially or ultimately rejecting him. Some will just reject him initially for his whining and inability to solve his own problems. Others, after having tried and repeatedly failed, will reject out of the frustration of being induced to feel exactly as the masochist feels—hopeless, incompetent, pessimistic, and angry. Unfortunately, therapists can often fall into either of these two groups.

So, what can be done? I believe the essence of the answer is in an accurate diagnosis as soon as possible. Often, this diagnosis will have to be obtained the hard way, by suffering the depressive affect and pessimism that the masochist is expert at eliciting in others and by suffering the inevitable defeats to any attempted therapeutic regimen. Once the diagnosis has been made, however, the therapist can from then on welcome what would otherwise have been unwelcome. A considerable degree of enlightenment is required to do this. One's human responses to the masochist are usually necessary to really experience how he feels, to understand the effect he has on others, and to grasp the self-perpetuating and cyclical nature of his problem. However, it is necessary, as soon as possible, not to respond or act out in these conventional ways for there to be any chance of ameliorating rather than reinforcing the pattern. In tackling this same point, Herbert Gross (1981) writes, "The dilemma would be to respond to the miserable patient rather than the misery of the patient." By this, I believe Gross is suggesting the same thing I am suggesting—to notice but not catch the misery one may so easily catch from the patient. Catching is useful diagnostically but it is not useful to respond from that caught place. The misery is essentially the patient's problem. How the patient becomes miserable is something the doctor can do something about by providing insight into how and why the patient makes herself so miserable. The therapist can also teach alternative strategies to deal with the conflicts and deficits that the patient experiences. But, the choice whether or not to use any of this remains with the patient. The therapist, coming from the position of neutrality, curiosity, separateness, and analytic attitude, allows the client to more consciously perceive this choice and take responsibility for making it. The therapist loses whenever he takes responsibility for the client's misery, because the patient stays the same by giving this responsibility to others and then defeating them.

The strategic therapists (e.g., Watzlawick, Weakland, and Fisch, 1974) have a strategy that comes to mind here for clients that are both unable and unwilling to change. It is termed the "Why Change Paradox," and essentially involves outlining to the client all the payoffs or advantages of his style of living. It is then quite seriously suggested that the individual not change because the cost would be too high. The individual is deemed better off with the kind of adjustment he already has established. I believe that something like this would only work with the masochist if the therapist were coming from a very enlightened position wherein this intervention would truly be given without any attempt to manipulate or strike back with hostility at a defeating client. The presentation of this idea would obviously have to be altered to truly emphasize the life choice required to give up an adaptation that provides identity, family, rebellion, aggression, and escape from emptiness, heartbreak, risk, rage, and much much more. Personally, this is the only way I would use such an intervention as I see the classic presentation of "paradox" as manipulation with a hidden agenda. But, to the extent that the underlying true therapeutic stance is neither manipulative nor hostile, it does represent a response to the miserable patient as opposed to a response to the misery in the patient. It clearly signals who is responsible for what and eliminates the therapist's participation in the familiar social interactions, which serve only to perpetuate the problem. In classic ways of understanding, the masochistic patient is typically the most resistant and these are precisely the patients for whom such strategies have apparently proven the most useful.

I believe that the therapists from the analytic school (e.g., Gross, 1981) and the strategic therapy school are essentially suggesting the same thing in response to these clients. Once again, however, this is much more easily said than done, and one must truly be in the position to allow the client to make his choice and live with the consequences, whatever they may be. Having made this clear, it now is possible to outline, in what would otherwise seem a very naive fashion, the cognitive, affective, and behavioral objectives for the masochistic character.

Cognitive Objectives

It can be ultimately useful for both therapist and client to truly understand the particular configuration of prior experiences that caused this client to adopt this particular lifestyle, including the script decisions or pathogenic beliefs, self-identifications, and so on. In this process, however, there may not be the same kind of truly collaborative therapeutic alliance that can occur in other structures. Even the compliance, which is obvious here, may be only superficial and part of a strategy to invalidate the therapist. However accurate his explanation, reconstruction, or interpretation, it doesn't help. Nothing helps, until the patient chooses the shift in responsibility. Yet, this knowledge can lead to clarity that there is a choice and explicate exactly what that choice is.

Beyond reconstruction of the past, the client may also be *ultimately* helped by interpretations of his affects, behaviors, and cognitions following the four paradigms of the underlying internal object relations. For the masochistic character, paradigms 1, 3, and 4 are usually more useful initially than 2, since the masochist has essentially given up conscious hope. The therapist can give the masochist an opportunity to learn how he has been programmed to maintain this depressive, self-defeating lifestyle. He can be given a chance to learn why he works to maintain a depressive state. He can learn how his self-defeating behavior helps to maintain and justify this state. He can begin to appreciate how his infusing others with this state works to maintain it either through the mirroring and collusion he achieves or by the provocation that results in his rejection. The masochistic client can be given the opportunity to change his view of his core experience from intrinsic and self-sustaining to alien and the result of circumstantial programming.

The therapeutic process will provide many and recurring opportunities to explore and understand how masochistic patterns play themselves out interpersonally. This can lead to similar understandings involving the client's current relationships. Analysis at this level will include such things as greater self-awareness concerning his subservience and provocation of others, his passive-resistance to control, his use of others to maintain depressive stasis, his hidden rebellion, aggression and spite, his maneuvers to escape personal responsibility, etc.

Affective Objectives

Successful treatment of the masochistic character will essentially involve her experiencing and taking responsibility for conscious rage and pleasure. Historically, the rage at abusive treatment, particularly overcontrol, has been suppressed and eventually repressed. Pleasure threatens the depressive defense and the depressive self-definition. Thus, both rage and pleasure create anxiety. These individuals need to learn to access these forbidden feelings, bear the anxiety that initially accompanies them, and eventually be desensitized to them. The spite, of which the masochistic person may be somewhat conscious, can be a beginning to this process as it may be the only residual expression of the real self. In this spite, there is both rage and pleasure, though the latter is often even more unconscious than the former.

The therapist may only give the client the opportunity to find himself in these ways. Even where the resistance is experienced as entirely automatic, the client may still choose whether or not to fight it. Of course, the client can consciously or unconsciously undermine the authenticity of this decision. But, this undermining provides further content for the therapy. In this representative pattern of resistance and analysis, there needn't be a battle between patient and therapist if the therapist doesn't need to help too much. People don't relinquish survival patterns, which have worked, until they have better survival patterns, which work just as well. When the client sabotages himself, he does so because he doesn't feel there is a viable alternative.

Any treatment of rage and pleasure in the masochist will, of course, involve the issue of guilt. This is one area in which I believe the therapist can be productively a bit more active with the masochistic person. She can give the patient permission to experience these affects without guilt though, once again, one has to be careful about opening the door to a struggle. Permission must be just that—not requirement. When the client changes permission to requirement and then resists it, this becomes more grist for the mill in the masochist's treatment.

Should the masochistic client decide to really risk change, she will experience anxiety and fear. Essentially, it is the fear of being beaten and heartbroken again. If we never get our hopes up, we can never be disappointed; if we never trust, we can never be betrayed; if we never risk, we can never lose what would have been bet on the risk. When the masochistic person hopes, trusts, or risks, the anxiety is great because prior costs have been heavy. Here, the therapist can help modulate the anxiety by just being there, by helping the client to evaluate the risk level with a wary eye for self-defeating set-ups and by always helping the client take full responsibility for the risks that she does take. Again, it is particularly important with these patients that the therapist not need to succeed, that he separate himself from the patient, and that he be continually clear about responsibility.

Finally, as with the therapy of all characterological issues, there will be grief—grief over the initial tragedies that created these painful strategies for living, grief at the loss of identity and family that must come with any true characterological change, and grief at the lost time and opportunities resulting from this self-destructive lifestyle. The therapist's main role in this is to simply be there as the client bears this grief. If the masochistic client ever gets this far, there is also a great deal to be happy about.

Behavioral-Social Objectives

The objectives in this category are, of course, to help the client desist self-defeating behaviors and concomitantly learn new behaviors, which can fulfill the necessary functions served by self-defeat. This is a challenging task because, in this character structure, self-defeat is defensive, self-defining, a mediator of contact with internal and external objects, rebellious, and retaliatory. A direct behavioral tack is usually quite ill-advised, particularly initially, because these clients are particularly prone to ask for, and then defeat, suggestions. For this reason, I think it is advisable to eschew direct behavioral work until one is reasonably sure that there is insight about the self-defeating process and a commitment to work through it. Even then, it is often useful to suggest any behavioral changes in a more self-consciously oblique way than might ordinarily be the case. For example, once insight and commitment have been achieved, it might be useful to wonder out loud, "I wonder what would happen if you were to just stop yourself from complaining to your friends?" For, although much self-defeating behavior can be entirely unconscious and beyond the client's conscious control, there are a number of patterns, such as complaining, which are more or less voluntary and therefore under conscious control. When the client is able to stop them voluntarily for a period of time, he can become increasingly aware of the functions they serve. Complaining, for example, often serves to structure social interactions and is felt to obtain intimacy in ways that nothing else really can. Experiencing the discomforts involved in giving up complaining can lead to insight concerning the functions it serves and the need to establish other methods of performing these functions. Complaining, for example, may well have been an historical conduit for closeness, particularly where one's parents are masochistic themselves. Such awareness can then naturally lead into discussion of other ways of achieving and maintaining intimacy. Wherever the primary function of the self-defeating behavior is to indirectly express aggression, the objective is to make this conscious and then give permission for and encourage direct expression.

As in every other character structure, perhaps the most basic objective of treatment is to work through the child abuse that the client experienced. In the case of the masochist, the abuse was intrusion, overpowering, and a breaking of the will. The anger that this engenders is profound. It must be claimed or owned, aimed at the appropriate source(s), and only thereby tamed. Since, in masochistic clients, these natural anger responses were disallowed and consequently repressed, they will need to be slowly reintroduced and their experience and expression even relearned. The direct release processes associated with bioenergetic, gestalt, and other expressive therapies can be most useful once there is insight and commitment. Once again, these strategies must be undertaken in a way that minimizes the pull for power struggles and authority battles.

Finally, for masochism to ever be transformed, there must be behavior that is an expression of the hope that has been lost. To some degree, this hope will be evidenced by the more direct expression of aggression in a close relationship, or by any behavior that is intended to establish closeness, other than the self-defeating behaviors that are so habitual. In addition to these "trusting" behaviors are those that betray even the most anxious trust in one's right to self-determined accomplishment or risk.

To be a good enough therapist for a person with these issues, you need to appreciate what you are asking, either explicitly or implicitly: that this person trust. If your will had been repeatedly overwhelmed and defeated and crushed, to reach out for intimacy directly, to express aggression directly, or to have hope for the positive result of your ambitions would make you very anxious. This anxiety will automatically trigger those defensive maneuvers which will escape it. This is to be expected. Wherever the therapist even supports such activity let alone directly suggests it, the therapist will automatically be setting himself up as a target for these defensive maneuvers. This, too, is to be expected, and, it is the therapist's enlightened gullibility that is necessary for the therapeutic process to play itself out.

Essentially, the client will defeat the therapist in the way he was defeated. This is the therapeutic test (Weiss & Sampson, 1986). To pass the test, the therapist must react differently from the manner in which the client reacted then and how others typically react now. He must not give up hope and resign himself nor should he act out his very understandable and human anger at the client's self- and therapist-defeating behavior. The most reliable, but not the only, therapeutic response in this situation, is interpretation. This includes the "test" interpretation that I have just provided. This persistently analytical response was, of course, not one that the patient had available to him as a child. But, the therapist has this response available to her and it is a response that the patient can increasingly have available to him in the present. Repeatedly traversing this present to past connection in all its permutations will be an essential if not sufficient ingredient of the therapeutic process. With this type of client, more than any other, the therapist's commitment to this process, paired with a relative detachment from the outcome, will be necessary to effect any change.

CHAPTER 10

The Exploited Child: Hysterical Defenses and the Histrionic Personality

ETIOLOGY

LOVE, SEX, RIVALRY, BETRAYAL, incest — these are the themes we encounter when we explore what has come to be called the histrionic personality disorder or the hysterical style. These are the same themes that Breuer and Freud encountered approximately one hundred years ago as they explored the problem of conversion hysteria. In 1896, only one year before proposing the Oedipus complex, Freud repeatedly noted the uniform currents of childhood sexual abuse, and particularly incest, in the histories of his hysterical conversion patients. Eventually, he came to say that "almost all my women patients told me they had been seduced by their fathers" (cited in Rush, 1980, p. 83). Earlier, he had written:

I therefore put forward the thesis that at the bottom of every case of hysteria there are *one or more occurrences of premature sexual experience*, occurrences which belong to the earliest years of childhood but which can be reproduced through the work of psycho-analysis in spite of the intervening decades. (Freud, 1896, p. 202) . . . In all eighteen cases (cases of pure hysteria and hysteria combined with obsessions, and comprising six men and twelve women) I have, as I have said, come to learn of sexual experiences of this kind in childhood. (p. 207)

He then goes on to indicate that these occurrences of childhood sexual abuse were divided into three classes, the first of which was stranger sexual abuse. The second group involved sexual contact with some adult caretaker, such as a nursery maid or governess and "unhappily, all too often, a close relative." The third group involved sexual relations between children of different sexes, generally a brother and sister. In most cases, he stated that individuals received abuse in two or more of these categories. He posited further that all cases of child sexual abuse were initiated by an aggressor child who himself had been sexually abused. As we know, Freud later repudiated this "trauma" or "seduction" theory, attributing the *fantasy* of being seduced by the father to the expression of the typical Oedipus complex in women. This repudiation is even more difficult to swallow once one has read Freud's earlier defense of these reports of sexual abuse:

. . . the general doubt about the reliability of the psycho-analytic method can be appraised and removed only when a complete presentation of its technique and results is available. Doubts about the genuineness of the infantile sexual scenes can, however, be deprived of their force here and now by more than one argument. In the first place, the behaviour of patients while they are reproducing these infantile experiences is in every respect incompatible with the assumption that the scenes are anything else than a reality which is being felt with distress and reproduced with the greatest reluctance. Before they come for analysis the patients know nothing about these scenes. They are indignant as a rule if we warn them that such scenes are going to emerge. Only the strongest compulsion of the treatment can induce them to embark on a reproduction of them. While they are recalling these infantile experiences to consciousness, they suffer under the most violent sensations, of which they are ashamed and which they try to conceal; and, even after they have gone through them once more in such a convincing manner, they still attempt to withhold belief from them, by emphasizing the fact that, unlike what happens in the case of other forgotten material, they have no feeling of remembering the scenes.

This latter piece of behavior seems to provide conclusive proof. Why should patients assure me so emphatically of their unbelief, if what they want to discredit is something which—from whatever motive—they themselves have invented?

It is less easy to refute the idea that the doctor forces reminiscences of this sort on the patient, that he influences him by suggestion to imagine and reproduce them. Nevertheless it appears to me equally untenable. I have never yet succeeded in forcing on a patient a scene I was expecting to find, in such a way that he seemed to be living through it with all the appropriate feelings. Perhaps others may be more successful in this.

There are, however, a whole number of other things that vouch for the reality of infantile sexual scenes. In the first place there is the uniformity which they exhibit in certain details, which is a necessary consequence if the preconditions of these experiences are always of the same kind, but which would otherwise lead us to believe that there were secret understandings between the various patients. In the second place, patients sometimes describe as harmless events whose significance they obviously do not understand, since they would be bound otherwise to be horrified by them. Or again, they mention details, without laying any stress on them, which only someone of experience in life can understand and appreciate as subtle traits of reality. (Freud, 1896, pp. 204–205)

Any clinician who has participated in the discovery of early physical or sexual abuse with a client will recognize the truth and wisdom of this account and argument. It was only in his letters to Wilhelm Fliess that Freud ever discussed his reasons for his change of heart. What he wrote to Fliess was that he just couldn't believe sexual abuse in general and incest in particular could be so prevalent. Apparently, on the basis of this disbelief, he came to discount these reports and attribute them to fantasy. The foregoing passage, however, makes quite plausible the hypothesis suggested by both Masson (1984) and Miller (1984) that Freud lost the necessary courage to reveal these findings. Whatever his motives, it seems clear today that Freud was in error. Contemporary data, which will be reviewed presently, indicates that sexual abuse is fairly common and incest is common enough to have profound public health consequences. Furthermore, the rates are considerably higher for clinical populations (as high as 50–70% for sexual abuse according to Briere & Runtz, 1991) and the level of psychic damage is documented to be quite considerable.

It is also quite plausible that sexual child abuse was even more prominent in Freud's time than it is in our own. This plausibility rests on two counts: First, as Miller (1983, 1984) has so thoroughly documented, abusive treatment and use of children was far more sanctioned in the 1800s than it is today. Second, sexual child abuse has increased incidence in families that are highly patriarchal and characterized by repressive and puritanical attitudes towards sex

(Thorman, 1983)—conditions that were predominant in Victorian-era Europe.

So, essentially, I believe Freud was right the first time when he wrote with Breuer their classic formulation: "hysterics suffer mainly from reminiscences" (Breuer & Freud, 1893–1895, p. 7). These reminiscences were, according to Breur and Freud, "psychic traumas," which were so upsetting that one would choose not to remember them in order to keep one's psychic equilibrium. In Freud's words:

For these patients whom I analysed had enjoyed good mental health . . . until their ego was faced with an experience, an idea or a feeling which aroused such a distressing affect that the subject decided to forget about it because he had no confidence in his power to resolve the contradiction between the incompatible idea and his ego by means of thought-activity. . . . In hysteria, the incompatible idea is rendered innocuous by its *sum of excitation* being *transformed to something somatic*. For this I should like to propose the name *conversion*. (Freud, 1896, pp. 47–49)

Freud termed this process a "splitting of consciousness" (p. 46). Later, he came to call one side of the split unconscious and the other conscious. This splitting of consciousness later became modeled as repression, which required psychic energy to maintain. Furthermore, this psychic energy could be manifested in somatic conversion, affective expression, cognitive obsession, or observable behavioral compulsions. This splitting of consciousness with consequent memory loss has been repeatedly demonstrated in the area of sexual child abuse. Research estimates range from 70–95% regarding the proportion of those with multiple personality disorder who have experienced severe sexual or physical abuse as children (e.g., see Putnam, 1989, pp. 46–50). Other research by Briere (1992) indicates that 60% of those who remember childhood sexual abuse did not remember it at one point in their lives.

Early descriptions of the hysterical character (i.e., Reich, 1961; Wittels, 1930)* do not substantially differ from the somewhat more developed descriptions given today (e.g., Horowitz, 1991; Kernberg, 1988). I believe the use of the hysteria label was appropriated for this characterological entity because of the similarities in the underlying issues and the similarities in the cognitive defenses and affective

---

*Reich's work was first published in German in 1933, and in English in 1945.

styles—(i.e., reliance on repression and affect defense). Consider Reich's (1965) statement, "the hysterical character . . . represents the simplest, most transparent type of character armor. . . . the most conspicuous characteristic of both male and female examples of this type is an importune sexual attitude" (p. 226).

In 1959, Rangell made a persuasive argument for separating hysteria from conversion. Rangell thoroughly documented his conclusion that conversion "is employed to express forbidden wishes throughout the entire gamut of psychopathological symptomatology" (p. 636). In so doing, Rangell helped the evolving diagnoses of hysterical "character neurosis" or "personality disorder," which have always involved complexes and conflicts of a sexual nature together with particular affective and cognitive styles for dealing with sexual and other conflictual topics. Pollack's (1981) review of empirical research on hysterical personality substantiates that conversion and hysterical personality are separate though perhaps related entities.

Writing within the psychoanalytic framework, Marmor (1953) and, later, Sperling (1973) argued that pre-oedipal issues played a much larger role in hysterical personality than had been previously recognized. Marmor believed that the hysteric's sexuality was used primarily to get the holding and attention of the opposite sex parent rather than to achieve any genital aim. Later writers have incorporated Marmor's revision of classical theory, emphasizing the pre-oedipal and particularly oral arrests of the hysterical personality and proposing a spectrum of hysterical functioning. At one end of this spectrum are individuals in whom oral conflicts predominate and whose structural functioning is in the range of personality disorder as defined in this volume. At the other end of the spectrum is the oedipal hysteric who is high-functioning or in the neurotic character to character style range as defined here. In these individuals, oedipal conflicts predominate, sexual issues are transparent, and interpretive psychotherapy is useful. Tupin (1981) gives a thorough summary of this continuum, illustrated by the two extreme polar positions. This spectrum approach is endorsed by a number of experts in the hysterical or histrionic personality field (e.g., Blacker & Tupin, 1991; Easser & Lesser, 1965; Horowitz, 1991; Kernberg, 1967; Lazare, 1971; Mueller & Aniskiewicz, 1986; Zetzel, 1968). Blacker and Tupin (1991) summarize what I believe to be the current predominant psychoanalytic position on this spectrum approach, which mirrors almost exactly the approach of this volume on this and every other basic personality issue.

Hysterical personality is associated with characteristics arising from both pregenital and genital psychosexual levels. The more infantile personality organization arises as a result of inadequate mothering, sexual and physical abuse, and deprivation during infancy and results in chaotic, extreme and unstable behavior as an adult that is highly resistant to psychotherapeutic, psychoanalytic intervention. This is contrasted with the genital, or mature, hysterical personality organization, which has experienced less early deprivation, exhibits more intact object relationships, has experienced more success in vocational, educational, and social areas, and has symptoms amenable to the present armament of psychotherapeutic intervention.

This is the position that I endorse and elaborate here but, in most respects, it is not all that different from my position on any characterological issue.

I believe what is distinctive about the hysterical adaptation is what Reich first identified—the presence of distinctly sexual issues, which are, most importantly, occasioned by some form of child sexual abuse. At the higher end of the structural continuum (i.e., character neurosis to character style), there is commonly a family pattern that includes a seductive father and the presence of rivalry between the mother and daughter for the father's attention. I believe this family pattern is far more common than actual contact incest, and I believe that it far more commonly involves female as opposed to male children, as does contact sexual abuse. The histrionic personality is simply the most identifiable syndrome associated with these classic "oedipal" issues.

The terribly crucial yet only real difference with Freud is the belief that these issues become problematic not because of the children's wishes and fantasies but because of adults' behavior and attitudes toward children. In these cases, adults exploit natural and basically innocent child needs and attitudes, including early sexual curiosity and arousal, need for physical contact and contact pleasure, needs for nurturance and attention, jealousy of the exclusive aspects of the parent's relationship, etc. It is because these natural human inclinations have been exploited (i.e., used in the service of adult needs) that the child experiences what have been called "oedipal" conflicts. Even in cases of clearly unwanted and intrusive contact sexual abuse, adult victims will typically remember valuing the special position they had with the offending parent, some positive aspect of the physical attention or contact, or some aspect of winning out over the same sex parent. These are human motivations, which may be exploited. Children certainly do go through a period of heightened interest, fascination, and curiosity concerning the opposite sex. All of this too, is eminently exploitable.

Such exploitation and the conflicts it engenders are highly overstimulating to children and cannot be productively integrated by them. As a result, they are split off from ordinary consciousness and are "repressed" just for the reasons that Breuer and Freud initially posited. This is why sexual abuse is so often forgotten, why it is so common in the histories of multiple personality disorders who are remarkable for their ability to dissociate, and why methods such as free association, hypnosis, dream interpretation, etc., may revivify the memories.

The hysterical personality style is partially defined by an overemotionality that has an "as if" quality and a cognitive style that is global and diffuse. Such a style serves repression by preventing the depth of either thinking or feeling, which could lead to resolution. So, the memories and the conflicts they engender may never be fully experienced or resolved. In Western cultures, the hysterical "caricature of femininity" often becomes a workable defensive style for women who have experienced this exploitive etiology. Particularly when these women have had seductive fathers, the demand to remain "Daddy's little girl" has been relatively overt and approved.

The hysterical character structure has so often been identified with women because little girls are the primary targets of every form of sexual abuse and because this style of maintaining repression is prescribed by the family and supported by the culture. Furthermore, what we are talking about here is truly a syndrome—a common confluence of etiology, resulting issues, and typical styles for handling affect, behavior, and cognition. As with all psychological syndromes, not all common characteristics are seen in each and every case. I have seen cases, for example, where all the sexual, rivalrous, and conflict issues are associated with the very etiology I am describing but where there is little if any apparent histrionic behavior. Other strategies, such as drug use, have been employed to maintain the repression. For this reason, it is somewhat unfortunate that these particular histrionic characteristics have been used to name the character structure. For me, it is not these behaviors that are definitional of this character. Rather, it is the presence of some form of sexual abuse and dysfunctional family history and the consequent conflicts, which that engenders concerning love, sex, and competition. For these reasons, I will, from now on, use the older term, hysterical character or personality, to refer to this syndrome because it lays a bit less emphasis on one characteristic of the syndrome. Just as we can separate conversion from hysteria as Rangell (1959) did, we can separate histrionic behavior from the hysterical personality syndrome.

Wherever the normal needs for nurturance and affection have not been adequately met, the child enters his or her "oedipal" stage with more damage and need and, as a result, is more vulnerable to exploitation. But, there must be sexual exploitation and the resulting "oedipal conflicts" for the underlying characterological issues to be what we are now calling hysterical. In the framework of the theoretical structure given here, one can have oral issues or hysterical issues or both. Oral issues depend on deprivation of nurturance whereas hysterical issues represent exploitation of human need, sexual interest, and normal rivalry. There are certainly cultural differences concerning the acceptability and commonality of histrionic behavior. It is possible to show histrionic behavior without exhibiting a hysterical personality in the sense defined here.

There are certainly histrionic men, and it's very possible for men to establish the same hysterical style in defense of the conflicts occasioned by sexual exploitation. In my experience and in my reading of others' work, however, this does not appear to be very common. It's very likely that a male in Western culture will respond differently to exploitation than will a female. In this connection, it's interesting to note that Freeman-Longo (1987) found that 40% of the rapists he studied had experienced childhood sexual abuse at the hands of a woman.

All that follows on the dynamics and description of the hysterical personality has to do with the female expression because this is where I have personal experience and where the literature offers some help in contextualizing that experience. I suspect that this is a uniquely Western female solution to what is a primarily female problem. Some of the factor analytic studies of personality support this view in that they have isolated an hysterical personality for the women studied but not for the men (Magaro & Smith, 1981; Torgersen, 1980).

Wherever I have seen the hysterical personality issue clearly differentiated from oral, narcissistic, symbiotic, and masochistic trends, it has always involved a woman who has a special sexualized relationship with a seductive father figure. Up until writing this chapter, it has also been my impression that my experience was reflected in the literature on the hysterical personality. As I undertook this chapter, I saw an opportunity for some rather obvious research. I decided to search the literature over the past thirty years and determine the proportion of hysterical personality case reports that included a description of such a father-daughter relationship or overt incest. I also decided to gather the same proportional information on the description of a cold, neglectful, or rivalrous relationship with the mother. Herman (1981) compared her original sample of 40 cases of father-daughter incest with 20 cases in which the father could be described as "seductive." I adopted the following definition by Herman of such seductiveness:

We defined seductiveness on the part of fathers to mean behavior that was clearly sexually motivated, but which did not involve physical contact or requirement for secrecy. For example, some fathers constantly talked about sex with their daughters, confiding the details of their love affairs and ceaselessly interrogating their daughters about their own sexual behavior. Others habitually left pornographic materials for their daughters to find. Others exhibited themselves to their daughters or spied upon them while they were undressing. Still others courted their daughters like jealous lovers, bringing them presents or flowers, expensive jewelry, or sexy underwear. Although all these behaviors stop short of genital contact, they clearly betray the father's intrusive sexual interest in their daughters, which was a form of covert incest. (Herman, 1981, p. 109)

For my research, the published case reports were obtained by four separate search procedures: *Psychological Abstracts* 1962–1991, two University of California computer-based journal article searches, and all relevant books held by the University of California at San Francisco.*

*I would like to thank Richard Litwin, Ph.D., for executing this search. Both he and I are responsible for the resulting judgments. See Appendix C for case study references used and results from each case study.

In 34 cases wherein the father-child relationships were adequately described, we found that 77% of them clearly described a father-daughter relationship that could be characterized as seductive. In several of the cases in which this was not so clearly demonstrated, there were descriptions of unusually intense father-daughter relationships. In one of these cases, there were sexual fantasies concerning the father, and in another there was the classic pattern of father-daughter estrangement during puberty after a prior positive and intense relationship. Interestingly, in only two of the 34 cases classified as seductive was there a clear-cut report of contact sexual abuse. In 61% of the same 28 classifiable cases, a mother-daughter relationship that could be characterized as cold, neglectful and/or rivalrous was also described.

Related to this question, we discovered a report of 21 other cases of hysterical personality seen by the same therapist (Blinder, 1966). In characterizing his cases, this therapist reported that 17 of his patients described their mothers as cold, ungiving, quarrelsome, or remote. These patients had "variable opinions" of their fathers, though these were generally more favorable and fathers were seen as more emotionally available. This report obviously gives support to the hypotheses concerning mothers' influence but does not support the seductive father hypothesis. Since all these cases come from one observer, we decided to note this report separately from the others.

While we have no control group for our survey of cases, I am confident that the observed proportion of father-daughter seductive relationships far exceeds that present in other personality issues. Thus, I feel that my clinical impressions have been confirmed by this research and that it will be instructive to explore more fully the dynamics of this etiological family constellation.

Family Patterns Associated with Hysterical Personality and Sexually Abused Children

A review of the literature on sexual child abuse reveals consistent family patterns associated with its occurrence. These patterns are strikingly similar to those observed in families that produce women with characteristics of hysterical personality. The following summary by Haugaard and Reppucci (1988), in *The Sexual Abuse of Children*, is typical.

One dynamic of the incestuous couple appears in many clinical descriptions: a marked difference in the authority of one parent over the other and a resulting blurring of role boundaries as the nonpowerful parent aligns more with the children than with the other parent. One family pattern has been described as representing a "pathological exaggeration of generally accepted patriarchal norms" (Herman, 1981, p. 83). It involves a dominant, often physically abusive father who is in clear command of the home and a submissive mother who is usually withdrawn because of a physical or emotional disability and who acts and is treated much like one of the children (Browning & Boatman, 1977; Finkelhor, 1979; Herman, 1981). . . .

Another pattern is, in many ways, the mirror image of this one. The mother is described as angry, dominant, and hostile, and the father as passive and dependent. The mother nurtures not only the children but also the father (Greene, 1977). Families with either of these structures appear to be at greater risk for incest than are those with different structures because of the overinvolvement of a parent with the child subsystem. This overinvolvement blurs the boundaries between the two subsystems, making it easy for the sexual boundary to be blurred also. In addition, one parent is left alone in the parent subsystem and this increases the chance that a child will be taken into the parental subsystem to fill the void. (Haugaard & Repucci, 1988, p. 124)

Compare this with the summary statement of Mueller and Aniskiewicz (1986) in their book, *Psychotherapeutic Intervention in Hysterical Disorders*.

Two patterns of family relationships can be used to illustrate the potential for varying hysterical styles. The first representative parental theme consists of a parental figure who is manifestly dominating, self-centered, and self-sufficient. He is complemented by a weak, ineffectual, inadequate mother. In the second theme, father emerges as manifestly passive in relation to the mother and overtly responsive to and collusive with the daughter. The mother is perceived to be competitive, nagging and controlling . . . the underlying theme common to the two representative pictures is one of inadequacy in both parents to meet their respective parental roles and relate as such to the hysteric. . . . Whether the mother is resigned to a weak, ineffectual role or is threatened by the child and reacts competitively, the basic issue remains of not having achieved a mature mutuality as wife and the generativity of mothering. Similarly, whether the father's adequacy conflicts are expressed through a brittle, pseudo-masculine exterior or directly in warm, sexual, or collusive ways with the daughter, he indicts himself and reveals his own immaturity. (p. 15)

In developing our understanding of these dynamics more fully, it is useful to briefly review the data on incidence of incest and the circumstances associated with it. Then we will move to reviewing Herman's (1981) results, where she compared families in which incest occurred with families characterized by a seductive father-daughter relationship.

Estimates of father-daughter incest have been fairly consistently reported at around 2%. Russell (1986), for example, found that "one out of every 43 women who had a biological father as a principle figure in her childhood years was sexually abused by him" (p. 234) before the age of 14. This translates to 2.32% and to over 2.9 million women in the United States, based on current population estimates. However, "women who are raised by a stepfather are over seven times more likely to be sexually abused by him than women who were raised by a biological father" based on the fact that "one out of approximately every six women who had a stepfather as a principle figure in her childhood years was sexually abused by him before the age of 14" (p. 234). We can be fairly confident that these are underestimates because of the forenoted tendency of sexual abuse victims to forget their abuse and because we can safely assume a reluctance to report these instances when they are remembered. For sexual abuse more generally, Peters, Wyatt, and Finkelhor (1986) reviewed 19 prevalence studies with abuse rate results from 8% to 62%. The mean of all these studies was approximately 23% and might serve as a conservative estimate of the prevalence. Finkelhor and Baron (1986) cite a ratio of 5 : 1 when comparing the incidence of sexual abuse of female as compared to male children. This converts to a 4.5% prevalence rate for male sexual victimization. Adult males are by far most often the perpetrators of sexual child abuse. Russell and Finkelhor (1984) report that 95% of the girls and 80% of the boys who were sexually abused by adults were abused by men.

In addition to the family dynamics associated with father-daughter incest cited earlier, there are several other factors that are commonly associated with it. In considering these factors as well as those already listed, it is important to remember that they all have a noticeably high association with the occurrence of incest, but they are not present in all cases. Rather, these are only factors that may help us construct a general theory concerning what might be happening in these families. The factors are as follows:

Mother Absence (Physical or Psychological). Maisch (1973, p. 136), for example, found that 33% of the mothers in incestuous families had suffered from serious physical illness. Herman (1981, p. 77) reported that 50% of the women she interviewed who had experienced incest with their fathers remembered that their mothers had disabling illnesses that resulted in frequent hospitalizations. Herman concluded that "the families in which mothers were rendered unusually powerless, whether through battering, physical disability, mental illness, or the burden of repeated child bearing, appeared to be particularly at risk for the development of overt incest" (p. 124).

Role Reversal. Most studies of incestuous families report that mother-daughter role reversal is common. The daughter has often taken on many of the mother's duties while she has become more dependent and/or less involved with the family. This pattern often accompanies serious physical or mental illness in the mother as noted above. Justice and Justice (1979) cited this as one of the most frequent characteristics of incestuous families. "The mother wants to become the child and the child wants to become the mother. This basic symbiotic quality is reflected in nearly all the characteristics of the mother whose husbands and daughters engage in incest" (p. 97). These same authors concluded that many mothers in incestuous families are frigid or want no sex with their husbands. According to these authors, this invites an extension of the role reversal to the sexual sphere.

High Stress. Justice and Justice (1979) also assessed the level of stress families had experienced by using the Social Readjustment Scale on their sample of 35 abusing families and compared that with the scores of a group of 35 non-abusing families. The differences were profound in that the abusing families had an average score of 234 as compared to an average score of 124 for the non-abusing group. Scores for the incestuous families (a subset of abuse) averaged 240, indicating that these families had experienced very high levels of important life changes over the year prior to the incest occurrence.

Altered Sexual Climate. Studies and clinical reports frequently observe that the sexual climate in incest families is either overly repressed or unusually high in erotic stimulation. Weinberg (1976), for example, found that the incestuous families he studied had unusually high levels of sexual stimulation. Children often were shown pornographic materials, were exposed to obscene language, and often observed their parents having sexual intercourse. Conversely, puritanical attitudes and repressive parental behaviors have been noted by other investigators (e.g., Thorman, 1983).

Social Isolation. The families in which incest takes place are often noted to be relatively detached from the outside world such that the members must seek gratification of all their needs from one another. This social isolation has often been seen as reinforcing the father's iron-clad control. Alternatively, it has been used to explain the father's turning to his daughter for sexual gratification when his wife is either unavailable or undesirable. Associated with this social isolation, investigators often find that many parents in incestuous families have low social skills thereby restricting their ability to meet their needs outside the family.

Since I believe that particularly the pure or "oedipal" hysteric is often associated with a family background including a seductive father and a cold, absent, or rivalrous mother, it is very instructive to explore Herman's findings, which compare incestuous families with families characterized by a sexualized father-daughter relationship. In so doing, it is well to remember that Herman found only the father-dominant family pattern in her sample of incestuous families.

The families were similar in many ways. Both groups were characterized by more puritanical and negative sexual attitudes. Like the incestuous families, the daughters of seductive fathers perceived the parental relationship to be tense and cold; indeed, the entire family was experienced as chilly, distrustful, and characterized by scarcity of emotional supplies. Traditional sex roles prevailed, wherein the mother's primary role was as wife and homemaker and the father was clearly dominant. These daughters saw their parents as unhappily married and feared their father's desertion just as did the incest victims. Fathers in both groups showed a relatively high proportion of excessive drinking (35% in both groups). The mothers in both groups were described as dependent on their husbands and "grimly determined to preserve their marriages at all cost" (Herman, 1981, p. 112), even though they were subjected to considerable verbal abuse. Like the incest victims, many of these women described their mothers as cold and hostile and indicated that overt competition characterized the relationship with their mothers. The mothers in the seductive families conveyed to their daughters that getting and keeping a man was a woman's primary objective and the mother-daughter rivalry for the father's attention was intense.

Herman writes "like the incest victims, many of these women felt that their mothers had in some degree sacrificed them to their fathers. While overtly the mothers resented the special relationship between father and daughter, covertly, the daughters felt, the mothers promoted or at least acquiesced in the relationships" (Herman, 1981, p. 114). While the daughters enjoyed their special relationship with their fathers, many of them, just as in the incest group, longed for a closer and more supportive relationship with their mothers. The daughters were often used in the marital struggles by the fathers, who were seen as revenging themselves on their wives. Herman writes "because the daughters were drawn into the marital conflict in the role of mother's rival, they often felt deeply torn. In effect, they felt as though they could please their fathers only at the expense of alienating their mothers. They paid for their special status in the family by suffering the jealousy and resentment of their mothers and often of other siblings as well" (p. 115).

This is exactly the pattern I have repeatedly seen in cases of hysterical personality in women. This is the "oedipal conflict" all right, but it is not a fantasy. It is imposed by the parents. The fathers in the families studied by Herman reacted to their daughters' emerging sexuality either with attempts to completely control their social and sexual behavior or, alternatively, by total rejection.

The differences between families characterized by seductive fathers and those in which incest occurred are also of interest. While these seductive fathers were dominant, only 20% of the daughters characterized their fathers as habitually violent as compared to 50% of the fathers who committed incest (Herman, 1981, p. 111). These fathers were seen to control more by withdrawal than intimidation. Unlike the incestuous fathers, they were more often womanizers. However, their affairs were either not secret within the family, or if they were, these daughters were made aware of their father's infidelity and were thereby involved in it.

The mothers differed in these nonincestuous families in that they were physically healthier, more assertive, competent, and socially involved. Only 15% had been seriously ill as opposed to 55% in the incestuous families. These mothers also bore fewer children and there was less functional role reversal between mother and daughters.

While the daughters in these families were significantly damaged by their dysfunctional families, they were substantially less damaged than the incest victims. Unlike the incest victims, these women did not go to extreme lengths to escape their families. Only one of the 20 (5%) made a runaway attempt as compared with 13 of the forty (32%) incest victims. None escaped to a residential school or foster care, only three became pregnant as adolescents (15% as compared to 45% of the incest victims), and far fewer escaped into marriage. Their academic achievements were considerably higher, with 30% obtaining graduate degrees compared with only 8% of the incest victims. Though many suffered depression, their symptoms were not as severe, and only one of the 20 abused drugs or alcohol as opposed to 35% of the incest victims. Also, only one ever attempted suicide as opposed to 38% of the incest victims. None of these women reported a beating from a husband or lover as compared with 28% of the incest victims.

"Though they were not, on the whole, as severely depressed as the incest victims, the majority (55%) did have major depressive symptoms. And though only 10% had a predominantly negative self-image as compared to 60% of the incest victims, a similarly low percentage described themselves in predominantly positive terms. The majority (80%) had a dual or confused self-image; they fluctuated between thinking of themselves as 'good girls' and 'bad girls.' On the one hand, they saw themselves in the idealized role as 'Daddy's princess'; on the other hand, they were never entirely able to suppress the covertly incestuous elements in their relationships with their fathers, and they saw themselves as little temptresses who had aroused their father's prurient interest and their mother's jealous hostility" (Herman, 1981, pp. 119–120). Herman indicates that "many of these women look at themselves as leading double lives and some develop secret sexual lives." Herman gives many examples of ways in which these daughters seem to continue to play out somewhat dissociated or at least unintegrated "good girl" and "bad girl" roles.

Many of the women from seductive families had difficulty in their relationships with men. One recurrent difficulty was "a repetitive pattern of romantic infatuation followed by disappointment and anger" (p. 122). Another pattern involved what appeared to be repeating the behavior of their mothers in that they concentrated their efforts on trying to attract and keep a difficult man. Another pattern involved seeking unstable or unavailable men with the objective of maintaining a relationship with the seductive father. Yet another pattern involved becoming engaged in a triangle with a man and a rival. Another pattern involved being "attracted to men who were either distant and aloof, or controlling and domineering" (p. 122). Few of these women were "able to establish relationships with men based on mutuality" (p. 122). Fully one-half of the daughters of seductive fathers also complained of sexual difficulties.

Like the incest victims, these women tended to overvalue men and undervalue women and often had superficial relationships with women. Daughters of seductive fathers had much more difficulty separating from the sexualized relationships with their fathers and some never negotiated a satisfactory separation.

In short, the incest victims were thoroughly defeated and confirmed in their negative identity, describing themselves as "witches, bitches or whores" (p. 119) or "irredeemably evil" (p. 124). Like the strong or "oedipal" hysteric, daughters of seductive fathers most often "tried to live up to the image of good girl, often imposing upon themselves impossible standards of achievement. All were haunted by the fear that beneath the facade lurked a contemptible person who would eventually be exposed or gain the upper hand" (p. 120). Thus, these women, like the strong hysteric described earlier, appear to adopt a winner's position, particularly as compared with the incest victim, whose eventual position has more masochistic features. This winning position is, however, very tenuous and must be continually supported by maneuvers that either suppress or vitiate the "bad" identity.

Comparing the two family patterns, Herman concludes, "the two types of family differed not in kind but in degree, the overtly incestuous family representing a pathological extreme of male dominance, the covertly incestuous family representing a more commonplace variety" (p. 124). It is also plausible that families with seductive fathers could revert to the incestuous pattern with occurrences of severe mother absence and/or high levels of stressful life change.

Dynamics and Internal Object Relations

In the present view, these "oedipal" issues may exist along a continuum of profound to relatively mild depending on the extent and intrusiveness of exploitation in the sexual realm. Furthermore, these issues may and usually do coexist with one or more of the other basic existential personality issues outlined in this volume. Viewing sexual exploitation singularly, the most severe and intrusive forms of sexual abuse will more commonly result in a personality structure that is more self-defeating or masochistic, whereas the relatively lighter etiology described here is more likely to result in a personality pattern associated with the "strong or mature" hysterical personality.

Hysterical signs and symptoms, then, are all attempts to deal with this family corruption. Corrupt systems always exploit the needs of their less powerful members in order to involve them in the corruption. Then, with the corruption so established, it is denied by all who participate in it, rationalized as somehow justified or necessary and eventually covered up. Whoever participates in the corruption and in its ultimate cover-up is always compromised. And, whenever possible, the most powerful in the system blame the least powerful whenever the cover-up fails and blame must be assigned.

Thorman (1983), in his discussion of incestuous families, makes it clear how this sacrifice of the daughter is built into the initial corruption.

She is told that there is nothing abnormal about incest, but she is also told never to disclose the secret relationship. . . . She is made to feel that she is behaving wrongfully but that her father wants her to continue to carry on the relationship but remain silent about it. She is caught in a double bind. If she reveals the secret, she will have disobeyed her father's instructions. If she does not reveal the secret, she must continue in the wrongful behavior. No matter which course she chooses, she will have to pay a price. (p. 73)

It may be important to add that, if the daughter reveals the secret, she is also often disbelieved; if believed, she is blamed for the illicit relationship and for the consequences to the father and the breakdown of the family, should that occur. It is clear that this same general dynamic also operates in those families we've described as having seductive fathers.

Once again, we can use Fairburn's universal model of the child's response to bad parenting—internalization of the bad self-object relationship with splitting (for a diagram of this, see Figure 1, page 204). The modelling for the hysteric becomes more complicated because there is usually more than one bad object. In addition to mother and father figures, there also may be siblings, members of the extended family, or others.

In discussing conversion hysteria, Fairburn outlines the universal distracting quality of hysterical defenses, which take attention from real interpersonal problems. "Its essential and distinctive feature is *the substitution of a bodily state for a personal problem*; and this substitution enables the personal problem as such to be ignored. All personal problems are basically problems involving personal relationships with significant objects; and the objects involved in the conflicts of the hysteric are essentially *internal objects*—and more specifically the exciting and frustrating objects . . . " (Fairbairn, 1954, p. 117).* In working with this model, I have found it most useful to think of the libidinal or "exciting" object as that object that the child needs in order for a particular developmental issue to mature optimally. In the case of these "oedipal" issues, a female-child needs a father who can be the safe target of her developing awareness of sexual excitement, fascination with the opposite sex, and emerging attraction to the wonders of a wider world. In the case of many females with an hysterical personality, the girl also turns to her father for gratification of earlier unmet needs for nurturance, holding, and support. This constitutes the oft noted orality in the hysterical personality (e.g., Blacker & Tupin, 1991; Marmor, 1953). Thus, dad is turned to as a combination of the sex object for immature sexuality, rescuer, and guide to the outside world.

In the case of the emerging hysteric, however, what is found is not this optimum figure but rather a father who exploits, becomes sexually excited himself, and thereby overexcites and corrupts her. To make matters worse, he exploits his daughter to get even with his wife.

This bad male object is internalized out of this extreme frustration and split into its exciting and rejecting parts. The "bad" side of the

*The reader may wish to know that my use of Fairbairn's model is somewhat different from his own use of it in his analysis of conversion hysteria, particularly with regard to my use of the libidinal or "exciting" object.

antilibidinal object is that corrupted seducer who uses the dependency and early sexual needs of his daughter to corrupt her. The antilibidinal self is that self that has been corrupted, seduced, and tricked. As a result of this corruption, she is herself a seductress responsible for arousing the prurient interests of her father and hurting her mother by so alienating her father's affections. The secretiveness of this special relationship reinforces this antilibidinal connection between the self and bad object.

The ideal mother figure in this drama is one whose primary relationship and sense of self is secure and mature enough to permit and enjoy the daughter's excitement, curiosity, and overall libidinal involvement when she turns to the father. In this more ideal situation, the bonds and identifications with mother are strong and secure so that other autonomous activities and other significant relationships and passions can be freely pursued. This mother will protect her daughter from overstimulation in such pursuits and is there for the daughter to turn to should there be occasions of overstimulation or exploitation. In the case of the hysterical personality, these built-in expectations are also massively frustrated, often in the prior "pre-oedipal" phases and always in the oedipal phase or in subsequent developmental phases.

This frustrating bad object is then internalized. At the antilibidinal pole we often find a mother figure who has colluded with the corruption, failed to protect, failed to be there for the daughter when reached for, and throughout proved to be threatened, retaliatory, and blaming. In this unconscious relationship, then, the antilibidinal self is the evil, sexual, corrupt other woman who damages the woman she loves with her sexuality, competition, and corruptibility. These, then, are some of the "personal problems" of the hysteric, and her symptomatic characteristics may be productively viewed simply as ways of dealing with them. All other characteristics of the hysterical personality involve those interpersonal situations in which the individual acts out her internalized personal problems in the external world through transference. In short, hysterical personality features involve either defense against the repressed "personal problems" so that repression is maintained, or the manifestation of these problems in the individual's relational life.

The hysterical person is notorious for playing alternate roles or involving herself in alternating relationships, which act out various aspects of these unconscious, internalized self-images or role-relationship models. The woman may, for example, be the naive nice girl in one setting or period while in another be the sexually provocative and exploitive bad girl. Or, she may invest in a love relationship with an often older, supportive, gentle man where she is relatively asexual and unexcited and then alternately with a man who is not at all kind to her but is sexually exciting, etc. Very often, the hysteric's defensive maneuvers serve to block awareness of the inconsistencies or problems of these roles and relationships. This maintains the ability to keep cycling through them without completion, resolution, or integration. With these underlying "personal problems" in mind, let us now review the affective, behavioral, and cognitive characteristics of the typical hysteric personality.

AFFECT, BEHAVIOR, COGNITION

Affect

In considering the characteristic affects of the hysterical personality, it is well to remember that the etiological situation just described is always overstimulating and confusing in its presentation of unresolvable double binds with powerful primal forces. The situation, the affects and conflicts they stimulate, are all overwhelming. Thus, an affective overwhelm is always a possible reality for this person and an unmetabolized blow-off of some of this affect can serve to reduce some of the tension as well as interfere or distract from any fuller awareness of what all this feeling is about. These emotional outbursts typically get other people involved, often in an ongoing melodrama that provides continual distraction. The histrionic elements of the hysterical character can most simply be understood as exhibition of an affect defense or, in Eric Berne's language, a racket feeling. The racket exists in that the displayed feeling covers or defends against feelings that, if felt in their true depth, would be overwhelming, revealing as they would the self-object relationships described earlier. With feelings serving these defensive functions, they are often experienced by others as phony or as having an "as if" quality. Their overly dramatic nature, their inappropriateness both in context and intensity, and the fact that they are so characteristic and do not resolve lead us to see them as not quite ringing true. Even positive affects can be expressed and experienced in this same way as this style helps to maintain repression of what would be encountered should this person enter into a more genuine state with herself and more true intimacy with others.

The hysteric's unconscious affects are those that hold together the repressed self-object relationships. In relation to the mother figure, there is a libidinal longing for the kind of nurturing and support that was not there, at least in confronting the seductiveness of the father and very often in the dependent phases prior to that. The greater this maternal deprivation, the lower the individual's functioning level and the greater the accompanying disorganization in response to these powerful feelings.

On the other side of the split, the self relates to the antilibidinal mother figure. Here, there is a good deal of unconscious rivalry, fear of retaliation, guilt for injuring the mother figure, etc. When these antilibidinal concepts about the self break through, they often cause depression. But here, too, the depression is usually used as an affect defense. In their research, Slavney and McHugh (1974) found that their histrionic inpatients were most clearly differentiated from other psychiatric patients by the presence of a suicide attempt as a reason for hospitalization ($p < .02$). This difference was made even more dramatic when this reason for hospitalization was added to depression but without a suicide attempt ($p < .001$). Furthermore, these authors note that most of the suicidal behavior by these patients with a histrionic personality diagnosis could best be characterized as suicidal gestures as opposed to serious suicidal attempts. There was in these cases, then, a dramatic but superficial acting out, which drew urgent attention and involvement from others.

It is very interesting to note in this rare objective study of histrionic personalities that, of a large number of variables studied, the only potentially causal variables that separated these groups were difficulties in family of origin and in adult love relationships. Significantly more of the histrionic personalities reported poor home atmosphere (72% versus 37%, $p < .01$) and unhappy marriages among those currently married (75% versus 20%, $p < .05$). Though not statistically significant, the authors found the frequency of fathers' alcohol abuse noteworthy (44% in fathers of histrionic personalities versus 19% in the control cases).

Turning now to the repressed relationship with the father figure, the hysteric still longs for that libidinally exciting but safe male figure who will take care of and rescue her. This paradigm is often represented in consciousness but her sexuality has been corrupted to be elicited in relationships of intrigue with concomitant exploitation. So, this longing may be repressed when these exciting relationships of intrigue are pursued, just as evil sexuality is repressed when the longing for rescue is pursued.

On the antilibidinal side of the split, the father is experienced as the male defiler, seducer, and corruptor. There is tremendous unconscious hostility toward the male for this exploitation. This hatred is fundamentally healthy and derives from the libidinal self. But, the antilibidinal self is experienced as colluding with the secret and corrupt relationship. As a result, the hysteric feels she has done something wrong and is herself the evil seductress. This view of the self also leads to depression, and the individual will marshall extreme affective states and behavioral maneuvers to defend against this more deeply felt experience (suicidal gestures, for example). There is also tremendous hostility toward men who are seen as weak and unable to meet the arrested libidinal expectations of the hysteric. Structurally, I see this hostility coming from the antilibidinal self and object and directed toward the imperfect, libidinal object. These hostile feelings toward men may well be acted out particularly where there is significant external justification for doing so.

Cognition

"Don't even think about it."
— Anonymous

Just as the hysteric cannot feel fully and deeply through her "personal problems," she also cannot think through them. She uses cognitive strategies that accomplish this objective by deleting information and blocking or blurring the thought process. Shapiro (1965) has been particularly helpful in emphasizing the global and impressionistic style in perception, the limitations of available memories, and the simplicity of cognitive categories for determining the meaning of events or the actions of others. Through dissociation, the hysteric can quite effectively separate thoughts, feelings, and actions. For example, she may act quite provocatively sexual, but be unaware of any sexual thoughts or feelings.

The hysteric is similarly notorious for the displacement of feelings or thoughts from the setting in which they belong but in which they would be threatening to an alternative setting where they are less threatening but where they really don't belong. This is particularly obvious in psychotherapy with this type of client in that she will often rather transparently displace ideas or affects, which belong in therapy, to other relationships and vice versa. The hysteric's tendency to act out these displacements can be a particularly tense part of her therapy, especially when she acts out either positive or negative transference belonging in the therapeutic relationship to other relationships in her life. Particularly at lower levels of functioning, the hysteric may act out such negative transference by perpetuating conflicts in her love relationships or actually leaving them. Alternatively, when positive transference is involved, she may become engaged or married to an inappropriate partner. The hysteric thus brings to mind the expression, "The right hand doesn't know what the left is doing." The hysteric can often see this about herself and certainly others see it.

The impressionistic and global nature of the hysteric's thought processes are particularly obvious in her speech. She talks about things in vague and global terms and will often resist verbal clarification. In his report of a prototypic case, for example, Horowitz (1991) noted that his client did not even have words for conflictual sexual topics and consequently was unable to discuss them with any specificity. This same client did not see herself as having a vagina and so did, in the visual realm, the same thing she did verbally. That is, she did not think about threatening topics. In this case, there was also dissociation of one cognitive system (i.e., visual, affective, or verbalized thought) from the others.

Another strategy, which hysterics often use, most obviously in the psychotherapeutic encounter, is simply bringing a threatening topic to premature closure. This strategy is often accompanied by an affective expression of discouragement or hopelessness. Thus, problems that are threatening are insoluble, and this inability to solve problems contributes to the hysteric's view of herself as incompetent and insubstantial. In lower-functioning individuals, many of these defensive cognitive operations are quite unstable and unreliable. When this is true, the hysteric is particularly prone to induce altered states of consciousness, either involuntarily or voluntarily through drug or alcohol abuse. A conversion symptom or hysterical fit can certainly achieve that outcome, as can self-mutilation, bingeing and purging episodes, suicidal gestures and their aftermath, etc.

The hysteric is also notorious for her tendency to see herself as not responsible for what happens to her and for her attempts to elicit sympathy, support, and rescue. This passive view of the self is defensive of the bad self representations effected by the internalization of both the bad mother and the bad father. This defensive cognitive style can unfortunately produce considerable deficits in her abilities to plan and execute her life so that she gets what she wants. Furthermore, it inhibits the learning that could take place as a result of accurate reception of feedback about her contribution to her life's outcomes. This increases both her own and others' tendencies to see her as insubstantial and irresponsible.

Appropriate therapy with an hysteric involves helping her to finally feel deeply and think clearly and completely by slowly defusing all the cognitive and affective defense maneuvers outlined thus far. As this is done, however, repression breaks down and the underlying "personal problems" are evermore exhibited both in the therapeutic transference and in the patient's life. These personal problems are then expressed in relationships where they belong. We will now turn to the client's behavior in such relationships.

Behavior

Historically, there have been two major sources of confusion in describing and understanding the hysterical character. The most pervasive source of this confusion involves equating the hysterical personality with conversion reactions. This has led theoreticians to group together patients who share a particular mechanism of defense but who do not necessarily share a similar etiological constellation, a core set of issues, or overall personality style (see Rangell, 1959). The second source of diagnostic and theoretical confusion has existed in the oral characteristics of many suffering from hysterical personality. Employing the present conceptualization, children who have suffered disappointment in nurturance will be far more susceptible to sexual exploitation in the first place and to the resulting self-recrimination in the second place. Oral deprivation helps to set up the sexual exploitation that underlies these "oedipal" issues. It seems to me, however, to be much clearer conceptually and practically, to separate these two etiological sources of psychopathology. Thus, oral and hysterical issues may frequently coexist in the same person but they are conceptually separate issues and should be viewed as such.

When these two sources of confusion are removed, one arrives at a much cleaner definition of this personality disorder, neurosis, or style. It is an identifiable syndrome associated with adults who, as children, were sexually or otherwise exploited in a family system in the area of "oedipal issues"—i.e., sexuality, love, and competition. This syndrome is certainly not the only adaptation to this kind of etiology but there is reason to believe that this particular syndrome is more likely to occur with sexually exploited females in European or North American cultural contexts. Behavior that is histrionic in nature—overly dramatic, emotional, and attention-getting—is strongly associated with this syndrome. This kind of behavior is, however, only one element of the syndrome and, as in every psychiatric syndrome, any one indicator is dispensable. This is why I have, as much as possible, eschewed the label of "histrionic personality disorder." Individuals with this personality disorder may very well not be histrionic just as they may not show conversion symptoms. They do, however, invariably show relational problems particularly where the relationship is both sexual and intimate.

In understanding the characteristics of any particular character type, one can conceptualize then as (1) transference behaviors in the broadest sense, which reflect the underlying and unconscious self-object relationships, or (2) the defenses against those transferences. The defenses themselves are typically not experienced as symptomatic by the individual in that they are generally seen to serve a constructive purpose. To the extent that their defenses work, as they often do in more highly functioning individuals, hysterics will usually not come for psychotherapy.

The hysteric's defensiveness is evidenced most clearly in her affect and cognition where, as we have seen, she blocks herself from feeling fully and thinking fully through her personal problems. In the behavioral realm, her histrionics are similarly defensive, but it is in her behavior in relationships that we begin to see the transference of unconscious role-relationship models on to her day to day life. With men, for example, she can behave in a very coquettish, coy, dependent way so as to provoke the kind of dependency gratification that she still seeks. Alternately, or with other men, she may be sexually seductive or verbally aggressive initially or after her seductiveness has provoked a sexual response. She may use herself as a sex object just as her father did. Alternatively, she may relate to men as sex objects, discarding them after that function has been used just as her father may have done to her. This playing out of internal self-object relations is not unusual; it happens in every character structure. But noteworthy in the hysterical personality are the rapid shifts from one kind of relationship to another, either with the same person or with different people. There may, for example, be simultaneous relationships, which play out each of these rather simplistic role relationship models with others whose psychology allows them to play the reciprocal part. Furthermore, all of these relationships will often have a rather dramatic, soap opera quality to them as opposed to a more genuinely felt humanity. Relationships, like affects, are "as if."

Relationships with women can be similarly simple, polarized, and fluctuating. These women often do not have close relationships with other women. They "prefer the company of men" and often see other women as boring, intellectually inferior, and/or hostile and competitive. Alternatively, they may have relationships with their mothers or "best friends," which appear regressive in nature. They behave in a little-girl-like fashion with these women, keep secrets, especially from men, and behave in other preadolescent or adolescent ways.

Not infrequently, hysterics involve themselves in triangles, both as the "other woman" in the triangle as they were in their own families or as the center of the triangle where they can typically play out one type of role relationship with one man and an alternative type with the other man. The turmoil created by these triangular relationships, as well as the turmoil in their lives generally, also serves a defensive function. Arousal is kept at such a high level that the real personal problems cannot be felt, thought, and worked through. In this same vein, the hysteric's oft noted obstinancy, exhibitionism, vanity, promiscuity, and jealousy are all defensive in occupying attention, keeping attention externally focussed, and keeping the attention of others on such externals. If one keeps things sufficiently stirred up and dramatic, one's attention is diverted from deeper feeling and thought.

In the service of repression and defense, the hysteric's interpersonal behaviors are kept superficial. Contact that is on the surface, showy, and "as if" allows the individual to avoid the reality of the bad self and object representations and to live in the fantasies of the good. "Nothing bad has happened. I've done nothing wrong. Someday my prince will come."

In the service of repression and defense, the hysteric's love relationships are also kept superficial. Deep contact is not safe for the hysteric. Getting father's attention was, of course, something she wanted. But she got much more and much less than she really wanted. Her father's attention was sexual and up to a point may have felt good. But it went beyond that good feeling point and was not accurately mirroring because it was determined more by the father's sexual interest than by his interest in his daughter as a person. Furthermore, this sexualized relationship with father seemingly damaged her relationship with her mother. As children do, she blamed herself for all this. As a result, it may be quite difficult for her to give herself a good relationship with a man because, then, she has what her mother did not. Indeed, she then has what she deprived her mother of. Unconsciously, that damages the mother again and evokes guilt. Hidden guilt comes in many forms (see Engel & Ferguson, 1990).

Sexual behaviors are also conflictual in a number of ways. Often, for example, there is a great deal of dependency experienced in relation to the man in her life just as there was toward her father. She is inclined, from this position, to see the man and his needs as far more important than her own, defer to him almost reflexively, and allow herself to be used sexually and otherwise. And, of course, she will resent all of this and the man will become the target of all her hostility both deserved and undeserved.

In the sexual as well as the social realm, the hysteric often engages in inauthentic, manipulative, or "gamey" behavior, which produces a repetitive drama, allowing her to cyclically act out reciprocal role relationship models and the affects that go with them. In the sexual realm, for instance, provocative seductiveness prompts sexually aggressive behavior, which is or can certainly appear to be insensitive, exploitative, or abusive. This behavior on the part of the other then justifies the underlying hostility directed at just these behaviors. In the social realm, helpless and irresponsible behavior activates patronizing and controlling behavior in others. But, the hysteric resents being treated as an irresponsible, helpless person and often won't be controlled. This engenders frustration and helplessness in the other. Conflict and anger are now imminent on both sides and eventually the hysteric has again the legitimate *external* excuse to indulge her rage.

It is well to remember again in reading these characterizations of character that what we are dealing with here is an archetype, a prototype, a stereotype. There is no such thing as an hysterical character. This, rather, is a general case scenario, which emphasizes the most central and common themes of a particular human dilemma. Any given human situation is fully more variable and complicated than the characterization. The characterization is a map, a way of getting our bearings by having a point of reference when dealing with a specific individual who exhibits some of these characteristics or themes.

THERAPEUTIC OBJECTIVES

Using the present theoretical model, the hysterical personality differs from all those we have considered thus far in that, if psychopathology exists in the lower structural range (i.e., personality disorder) it derives from earlier developmental issues. This difference is somewhat more theoretical than real, however, since nearly all individuals in the personality disorder range typically have serious etiological factors from two or more of the basic existential life issues underlying these character types. For outlining the therapeutic objectives, however, this fact has implications in that I will discuss only those strategies necessary for the "oedipal" issues. Thus, the remarks below do not take into account the necessary adaptations for those who suffer the structural deficits outlined in all the previous chapters based on these "pre-oedipal" injuries.

Psychotherapy for this hypothetically pure "oedipal" character can more closely approximate that associated with more traditional psychoanalytic thought. Initial work is directed toward building a therapeutic alliance, followed by interventions primarily aimed at dismantling the defenses to repressed or warded-off thoughts and feelings. Among such defenses, however, there is splitting, especially of the role relationship models, together with their associated affects and behaviors, as described above. As this defense analysis is accomplished, problematic thoughts and feelings begin to reach consciousness and find expression. This can only occur, of course, if a sufficient therapeutic alliance has been developed and the therapeutic context is experienced as fundamentally safe. These conflictual thoughts and feelings are then worked through in the therapeutic relationship. This working through is believed to be particularly powerful when the thoughts and feelings are transferred onto the therapeutic relationship and can, in this sense, be worked through in "real time." I believe this is a fundamentally adequate model for conducting psychotherapy with "oedipal" issues, though it has rather little to say about the substitution of newer and healthier self-object relationship models, which also must occur.

Cognitive Objectives

Cognitively, the therapist will need to stop those maneuvers that prevent the individual from either accessing or fully developing thoughts and feelings. Free association is a good example of a method that facilitates this. The basic instruction demands free-flowing thought centered on those topics about which the client is most resistant. The blocks to free thought are thereby brought to the fore. Attempts at self-distraction, premature closure, and out-and-out cognitive blocking are highlighted by this method, often without the therapist doing anything. Adding interpretation highlights the particular nature of the block and points to the underlying dynamic, which presumably created it. Such interpretations call for and model the desired introspection. As thought begins to flow more freely, memories relevant to the themes in question usually emerge. These may be new memories or memories that are experienced with greater clarity or with greater connection between feelings, thoughts, and behaviors. Where this does not occur, the therapist may prompt such memories or connections between representational systems.

In psychotherapy, which is more face to face dialogue, the therapist can both encourage and model clear and complete thinking, pursuing a topic to appropriate closure or resolution. Also a therapist can be particularly alert to patient behaviors, which are directed at him and give permission for or otherwise disinhibit such transferential behaviors and attitudes. As mentioned earlier, the hysterical personality is particularly characterized by a tendency to rather transparently transfer within and amongst all the relationships in her life. As a result, she is a particularly appropriate customer for the well-developed observational and interpretive skills of the more analytically oriented therapist.

It may be important to emphasize again that all this transference is not necessarily from past parental figures onto the therapist. The hysterical client is much more likely than most to transfer out of therapy those reactions that belong in it and to bring into therapy reactions that belong in the external social environment. Thus, the transference orientation as broadly defined can be very useful in helping this kind of client discover what she really thinks and feels. There is dissociation here but it is not as global as in some other structures such as the schizoid. Rather the dissociation is between representational systems or between the possible targets of her reactions.

The same cognitive slippage occurs when the hysteric sees herself as passive and thereby fails to take responsibility for her actions or their outcome. She prefers to attribute power and particularly blame elsewhere but denies her power and responsibility. Again, interpretation of this pattern as well as its underlying motivations is useful in helping the hysteric think clearly.

The therapist will also be called upon to help the hysteric increase her association, as opposed to dissociation, between thoughts, feelings, and behavior. Again, the therapist may be called upon to interpret seductive behavior, which is dissociated from sexual longings or feelings. Alternatively, the therapist may be able to assist the client in finding the words that go with feelings, particularly those that are overwhelming and dissociated from what elicits them.

The accuracy of the hysteric's self-perception also needs to be enhanced. She is inclined to see herself in polar self-representations, such as a naive, irresponsible child or as evil seductress who should be ashamed. In addition to modifying this polar self-concept, she also needs to more accurately self-perceive her helplessness, seductiveness, competitiveness, histrionics, and aggression. She also needs to clearly perceive and understand others' reactions to her. A reduction of shame in the negative pole ordinarily helps a great deal in achieving more accurate self-perception. Shame is one area in which an object relations model helps us to understand and facilitate the client's adoption of the therapist's more sane and mature view of self through internalization of the therapist and her attitudes toward the client.

Associated with these self-concepts are role relationship models that tend to be polarized. Men, for example, are seen as rescuers or defilers, whereas women can be seen as potential protectors or persecutors. These rather simplistic, immature, and sometimes romantic models of interpersonal relations need to be replaced by more mature, realistic, and balanced views.

Successful therapy with the hysterical personality will also result in the diminution of what we may call "hysterical states." These are states of mind in which the person is so overwhelmed by affect, either real or defensive, or by dissociation of threatening themes that she experiences a very real loss of self-control. Among other things, alternative methods of control or defense may be taught or encouraged to garner this outcome. Such strategies may be particularly useful while therapy slowly progresses to the more evolved goal of personal integration. The entire therapeutic process should result in the diminution if not the disappearance of such hysterical states.

Affective Objectives

For every characterological expression, it is instructive to delineate those affective characteristics that accompany the underlying "personal problems" or unconscious object relations. Such feelings may always be set in contrast to the more surface expressions of affect, which typically defend the underlying structure and the emergence of these personal problems and the painful feelings that go with them. In the hysteric's case, her labile, dramatic, and theatrical expression of feelings is defensive. One way or another, this defensive use of feelings must be relinquished before she will be able to feel her true nature.

The second most obvious affective characteristic of the hysteric is her tendency to become depressed, often in a very diffuse way. If her depression has content at all, it will usually involve repetitive self-recrimination. Such depressions are, of course, symptomatic and are tolerated particularly badly by the hysterical person, who is inclined to seek quick escape. Unpleasant as they are, the hysteric's depressions may also be defensive in that they depress the experience of more deeply disturbing but warded off feelings. Affect, as defense, is probably more common and obvious in the hysteric than in any other personality. As a result, an initial therapeutic objective with this personality must be the gradual relinquishing of the affect defense.

This initial therapeutic objective will in part be realized by enhancing the individual's capacity to tolerate the true experience of all the dreaded feelings. The hysteric can truly be desensitized to the experience of real feelings by gradually experiencing more and more of them, particularly in the context of the safe therapeutic relationship. This process can be enhanced by normalizing and understanding the feelings in question and by reframing their very experience as a positive, desired outcome. Because the hysterical personality is overwhelmed by feeling, and those of lower structure are literally thoroughly disorganized by it, it is natural that these experiences are avoided. Reversing this avoidant pattern is a necessary if not sufficient condition for transformation.

Underlying these more obvious and defensive affects, there is a whole complex of conflicting feelings, which must be brought to consciousness and worked through. These are the feelings of the "Oedipus" or "Electra" complex. Perhaps most accessible to consciousness are those negative feelings about the self that are at least dimly present during the hysteric's depressions. At the most superficial level, the hysteric often feels that she is somehow not good enough, and just beneath this she feels she is evil. At the more superficial level, she may tell you what others see about her — she is insubstantial, indecisive, dependent, and unsure of who she is or what she wants in life. At the deepest level, the hysteric blames herself for what happened in her family and to herself. Had she been better, her mother would have been better able or more willing to care for her. They would have had the mother-daughter relationship for which she still longs. She can come to know that she is guilty over her natural competitiveness with her mother and feels that this, along with her need and sexuality, caused her to fall from the grace she still seeks.

Conflicting with all this guilt and shame, while at the same time contributing to it, she is angry with her mother. Her mother was not there for her, did not protect her and was unable to satisfy her father so that she could have her own life free of the resulting corruption. In some cases, she will feel that her mother hated her and she will hate her mother in return. She will usually blame herself for this state of affairs, feeling that the mother's hate was engendered by her own basic badness and that her returned hatred is only evidence of how bad she really is.

She will also feel guilty in relation to the father, believing unconsciously that her coquettishness, seductiveness, and childish need for attention corrupted him. All of these feelings are enhanced to the extent that she colluded with the father in making aspects of their relationship secret. Further, any enjoyment she derived from this relationship will serve as further evidence of her guilt and her essentially evil nature.

She will, of course, also be angry with her father for exploiting her, leaving her imprisoned in this complex, which restricts her ability to be at peace with herself and develop a fully satisfying love relationship. So called "oedipal guilt" makes it particularly difficult to attain a satisfying adult-adult sex-love relationship. She is guilty for attaining the love of her father, which her mother could not attain. She may also be unconsciously guilty for abandoning her father to be involved with another. Furthermore, to have a satisfying relationship of her own would mean outdoing both her parents in having something they could not have, largely, she believes, because of the evil she herself brought into the family. This is the complex of personal problems to be brought to consciousness and felt through.

But there is much resistance. She is afraid of her needy, competitive, and sexual impulses. She is afraid of exploiting or being exploited, and she is afraid of being found out in her badness and rejected for it. Essentially, she is afraid of experiencing and working through what we are calling here the oedipal complex of threatening impulses, conflicting feelings, and unconscious ideas, which confirm her evil nature.

There is also, of course, the inevitable sadness, which the hysteric must face, concerning the reality of her family situation and her place in it. Realizing that she was sacrificed for the needs of others and that her natural need, sexuality, love, and competitiveness were exploited will relieve her guilt. But, she must come to terms with or feel through the grief that this realization uncovers. There will also be grief for the real losses of adult life occasioned by the history of corruption. Love relationships, in particular, have been damaged and damaging. People, those who have loved her most and even her own children, have been damaged. Life has been wasted.

Behavioral-Social Objectives

As outlined earlier, the hysteric's relationships often seem phony, disingenuous, or "as if." Should this defensive style break down, relationships become infused with the transference of the unconscious self-object relationships we have been considering. Both patterns will infuse the therapeutic relationship, and the therapist's management of them will determine the success or failure of any therapeutic endeavor. It is critical to initially establish a respectful, adult-adult relationship involving therapeutic alliance with appropriate limits. The hysteric will be inclined, initially at least, to continue in her pseudo-relating, which keeps distance on the one hand and simultaneously attempts to extend the relationship beyond appropriate limits. Early or abrupt confrontations of these patterns may result in the client's terminating treatment, or, because they signal a lack of safety, may further perpetuate greater defensiveness. The hysteric is narcissistically vulnerable because of her underlying poor self-esteem. So, the therapist will usually fare better by simply modelling a solid, respectful, warm, but boundaried relational style. In so doing, the therapist creates a safe and bounded environment, wherein the transference of underlying relational dynamics can be displayed and explored. Hysterics are notorious for using the transference channel in therapeutic work. The alliance, the appropriate limitations, as well as the warmth and respect, will allow that transference to be used productively. It will prompt more transference, disinhibit its sharing, and, finally, encourage its analysis.

The three most common transferences of the hysteric are erotic, dependent, and hostile. As with all transferences in higher functioning clients, it is well to allow, encourage, and welcome them, to limit acting out on them, and to understand them in the strengthened context of an adult-adult therapeutic alliance imbued with respect. Psychoanalysis, love affairs, and family life drive people crazy because they unleash unresolved, unconscious dynamics. Analysis, however, is unique in providing the best opportunity for limits to acting out as well as the best opportunity for understanding due to the neutrality and training of the therapist. Analysis cures not so much by the understanding provided as by the release and resolution of these powerful forces within a human relationship. As these transferences are successfully dealt with, the hysteric's relationships can be more and more real in that they can be loving when loving, sexual when sexual, competitive when competitive, dependent when dependent, and so on. All of these essentially human responses can then be uncontaminated by guilt, malevolence, self-attribution, or projection of hostility, exploitation, and the corruption of secrets and deceit.

Behaviorally, you know your work with an hysteric is coming to an end when she is straight with you and everyone else in her life. She no longer manipulates, cajoles, or flirts to get her way. She knows what she wants, accepts the validity of her needs, and meets them in a direct as opposed to an indirect manner. She acts like a grown-up with others and expects the same of them. Her feelings and thoughts about things are not characterized by naive simplicity and polarity but by ambivalence and complexity. She doesn't pick sugar daddies for partners nor does she become enraged at male vulnerability or weakness.

Similarly, any addictive behaviors that were used to avoid the pain of her personal problems will be handled. Most commonly, her addictions will have involved drugs and alcohol, compulsive spending, or eating disorders. While a great proportion of such change is a byproduct of working through, it can also be directly affected through modelling, instruction, and encouragement.

The relational objectives of therapy can be stated quite succinctly. They involve simply creating genuineness in relationships by welcoming into them those natural human propensities that have been corrupted, and decorrupting them by understanding, respect, and affirmation of their essential legitimacy. Most central to this process for the hysteric is legitimizing her sexuality, neediness, and competitive striving together with the rage, disappointment, and self-blame that resulted from her exploitation.

CHAPTER 11

The Disciplined Child:
The Obsessive-Compulsive Personality

He knows when you are sleeping,
He knows when you're awake,
He knows when you've been bad or good,
So be good for goodness sake.

— "Santa Claus is Coming to Town"

THE OBSESSIVE-COMPULSIVE AND the hysteric share many commonalities. The abilities required for both adjustments develop relatively late, and most theoreticians have speculated that both personality types develop in response to relatively more advanced life issues. Like the hysterical character, the obsessive-compulsive represents a complex syndrome. Yet, it gets its name from those behavioral elements of the syndrome that are most obvious but not most central.

Focusing on obsessive thought and compulsive behavior as central in this syndrome can lead to confusion due to the many other psychological and medical conditions that can lead to such expressions. The obsessive-compulsive personality syndrome is probably the best delineated, most researched, and most consistently validated personality type. Yet, it is not the condition associated with the most dramatic examples of obsessive thinking or compulsive behavior. This distinction probably goes to the obsessive-compulsive disorder (OCD), which, as I will document shortly, appears to be a separate condition. Dramatic obsessions and compulsions are also noted in cases

266

of anorexia nervosa, organic brain syndrome, head trauma, epilepsy, Tourette's syndrome, and Lesch-Nyhaus syndrome (Turner, Beidel, & Nathan, 1985).

Freud (1913) made a distinction between the personalty syndrome he called "anal character" and what he labeled obsessive-compulsive neurosis. This differentiation has persisted to this day, represented by the current distinction in the American Psychiatric Association's *Diagnostic and Statistical Manual* between obsessive-compulsive disorder and obsessive-compulsive personality disorder. But, while the distinction has always been made and is more justified by recent research than ever before, it has often been lost. Some of the best known and most useful works on the obsessive-compulsive personality have lost it. In common practice, it is even more reliably lost, as are other differentiations between this personality syndrome and the other conditions associated with obsessional thought and compulsive behavior. Before describing this personality syndrome, I believe it is necessary to delineate some of these other obsessive-compulsive etiologies, particularly OCD.

OBSESSIVE-COMPULSIVE DISORDER

Individuals diagnosed with obsessive-compulsive disorder display some of the most extreme examples of anxiety driven phenomenology together with ritualistic activities and repetitive thoughts or actions. In attempting to organize the literature on OCD, Liebowitz and Hollander (1991) distinguished three types.

The most common type is characterized by "an excessive fear of physical harm or danger to one's self, or others, or property" (p. 228). These individuals may continually worry about getting AIDS, for example, or become excessively obsessed with the danger of their hostile impulses. These concerns can then lead to compulsive behaviors such as rituals or excessive washing or checking. The second type involves "a vague sense of unease rather than actual danger in the face of normal exposures" (p. 228). This high level of psychic arousal, resembling generalized anxiety, can similarly lead to compulsive behaviors such as hoarding, excessive arranging, and cataloging. The third type is distinguished by continual striving for perfection and symmetry. Some such patients may need, for example, to have each shoe tied to the same degree of tension or need to walk through a doorway precisely in the middle. Religious or other rituals may have to be done with perfect attention to every detail and sequence, or one's desk may need to be arranged with complete orderliness and symmetry with every object at its exactly prescribed angle. For the most part, individuals with this diagnosis also find their compulsive behaviors to be irrational, ego-dystonic, and intrusive, yet they feel compelled to do them. A common exception to this generalization, however, is that their perfectionistic standards are often ego-syntonic.

The underlying anxiety or over-aroused psychic state is their most generally apparent characteristic and is often expressed through excessive checking, cleaning, ritualistic behavior, and/or continual obsessions such as those involved in hypochondriasis, continual worry over low-probability threatening events, or aggressive thoughts and fantasies. The course of obsessive-compulsive disorder is regarded as chronic with periodic exacerbation and diminution of symptoms.

A number of studies of OCD suggest that it has a genetic component. In reviewing the twin studies in which monozygotic and dizygotic twins are compared, Turner, Beidel, and Nathan (1985) conclude that the OCD concordant rates for monozygotic pairs far exceed the dizygotic rates, establishing a genetic link. This same review also documents the oft-noted relationship between OCD and Tourette's Syndrome, in that obsessive-compulsive disorder occurs in 33% to 89% of patients diagnosed with Tourette's. Obsessive-compulsive disorder also frequently appears in first-degree relatives of patients with Tourette's (Montgomery, Clayton, & Friedhoff, 1982). Furthermore, OCD symptoms have been reduced by surgeries, which produce ablations of sections of the lymphic system. Such surgeries have usually been conducted only in the most severe cases where other forms of treatment have been unsuccessful and where the OCD symptoms eliminate any possibility for a reasonable life.

In recent years, medications that inhibit serotonergic reuptake (e.g., clomipramine and fluoxetine) have shown impressive results in the treatment of OCD. On average, approximately 50% of patients are significantly improved on these sorts of medications. Several reports also give positive results for behavioral treatments with OCD (e.g., Beech & Vaughan, 1978; Marks, 1981).

In contrast to these treatment results, most investigators agree that psychoanalytic or insight therapy is generally ineffective with

OCD. Sifneos (1985) provides one exception to this generalization, but his cases represent very mild versions, so much so that their OCD status is questionable.

A number of studies have been done to investigate the overlap between OCD and obsessive-compulsive personality disorder (OCPD). One theory espoused most clearly by Salzman and Thaler (1981) posits that a continuum exists from normal obsessional and orderly behavior to obsessive-compulsive personality, to OCD. According to this theory, OCD represents a decompensation from the milder, pre-existing condition of obsessive-compulsive personality. Research results are somewhat inconsistent in documenting the relationship between OCD and OCPD but there certainly is no demonstration of any clear linear connection. Reviews by Pollack (1979, 1987) and Baer and Jenike (1990) would seem to lead to the following conclusion: While a few studies do document either a premorbid or concurrent diagnosis of obsessive-compulsive personality disorder in some significant proportion of patients diagnosed with obsessive-compulsive disorder, many other studies do not show such a relationship. These studies may indicate that a high proportion of OCD patients also quality for a personality disorder diagnosis but the obsessive-compulsive personality disorder is not among the most commonly assigned. The research taken as a whole does not persuasively argue for a direct link between obsessive-compulsive personality and obsessive-compulsive disorder. In view of all of the research, it appears that these conditions are essentially separate.

OCD is a fascinating problem and the increased understanding of this condition over the past ten years may very well help many whose severe symptomatology has not formally been recognized as emanating from a basic neurological condition. Jenike (1990) makes a very persuasive argument that many severe conditions are truly manifestations of OCD. These include some proportion of anorexia nervosa, compulsive self-mutilation, pathologic gambling, monosymptomatic hypochondriasis, trichotillomania (compulsive hair-pulling), and other obsessions involving the body or illness.

In reviewing the biological research on OCD, Turner, Beidel, and Nathan (1985) conclude that the available data point to "a chronic over-aroused state in the obsessive-compulsive." The obsessive-compulsive behavior can then be seen as a consequence or response to this over-aroused state — even as an attempt to gain control of it.

It may be that all obsessive-compulsive behavior of whatever origin has at its base the attempt to gain control of underlying affective states. The human being, along with other animals, may very well rely on such abilities to bring order to underlying affective disturbance. But for now, it is important to simply distinguish between OCD and obsessive-compulsive personality.

OTHER CAUSES OF OBSESSIVE-COMPULSIVE BEHAVIOR

In conjunction with the OCD distinction, I would also like to briefly discuss those cases in which I have seen obsessive-compulsive behavior, which is also distinct from both the obsessive-compulsive personality and the obsessive-compulsive disorder. People who have been raised in unpredictable or chaotic family situations but who have survived them by identifying with other models of behavior or ideology can show an obsessive-like commitment to values or a compulsive need for order. Some adult children of alcoholics, for example, or the more functional offspring of families dominated by drug addition may well show this pattern. Their devotion to a value system or a system of order and self-regulation has helped them escape the chaos engendered by their parents or guardians and has enabled them to establish a structure, which they cherish. These individuals do not display the other soon to be described characteristics of the obsessive-compulsive personality. In particular, these people are not usually so out of touch with their own feelings and they are usually more affectively labile than the obsessive-compulsive personality. They are more in touch with themselves but simply use values and order to establish stability.

Another group of individuals that may appear obsessive and/or compulsive are those who are compensating for an underlying lack of structure or self. Whatever characterological issues they are grappling with, their structural functioning is in the lower or personality disorder range, as described throughout this volume, and they require firm anchor points to bolster their fragile sense of self. They are similar to the group just discussed in that they need to compensate for personal experience that might otherwise be chaotic. So, the rigidity of their belief structure or routines create a greater sense of self and security. Similar to the group just discussed, these individuals do not necessarily show the other characteristics of obsessive-compulsive personality. While they may show some restriction in self-expression, they do not show the same ability to narrowly focus their attention and achieve the same level of pervasive self-control associated with the obsessive-compulsive personality. They are not as well-formed personalities and they cannot so exquisitely self-manage or over-manage themselves. Rather, they are hanging on for dear life to a value structure or organizational structure which gives them some semblance of self structure.

ETIOLOGY

There is considerable empirical research on obsessive-compulsive personality and a good deal of agreement in this research concerning the validity of the traits and symptoms associated with it (e.g., see reviews by Fisher & Greenberg, 1977; Kline, 1981; Pollack, 1979, 1987; Slade, 1974). Factor analytic studies show a consistent pattern across pathological and normal groups as well as across cultures. Furthermore, the predictive validity of this personality construct has been shown by a number of studies employing behavioral criteria (e.g., see Fisher & Greenberg, 1977). Nearly all of the research on the etiology of obsessive-compulsive personality find almost no empirical support for the Freudian proposition that these character traits derive from particular toilet-training practices (e.g., see O'Connor & Franks, 1960; Pollack, 1979, 1987). However, several studies do converge in finding similarities in the "anal" or obsessive-compulsive orientation of parents and their children (Adams, 1973; Beloff, 1957; Finney, 1963; Hayes, 1972; Heatherington & Brackville, 1963). Furthermore, there is a good deal of agreement, even among usually competing theoretical schools of thought on the etiology of obsessive-compulsive personality. The social learning perspective, as exhibited by Millon (1981), and the psychodynamic perspective, as exemplified by Fisher and Greenberg (1977), both emphasize the role of over-controlling, rigid, rule-bound, and exacting parenting, which disallows spontaneity and flexibility in socialization and moral development.

The fact that obsessive-compulsive personality seems to run in families, of course, begs the nature-nurture question. In a study comparing 419 pairs of monozygotic and dizygotic normal twins, Clifford, Murray, and Fulker (1984) found that just under half of the variance (44%) in the Latent Obsessional Trait Inventory was attributable to heredity with the monozygotic twin correlations approximately double those of the dizygotic twin correlations. This is one of several studies that gives support to what many have suspected: that a number of key personality dimensions are determined by hereditary factors and influence characterological expression in both the normal and pathological spheres. I suspect that, like introversion-extroversion, a tendency towards environmental and self-control, as exhibited in this character type, is one of those basic personality dimensions having a strong hereditary component. At the same time, however, I believe that these personality factors only cause trouble when they are influenced by an environment that is pathogenic.

One of the best ways to appreciate the functional as opposed to genetic etiology of obsessive-compulsive personality is to imagine what it would be like to be the child of two very obsessive-compulsive parents. In imagining this scenario, it's most instructive to think of the obsessive-compulsive family in its purest form. Often, an obsessive-compulsive etiology will include some of the sadistic parenting that results in masochism or the narcissistic parenting that leads to narcissism. While some such narcissistic injury is probably never reducible to zero in the kind of scenario we are now considering, it can be relatively minimal. The "pure" result of obsessive-compulsive parenting would be a neurotic adjustment involving conflict about such issues as love, sex, competition, and aggression. In other words, this pure obsessive-compulsive etiology would not lead to the kind of structural deficits associated with a basic self-disorder or borderline personality organization. There certainly are obsessive-compulsives who could be so categorized, but in the theoretical view presented here, these individuals would also have to have suffered more structurally damaging environments. These theoretical distinctions are necessary for differentiating the obsessive-compulsive etiology and personality from others—particularly narcissism.

The archetypal scenario that follows, then, is typical only for the upper half of the structural functioning continuum. I use this for illustration purposes to avoid the contamination of this issue with others. In real life, however, such contamination is more the rule, though this purer form of etiological factors certainly does occur.

A high-functioning obsessive-compulsive couple will approach child-rearing in the same way they approach everything else. They will take it very seriously and try, with all good intentions, to do it perfectly. Even more than most parents, they will be particularly concerned about doing something wrong; they will have very little trust in their own intuition or common sense and will rely a good deal on authority, common practice, or their own childhood for prescriptions of proper parenting. They will not attune their parenting very well to the peculiar or idiosyncratic characteristics of their child. This kind of parenting can be less narcissistically injuring than might be expected because, over time, the child will feel that his parents do truly love him and that they are clearly trying to do what is best for him. These parents will believe that about themselves and will present that to their child.

Whatever negativity they do exhibit will come out in their obstinacy, which will be framed as necessary and "for the child's own good." The parents' presentation of this stance, as well as the truth of it, makes it even more difficult for the child to rebel against parental authority or express any real anger against it. As a result, he is prone to assimilate it quite smoothly into his own self-structure. Just like his parents, the rebellion and negativity will be shown only in his obstinacy or stubbornness, which, particularly when it is righteous, will be quite pronounced and ego-syntonic.

These are conscientious parents who worry about their children and who typically provide them with what they need in a dutiful and well-meaning manner. The child's first eighteen months to even two years can be quite normal in such a family, and the child will thrive. Unless the culture prescribes inappropriate practices, these parents will appropriately indulge their children and not impose out-of-phase expectations on them. The parents may be a little hard on themselves about doing the proper thing, but their relatively solid structure will enable them to manage this anxiety well and insulate their child from it. As standards for right conduct become more and more necessary in the interaction of parent and child, these very well disciplined adults will be particularly conscientious in instilling the "right" codes of ethics, belief, and conduct in their offspring. They may very well not expect more than their children can deliver and, in that, they will be even more effective in instilling discipline and self-control.

As it becomes more and more possible due to the child's development, these parents will begin to impose the same standard of error-free performance on their children as they do on themselves. They then evaluate the child's performance quite precisely and reward and punish contingently. They may, for example, give their child an allowance. But the allowance will not be over-generous, there won't be many additional gratifications or surprises, the allowance may be quite contingent, and these contingencies will be rigidly managed. Yet, in all this the parent tries to be fair and reasonable at all times. This parent of rigid character essentially "goes by the book." And, of course, obsessive-compulsive parents are not much fun. They are not able to play, to appreciate spontaneous emotion, to understand, participate in, or learn from the child's ability to become engrossed in something for its own sake, to engage in an activity for the feelings it produces, to reach the heights of ecstasy or the depths of despair, to be silly, etc.

An obsessive-compulsive parent will also tend to deny hostility or any form of negativity, masking it by righteous necessity. The child is thereby encouraged, once again, to distrust his own perception and feelings while accepting his parent's "party line" of beneficent intent for treatment that doesn't feel very good.

These adults are essentially too adult and their often very effective parenting causes their child to follow too quickly and too completely in their footsteps. That which is childlike, animal-like, passionate, sensual, or self-indulgent is kept under tight control. These forces are harnessed, and the child is taught that this is the way to be. Particularly as this kind of training and treatment is phase appropriate and to the extent that it is accompanied by attitudes and behaviors that communicate caring for the child, the product is an exceedingly well disciplined child who, like his parents, always tries to do everything right.

The treatment outlined above engenders the well known rigidity of the obsessive-compulsive. To keep things under tight control, he begins to breathe less fully and to move less fluidly. Similarly, the value and belief structure of such a person rigidifies in the pursuit of perfection and the avoidance of any mistake.

The pathology resulting from the induction outlined above will, to a large extent, depend on temperament. A very active, strong willed, passionate disposition in the child will, of course, create much more conflict than would a more passive disposition. It is very difficult, however, to sustain continued rebellion in such a family. In these cases, one would expect a much higher level of underground hostility, resentment, or rebellion, which would be expressed through obstinacy and passive aggressive behavior. With more underground feelings of this sort one would also expect more symptoms such as obsessive worry, psychosomatic symptoms, intrusive thoughts of a forbidden nature, etc.

The other source of difficulty is that this kind of parenting is often out of phase developmentally. These parents are known for being unempathic with their child and as a consequence they often do not pace their socialization as smoothly as in the preceding scenario. In addition, there is often far more hostility and control exhibited by such parents together with rationalizations for such behavior and a loving external presentation. As control and discipline are imposed less appropriately and with greater masked hostility, they create more serious narcissistic wounds, increasing the child's anger, rebellion, and conflict over these intense disallowed emotions. Another way to say it is that the more disallowed passion the child has to subject to his will, the more symptomatic he will be. The obsessive-compulsive is a constricted, controlled, and inhibited personality. But the more there is to constrain the harder it is to function like the well-oiled machine that is the ideal of this structure. With more to be constrained there is more opportunity for leakage and/or breakdown in the dam that is holding it all back.

To understand the character structures presented in this book, I think it is most useful to apprehend them from an internal subjective point of view, which emphasizes the individual's experience and motivation, thereby making sense of all the resulting manifestations. In the present case, this essential subjectivity is that the individual is trying to please these very exacting parental figures with extraordinarily high and precise standards, which include the exquisite self-regulation of all spontaneous expression. Essentially the obsessive-compulsive is just trying to stay out of trouble and fears that if he should relax he will be in deep trouble. Everything that follows essentially derives from this.

AFFECT, BEHAVIOR, COGNITION

Behavior

Sigmund Freud identified this character structure in 1908, and his initial description still holds up well to decades of research and clinical experience. He emphasized the traits of orderliness, parsimony, and obstinacy in describing the "anal retentive" or "anal" character. Though the specific etiology implied by this label has not held up to research, the name has stuck and is used in popular parlance to describe the personality type we are considering. In some ways, it is a better label because it is so widely understood and because it brings our attention to defining behaviors other than the obsessive and compulsive. Parsimony, for example, refers to the well-known characteristic of frugality, avarice, or stinginess. Another way of saying it is that these individuals are tight. They hold themselves tightly in rein, and they hold on tightly to their possessions. Typically, they are at least as frugal with themselves, as waste of anything is viewed as sinful. They carry themselves tightly and are even tight with their expressions of appreciation and affection. Such people are seen as "tight assed," deriving, I believe, from the tight anal sphincter metaphor of the anal retentive character.

Freud's obstinacy refers to persistence and perseverance, conscientiousness and determination, willfulness and endurance. All of these qualities can be quite adaptive, particularly in complex bureaucratic societies. This characterization also, however, refers to less attractive traits, such as stubbornness, defiance, inflexibility, and other similar expressions of negativity, which could be characterized as holding on to one's position, one's anger, one's resentment, etc. It often appears that this is the only acceptable way for such a person to have or express angry feelings. This becomes even more apparent when the obstinacy is exhibited through a rigidly righteous stance, which may have to do with values or codes of conduct. From that righteous position, such a person can be quite controlling and critical and, in the extreme, wield cruel power over others without guilt.

These considerations lead directly to the obsessive-compulsive's relationship to authority. Almost every description of this personality type will refer to the fact that these people are often quite submissive to authority on the one hand and correspondingly authoritarian with those under their control or those perceived to be beneath them in status. Their reliability, conscientiousness, obedience to rules, etc., may be viewed as characteristics of their subservience to authority. Their stubbornness, obstinance, and defiance may be viewed as permissible rebellion against such authority, particularly where it is righteous. Their dominant, strict, and even sadistic exercise of authority can be viewed as an identification with authority, which provides a sanctioned way of releasing the hostility that is a consequence of being so strictly dominated by authority. These are the very same dynamics associated with the authoritarian personality (Adorno, Frankel-Brunswick, & Sanford, 1950).

Related to obstinacy is the oft-noted characteristic of body rigidity, inflexibility, or stiffness. These characteristics are noted even by those theoreticians who do not typically pay attention to energetic or body expressions of character. Those who get more specific about this point to a tightness or stiffness in the joints. Again, it is as if these people are holding on and holding back, particularly in their expression of both positive and negative feeling. In this connection, these individuals are typically experienced socially as formal, cold, standoffish, aloof, or distant.

Freud's orderliness factor is what we contemporarily think of as compulsive. In the classic presentation, these individuals crave order, precision, organization, cleanliness, and correctness in every detail. Often, they do not have a good sense of priority. Everything is of equal and usually grave importance. A misplaced comma, a tiny spot, a minute of lateness can spoil the sought-for perfection. Indeed, these individuals are known for their tendency to miss what is most important by concentrating on minor details. Compulsivity is where the drivenness of this personality is most obvious. There is a kind of ever-present tension in this, which is typically experienced as a little uncomfortable and which may result in the individual's asking for help if it gets bad enough. Those who are in more discomfort or those who are more psychologically sophisticated may begin to see their need for order and perfection as a bit silly and the underlying tension as undesirable.

A fourth characteristic that is often noted in these personalities, though not as reliably found in the factor analytic personality studies, is indecisiveness, inconclusiveness, or "obsessive doubt." Again, we are discussing a personality syndrome in which not every characteristic is always present. Indeed, obsessive doubt and the procrastination that accompanies it can be the most noticeable or problematic characteristic in some cases, while it is relatively absent in others. There may be a reciprocal relationship in that those individuals who are very absorbed and accepting of their compulsive need for orderliness and all the activities required to maintain it do not really have the time or psychic energy to engage in a great deal of internal debate. The underlying anxiety, insecurity, and uncertainty may be bound by this kind of driven compulsive activity. In any case, those who suffer these more obsessive-like symptoms vacillate or shift back and forth in their behavior and attitudes. They have a great deal of trouble in committing to one course of action or another. Like the OCD patient, they may repeat and check frequently. Imperfection and incompleteness bother them, and they have difficulty "leaving well enough alone," tending to ruin a project by continually over-correcting it.

When presenting this factor I'm often reminded of two individuals I have been told of. One was so insecure in his work that he proof-read all his Xerox copies. The other kept trimming his beard until he had to cut it off entirely. Both of these examples have the absurdity and extreme qualities associated with OCD, and because I haven't met these individuals I don't know which diagnosis they represent. They do, however, exemplify the extreme pole of this particular personality factor. In this factor there are the essential commonalities of the fear of error and the anxiety at imperfection.

Again, I think it is helpful to see these characteristics as essentially motivated by the individual's attempt to stay out of trouble. When it becomes obviously neurotic, we can so clearly see that these people are creating trouble for themselves by attempting to avoid trouble, which only they are creating. Here, we have the essence of neurosis wherein the organism is divided against itself, creating trouble for itself with the very maneuvers that are attempting to avoid it.

Cognition

Before going into the cognitive characteristics of the obsessive-compulsive personality I would like to briefly review an animal behavior model proposed in the study of obsessive-compulsive disorder. This model provides a useful heuristic metaphor for both describing and understanding certain aspects of obsessive-compulsive personality.

A number of students of animal behavior have observed "displacement behaviors," such as grooming, pecking, digging, head turning, or nesting occurring in apparently inappropriate contexts (e.g., Lorenz, 1966; Tinbergen, 1953). Such displacement behaviors are invariably triggered by conflict between two opposing response tendencies or drives. Particularly common are conflicts between defending territory and escaping potential danger (Tinbergen, 1953). Such behavior also is characterized by its "fixed action pattern" referring to its "all or nothing" quality and its apparent autonomous functioning once it has begun. It seems to keep going until the conflict between response tendencies or drives is either removed or replaced by a more urgent need. Holland (1974) has proposed this as an ethological model of OCD. I present it merely as a useful metaphor for understanding obsessive-compulsive defenses. If this metaphor is not already obvious, it should become so very shortly.

Horowitz (1986; Horowitz et al., 1984), Salzman (1980), Shapiro (1965), and Horner (1990) are all very helpful in describing and conceptualizing the obsessive-compulsive's cognitive style. Essentially, all of their models emphasize the shifting of attention from thinking and feeling through an issue in order to avoid those thoughts and feelings that are unacceptable. One such shift is away from the center of the issue to its periphery where sharply focused attention is given to relatively inconsequential details. One performer of my acquaintance, for example, manages her anxiety over an upcoming performance by focusing on the meticulous grooming of her eyebrows. This brilliantly talented woman behaves in a way reminiscent of the animals observed by Tinbergen and Lorenz.

Another form of shift is to the abstract to search for or profess certain principles or rules, which provide guidelines for dealing with the issue in question. One client, for example, attributed his difficulty in committing to his girlfriend to his belief that he should mate with someone culturally different thereby contributing to the cultural melting pot. In such an over-intellectualized preoccupation, the individual can avoid emotions that are threatening, such as rage, fear, lust, crushing disappointment, grief at loss, etc.

Another method of shifting involves the vacillation of "obsessive doubt." Horowitz writes, "Very often, a given theme has opposite poles of conflict, and the patient shifts rapidly from one to the other and back again . . . for example, a sense of impending guilt over being too strong is undone by a quick shift towards a sense of impending fear of being too weak and vulnerable. For the person who makes such shifts, one emotional propensity undoes another. Since oscillation occurs rapidly, no strong emotion is experienced. The result may be prolonged indecision or confusion. To avoid this expe-

rience, some compulsive patients make impulsive decisions. However, these choices are not based on rational completion of a train of
thought. Accordingly, the decision itself may then become a focus
for further undoing operations" (Horowitz et al., 1984, pp. 160–
161). These shifts, to the periphery, to the abstract, and to rapid
oscillation define the cognitive defenses of the obsessive-compulsive.

When you talk with such a person and experience how his mind
works, you are struck with how he tends to keep life at arm's length.
Particularly those strong elements of life that, at least temporarily,
can take us over and lead us to decisive action—such things as love,
sex, anger, hatred, need, etc.—are absent or severely muted. All of
this is kept at arm's length by holding to abstraction, minutae, and
vacillation. As a result, life is characterized by an intellectualized
aridness and a lack of color. It is as if these people are void of the
bright, primary colors of life and experience it in various shades of
gray. Whenever a primary color threatens, it prompts a shift to the
periphery, to the abstract, or to conflict.

The obsessive-compulsive has difficulty making decisions because
most decisions in life, particularly the important ones, require a
solidly felt kinesthetic sense. Without that, we are not playing with
a full deck. The obsessive-compulsive tries to do without that—
living as he should, marrying whom he should, working at what he
should, etc. He is, then, never in touch and thus never sure that he
is doing the right thing. Whenever he experiences getting in touch,
he gets too close to some forbidden feeling and then rapidly shifts
away. Optimal decision making may very well involve adding up all
of the pros and cons and imagining what could happen with each
alternative. What is also necessary, however, is checking in with
oneself about what feels right or what one truly wants. This is where
the obsessive's style of cognitive processing fails. By so desperately
trying to do the right thing and staying out of trouble, he obscures
what is right for him and creates trouble.

What is warded off can intrude. A not uncommon symptom of
obsessive-compulsive personality is intrusive thoughts. "Maybe I
should run down that pedestrian, drown my two-year old son, rape
that woman." Such thoughts in an otherwise extraordinarily well-
disciplined, good citizen, who is striving above all else to be correct,
can be quite alarming. Interestingly, such thoughts are just that—
they are thoughts as opposed to impulses with a strong emotional
component. They have more of a "what if" quality but still can

profoundly shake the obsessive-compulsive person. In a very general way they do signal what unacceptable emotions and thoughts have been warded off and can really be seen as bids from the unconscious to attend to that part of the deck that is not being played.

In the pure obsessive-compulsive personality, such thoughts do not represent any real danger to the community. When the obsessive-compulsive is in the process of liberating himself from his tight harness, he may "lose it" by his standards, have a temper outburst, or blurt out something inappropriately. But these are relatively minor errors and his fear of going berserk and losing complete control of himself is unwarranted. In its pure form, the obsessive-compulsive personality possesses a relatively strong underlying structure, which does not decompensate.

In this context, however, it is well to remember again that obsessive-compulsive behaviors and attitudes can be found in other less structured characters. A sudden breakdown of the social and belief structures, which keep these individuals together, can result in a disintegration that can lead to serious threats to self and others. The pure obsessive-compulsive personality discussed here, however, is really his own worst enemy, and while this person may never really live, he is not a killer or a rapist—he is a neurotic.

To balance this discussion of the obsessive-compulsive's potential pathology it is also well to highlight his strengths. These can be considerable, particularly at the character style end of the continuum and in areas that are conflict-free. This personality is particularly good at rational, detailed, and disciplined thinking and can excel in such things as accounting, law, technology, research, and certain areas of medicine where all these qualities are necessary for optimum performance. Indeed, a certain degree of obsessive-compulsiveness is necessary to function optimally in the complex modern age. But, even in the more or less well adjusted individual there is a sacrifice of spontaneous, deeply felt, connected living to the demands of order, efficiency, and accuracy. All these are attributes of a well-running machine, but are not enough for a well-functioning human being.

Affect

The most noticeable characteristic of the obsessive-compulsive in the area of feelings is their absence. The ideal for this character type is rationality, reasonableness, and correctness. As outlined in the last section, these individuals accomplish this in part by staying in the periphery, in abstractions, or in continual conflict so that the deeper, threatening feelings do not emerge. Where there is a temperamental predisposition to this way of functioning, and where parenting has been minimally frustrating, this apparent lack of emotionality may not be problematic. However, in cases where this character style is accompanied by any dysfunctionality, there are predictable underlying emotions, which are more or less well-covered by these more sophisticated defense mechanisms.

As with the masochistic character, the emotion that is usually most apparent to those around him is anger. Obstinance, stubbornness, persistence, and rigidity typical in this character structure all express anger, albeit indirectly.

Fischer and Juni (1982) completed an illustrative study of these phenomena. They took 65 college students and divided them into high versus low "anality" on the basis of a questionnaire. In general, they were confirmed in their predictions that the highly anal group would show more resistance to comply and disclose. This group was significantly less revealing of personal information (p < .0001), and they responded less well to the experimental condition requiring higher disclosure (p < .001). Predictions that these more anal-retentive subjects would more frequently fail to show up for appointments and would take more time to agree to participate were not confirmed. These results, and others like them available in literature, are striking in that such a small sample can provide such profound results using unselected normal subjects and predicting from questionnaires to behavior.

What underlies these kinds of rigid, passive-aggressive, and overly bounded behaviors is the far deeper resentment at the suppression of self, which was required to become so reasonable, rational, and precisely correct. The kind of excessive willpower exhibited by people of this character type is not natural, but the resentment that it engenders is. It is in his "anality" that the obsessive-compulsive character resembles the masochist. This set of stubborn, passive-aggressive characteristics operates with very much the same dynamic. The difference exists more in the degree of abusiveness or sadism in the suppression that results in resentment. In the masochist, there is more intrusive abuse, which results in defeat and retaliations through self-defeat. In the obsessive-compulsive, the self-discipline is acquired more gradually and more gently with the plausible and shared belief between parent and child that such training is for the child's own good. For the same reason, however, the obsessive-compulsive's anger, resentment, and rebellion may be even more difficult to elicit than it is with the masochist. Often, the well-functioning obsessive-compulsive is not so defeated as he is restrained in personal or self-expression. Working on more general and often physical release may productively lead to a direct expression of the underlying resentment.

Not infrequently this kind of person may be more easily freed by seeing himself and his restricting parent as essentially "in the same boat." When this is true, the individual can break these chains while retaining a compassionate attachment to the loved object and can see the release as symbolically releasing for the parents. Nevertheless, as this is achieved, there must be more personal owning of aggressive tendencies and greater direct expression of them. Active gestalt or body work is often very useful for these purposes. Continuing to hold the person to this theme of anger at the loved but restraining parent in spite of his attempts to shift away from it is an example of the necessary work with this character structure.

The other side of this anger and resentment is the love that is also held back, held in, or frozen. Particularly in these more high functioning cases, it was the love that made it possible for the parent to so effectively restrain the child. Love mediated the internalization of restraint. Through love, autonomy was stolen. The obsessive-compulsive is often reluctant to love deeply due to the unconscious fear that this will happen again. More of his autonomous real self will then be stolen in the interest of pleasing the loved one. This is the typical obligation of the obsessive-compulsive.

Behaviorally, obsessive-compulsive parents discourage effusive expressions of love and are more comfortable with sublimated deeds, which communicate caring at a safer distance. They tend to be embarrassed by too much affection, either verbal or physical. So, there are reasons to keep a well bounded distance from loved ones as well as modelling and reinforcement of that tendency.

As this character type softens in therapy or in life there is often revealed a reservoir of sentiment, which feels at once very sweet and threatening. Again, these individuals will tend to react almost reflexively in avoidance of such feelings or displays. Very frequently they will, if held to the feeling, report the fear of obligation that is tied to their love. They feel that if they love somebody, they have to marry them or put them through college or find them a job, etc.

Obsessive-compulsives need to learn to freely experience and express love without the obligation they feel must naturally go with it. Essentially, they've learned that if you love your parents you must do what they say. That fundamentally incorrect script decision or pathogenic belief must be repeatedly challenged before the individual can freely feel and express himself without feeling constrained by the attached obligations. He must learn that love is a gift whether given or received, and it does not imply any more than it is. When the obsessive-compulsive gets this, he no longer needs to be quite so obstinate and bounded. He owns himself and his love and neither can be wrested from him.

The obsessive-compulsive individual lives under a constant state of strain. Like the narcissist, perfection is a rather constant theme, but where the exhibitionistic narcissist says "I am perfect," the obsessive-compulsive says "I should be perfect." There is more apparent anxiety in the obsessive-compulsive's perfectionism. He is more afraid of getting into trouble and more conscious of the shame that he risks by self-activation. The obsessive-compulsive is not as sure of himself and, as noted before, is very prone to the vulnerability of indecision. The feeling that accompanies this indecision is an uncomfortable tension. He is caught in that he is fundamentally out of touch with his own feelings, preferences, and intuition while at the same time extraordinarily obligated to do precisely the right thing. This tension-filled state exists more or less continuously and affects every decision, from miniscule to major. The primary underlying affect here is fear—the fear of doing something wrong. And yet how can you do the right thing when you are so out of touch with yourself that you can never really know what is right. All you can know is what the church or the law or your family says is right. But, of course, they could always be wrong . . .

If the obsessive-compulsive ever gets to the point where he can admit to the foregoing possibility he will be even more anxious. For it is here that he dives headlong into the void of his fundamentally insubstantial condition. But, if his structure is sufficiently solid, the obsessive-compulsive can, especially with support, tolerate this anxiety and begin to find his substance. In this state, the anxiety is real and the void is real. This crisis is similar to the religious crisis for a true believer. It shakes one's very foundation. Yet this doubt, and the feeling that goes with it, may be the first authentically experienced experience in a very, very long time. Prior to such a crisis, he will always be asking the wrong question—"What should I do?" This question is at the periphery of the essential question "Who am I?" In cycling back and forth between one alternative and another he keeps himself distracted so as not to experience the much deeper question and the panic that it can engender. When the obsessive-compulsive finally begins asking the right question, he often fears he will lose control, go crazy, become violent or depraved. As I have indicated earlier, this result is highly unlikely in any but the most damaged people who are dealing with many other issues. Yet this fear of such loss of control is common in this personality. Expressed in this fear is the obsessive-compulsive's subliminal awareness of how much he really has been keeping under control and his essential unfamiliarity with what he's been suppressing.

Expressive or uncovering therapies are often most applicable to these individuals from the middle to higher end of the structural functioning continuum. Such therapies expose the individual to this warded off but necessary crisis, which will lead him back to himself. This character structure, at the middle to higher end, can certainly love, but he is terribly reluctant to soften to love. It puts him in touch with his truly human nature where mistakes are inevitable. The hate is at those same figures who are loved—those who have harnessed and restrained and caused the individual to cut himself off from his own humanity.

While the higher functioning obsessive-compulsive may be a great business partner, he is typically a very poor vacation, sexual, or love partner. Genuine interest and joy are necessary for these activities and, in the obsessive-compulsive, they have been effectively suppressed. Being part of human nature, however, they are still present in all of us. Reaching and then liberating them will be the ultimate payoff of the therapeutic work with this personality structure.

THERAPEUTIC OBJECTIVES

The essential objective of therapy with the obsessive-compulsive is to reconnect him with his basic human nature. The complexes of this character structure are the most suited to those modern psychotherapies that emphasize uncovering, expression, and release. The obsessive-compulsive is a human being imprisoned in his own rigidity. This rigidity exists in the tightness of his musculature, in the inflexibility of his belief systems, and in the excessive orderliness of his behavior. His id, his shadow, his warrior are all locked in this now self-maintained prison.

Cognitive Objectives

It is an oversimplification, but a useful one, to say that the characteristic cognitive style and behaviors of the obsessive-compulsive are defensive and the objective of therapy is to melt away these defenses so that the underlying feelings can come forth. Particularly in the narrow or pure obsessive-compulsive personality, the basic premises of classic psychoanalytic therapy apply rather well. This is an intact structure defending against anxiety, with much of that anxiety coming from the person's own repressed feelings. Such a person can tolerate a challenging, interpretive, and abstinent approach to therapy and benefit greatly from it. The approach of many short-term psychoanalytic therapists (e.g., Davanloo, 1980; Sifneos, 1979) can be quite successful with such high functioning clients.

In the cognitive realm, this work will be directed at describing and interpreting those cognitive maneuvers that avoid conflictual topics. In such work, the therapist will literally hold the subject on the conflictual topic as she describes the client's shifting maneuvers and interprets the underlying motivations for them. To review, the most common shifts are to the periphery of an issue, to abstractions about the issue, or to rapidly cycling vacillation over the issue. For example, the therapist might say, "I notice every time we begin to talk about your mixed feelings about your boss, you shift to some concern about the time or to that spot on your trousers" (periphery). Or "Every time we begin talking about the mixed feelings about your boss you won't stay with your anger but quickly shift to your admiration for him (rapidly cycling vacillation). Or "Every time we begin talking about your mixed feelings about your boss, you begin to discuss the necessity for hierarchy in organizations or begin to discuss alternative political systems" (shift to the abstract). Any such interpretation can then be followed up with a direct request, "Now tell me more about your anger at your boss."

Very often this kind of frontal attack on defenses will lead to here and now emotional reactions, which involve the therapist. This is excellent content for the obsessive-compulsive's therapy because the entire process of defense and over-modulation of affect can be observed and handled with the greatest immediacy. This is true in the therapy of most individuals but it is particularly important with the obsessive-compulsive to use every opportunity for work in the therapist-client relationship. He prefers the "Ivory Tower" for its distance, its pristine cleanliness, and its "broader view." But it is "in the clinches" of an ongoing affect-laden interaction that the obsessive-compulsive can really learn about relationship, feeling, and the acceptability of error.

The work described above will, of course, be complemented by understanding the personal history, which made necessary such perfection and control. How did this person become so reluctant to admit to hatred or resentment? How did it become so necessary to have such complete control both internally and externally? Where did he get the idea, for example, that it is so terrible to make a mistake, so intolerable to be anxious, or so necessary to protect against any possible criticism? Who are the internalized bad objects? And, perhaps most important, how much does he love them? The risk of this relatively more comfortable intellectual work is getting lost in cognitive exercise and diverting attention from the emotional work, which is far more threatening and essential. For this reason, it's often important with this personality to keep such interpretive work alive but, on any given occasion, to keep it brief. Generally, it is too comfortable and too fertile an area for doubt, obfuscation, exploration of irrelevant detail, and exercise of all the other obsessional defenses.

The combination of this here-and-now, affectively ladened therapy with reconstruction and interpretation will naturally lead to many opportunities for changing the obsessive-compulsive script decisions or pathogenic beliefs. It is well to repeat to him again and again that it is not necessary to have such perfection and such guarantees against criticism, failure, and particularly anxiety. All of these experiences are a necessary part of life. Learning that is completely error free is usually pretty limited. The obsessive-compulsive needs to learn that the price of trying to maintain such guarantees is too high. They rob life of variety, spontaneity, creativity, adventure, and discovery.

The obsessive-compulsive patient needs to learn that he can tolerate anxiety. This must, of course, be an experiential learning; but repeatedly encouraging this learning, particularly as anxiety is being tolerated, cannot but help.

Behavioral-Social Objectives

The behavioral objectives for this personality are almost too obvious to state. We seek to attenuate the overly orderly compulsive aspects of the patient's behaviors. These behaviors, which serve the function of binding anxiety, are to be relinquished.

In therapy with these individuals, prescriptions for stopping such behavior can be tried as experiments in the tolerance of anxiety and the uncovering of underlying emotions. Particularly once there is a good therapeutic alliance and a significant level of insight as well as experience of anxiety and direct emotion in the therapeutic hour, these behavioral strategies can be most effective. The client himself may join with curiosity to see what happens if he doesn't vacuum the carpet every day or straighten up his desk so regularly.

I believe all such behavioral prescriptions are best when they are undertaken in the spirit of experimentation providing further grist for the mill. Particularly in the obsessive-compulsive's case, the investigative nature of such assignments is critical in that they permit the individual to experience the anxiety, discover what it is about, and learn that it is tolerable. Anxiety for the obsessive-compulsive can be reframed from its usual function of signalling danger to a signal that can tell him what topics and feelings require further elaboration and investigation. The automatic aversive power of anxiety can, to some extent, be reversed by such an intellectual understanding, capitalizing as it does on the obsessive-compulsive's strong will.

Another overall behavioral objective of treatment is to assist the client in being able to commit to action and particularly to relationships. This is very much a higher order goal that must come out of the entirety of the therapeutic process. Much of it will rely on the ever growing ability of the client to trust the therapist, form a therapeutic alliance, and commit to the therapy itself. Some of this increased ability to commit will come from understanding a personal history in which a mistake was a sin and the resulting redecision allowing human fallibility, including making and correcting mistakes. Just as a person can stop compulsive behavior, live through the anxiety, and learn from the experience, so can he practice small commitments, learn to tolerate the anxiety so generated, and learn from these experiences.

Many obsessive-compulsive individuals need not only to relax the rigidity of their beliefs and compulsive behaviors but also the rigidity of their bodies. They need to relax, to breathe, to loosen in the joints and in their social manner. Successful treatment will result in the patient becoming less tight and more generous with himself and others. I believe this change will be affected most by a change in the affective sphere, particularly in the ability to experience anger and hostility more directly. But relaxation can be directly taught to compliment this affective work.

Affective Objectives

We hope for the obsessive-compulsive that he will finally come to really hear and feel the music of life and be able to play all its notes from his core. We hope to help him reconnect to all his feelings and we know that our therapy must involve those emotions that are most frightening or abhorrent to him. His tightness really comes from disallowing these feelings, and he cannot really loosen up and regain connection with himself until these disallowed emotions are reclaimed. Most central to all this is the deeply felt experience of love and hate, particularly love and hate for the same person. As I have indicated before, particularly with the higher functioning person, this is the essential emotional reality, which must be felt and accepted as truly human. When this is learned, the individual can love the confining parents, yet separate from them. In the profound experience of joining in with all the music of life, he can outdo them without guilt. Then there is no longer any need to rebel in stinginess or obstinance. There is no longer any jailer to identify with or resist. One merely lives freely because that is what is to be done with life.

To get to this point of liberation, the defenses must be sufficiently dismantled so that the underlying feelings can emerge. There must be a safe therapeutic environment in which they can be experienced and expressed. Measures must be taken to insure the generalization of this learning to life outside the consulting room. This usually takes much longer than it would seem it should with someone as structurally sound as the higher functioning obsessive-compulsive.

But, as in every other structure, it takes the time it takes and no matter how long it's always worth it. As I've stated, the body therapies, the affective therapies, the uncovering and release therapies all have strategies that are beneficial to this character problem once the defenses have been sufficiently relaxed.

The other prominent affective experiences that the person must repeatedly have include a free and even self-indulgent experience of his sexuality and a similarly guilt-free experience of his competitive nature. To experience all of these feelings cleanly, clearly, and without guilt is a human right. One can always argue about the advisability of certain innate human characteristics. Yet a *human* life is the one we have been given. We do much better if we're allowed to live it. Trying to live something other than a human life just doesn't work. Indeed, it leads to incredible difficulty on a personal as well as societal level.

The objective of good psychotherapy is to return one to his or her human life with all its particular dilemmas, limitations, and possibilities. I trust that if we are able to do this then any single life or human life in general will evolve optimally. The obsessive-compulsive illustrates so clearly that forcing life to live itself against its nature leads to a living death.

APPENDICES

Psychoanalytic Developmental Concepts: A Selected Glossary

accommodation (Piaget, 1936)—a process basic to learning, which involves the "changing or adjusting of preexisting structures (within the person) to accommodate reality." Horner (1979) feels that the working-through process in therapy is an example of accommodation.

agency (Stern, 1985)—the child's sense that he is the author of his acts, which he gradually achieves through the first few months of life. According to Stern, it is comprised of three parts: the sense of volition, which he sees as being present in the second month of life; proprioceptive feedback, present from birth; and predictability of consequences, which Stern feels develops gradually over the child's first few years.

ambivalence—the simultaneous experience of positive and negative feelings within oneself; the ability to be conscious of and to tolerate this experience is the hallmark of child development begun during the rapprochement phase.

antilibidinal object—*see* rejecting object.

antilibidinal self—*see* internal saboteur.

Appendix A was created jointly by Sue Hully and the author.

attachment — Bowlby (1969) used this term to describe a process by which the infant bonds with an early caretaker, most often the mother. Bowlby brought in ethnological research to show that humans have innate sets of attachment behaviors, which the infant uses to gain this bond.

assimilation (Piaget, 1936) — the process basic to learning whereby new experiences are taken into and modified to fit with a preexisting mental organization. Horner (1979) cites transference within therapy as an example of this process.

autism (Mahler, Pine, & Bergman, 1975) — the "normal autistic phase occurs in the first weeks of life after birth, during which the young infant appears to be an almost purely biological organism, his instinctual responses to stimuli being on a reflex . . . level." Mahler sees the child as attempting to maintain homeostatic equilibrium by avoiding over or under-stimulation, by the inability to distinguish between inside and outside, and by finding need satisfaction in "his own omnipotent autistic orbit."
This concept has been challenged by Stern (1985), who cites numerous studies that show that the child is, from birth, both aware of and interacting with the external world. Contrary to the picture painted by Mahler, Stern also feels that the child's maintenance of homeostatic equilibrium is inextricably linked within the primary caretaker, who functions to help the infant accomplish this by regulating the stimulus input to the infant.

boundaries — psychic demarcations of divisions between people (or objects). According to Mahler, the infant learns gradually about these boundaries throughout development.

differentiation (Mahler et al., 1975) — the first subphase of the separation-individuation process, occurring from five to nine months of age. The infant's total bodily dependence on his mother begins to decrease, and he begins a visual and tactile exploration of mother's face and body. Assured of "safe anchorage" (Mahler, 1968) and aided by locomotion and other maturational processes, the infant begins "expansion beyond the symbiotic orbit." Although the infant remains in close proximity to his mother during this period, he is also developing a primitive, but distinct, body image of his own.

enmeshment — a process whereby the realistic boundaries between people are not recognized or are violated. This involves one person's taking over what would normally be aspects of another's functioning or intruding upon what would normally be thought of as another's territory.

entitlement—the belief that one deserves to be given to without reciprocal expectation. Also believed to be exhibited in early life, with resolution beginning in rapprochement.

evocative memory—that form of memory made possible by the acquisition of object permanence. The individual may internally evoke the visual image or affective memory of an object or person in its absence. Adler and Buie (1979) argue that evocative memory is fragile in borderline patients and may be disrupted by intense affective states. They hypothesize that "person permanence" is particularly susceptible, especially given the borderline's relative inability to retain the affective memory of a significant other when experiencing a disruptive state.

exciting object (Fairbairn, 1958)—that repressed part of the original "bad" object that is split off from the "rejecting object." The libidinal self reaches toward this idealized object for the complete and unconditional gratification appropriate to an infant. The exciting object is, therefore, always ultimately disappointing. In this book, the exciting object has been labeled the libidinal object.

idealization (Kohut, 1971)—a type of archaic experience of the other by the person's "damaged pole of ideals," which searches for a selfobject that will warrant its idealization.

identification—a process of internalizing aspects of another to create psychic structure. The child begins to identify with the mother in the first year of life, and the resulting identifications contribute to ego and superego formation. These later combine with identifications with the father to round out ego and superego development. Identification may or may not include processes of assimilation and accommodation, which make what was another's, one's own.

internal saboteur—the repressed, introjected self that maintains contact with the rejecting object by colluding with it in life-denying or antilibidinal aggression toward the libidinal self. In this book, the internal saboteur is labeled the antilibidinal self.

internalization—a process spanning all of life during which the person takes into himself and makes his own, aspects of his significant objects, first by imitation, later, as he matures, by introjection, and finally, through identification. Through this process, regulation, which had previously taken place in interactions with the outside world, are substituted for by internal regulations. Internalization implies active processes of assimilation and accommodation, which result in making one's own what was once external.

introjection (Rycroft, 1973)—the process whereby the child incorporates the parents' attitudes in the form of multiple memory traces: The functions of the parents are thus taken over by the child's mental representations of the parents. In the analytic literature, introjection is usually seen as a relatively primitive form of internalization, in which the attributes of others are more or less swallowed whole and not effectively made one's own. "Incorporation" is also used to label this more primitive process. In this work, I have used "incorporative introjection" to communicate this idea.

libidinal ego (Fairbairn, 1958)—that repressed and developmentally arrested part of the self that retains the original organismic self-expressions. In this book, libidinal ego is labeled libidinal self.

libidinal object—*see* exciting object.

libidinal self—*see* libidinal ego.

magical thinking—a primitive form of thought based on primary process, lacking a knowledge of reality and true cause and effect. According to Freud, infants begin by thinking in this fashion and increasingly enlarge their capacity for secondary process thought, finally abandoning magical thinking. Stern challenges this developmental theory by arguing that the abilities needed for magical thinking develop later.

merger (Kohut, 1984)—seen as the patient's remobilization of a need from an early stage of development for fusion with "archaic idealized omnipotent selfobjects."

mirror—Kohut describes this as the person's need to be "mirrored," i.e., to be experienced with joy and approval by a delighted, parental selfobject. He describes this as "the damaged pole of ambitions seeking a confirming/ approving response of the selfobject."

narcissistic cathexis—cathexis (Freud) is the investment of energy in a mental mechanism or an object. Narcissistic cathexis refers to investment in another person without an appreciation of the other as the source of his/ her own initiative.

object constancy (Burgner & Edgecumbe, 1972)—"the capacity for constant relations, the capacity to recognize and tolerate loving and hostile feelings toward the same object, the capacity to keep feelings centered on a specific object, and the capacity to value an object for attributes other than its function of satisfying needs." Or, as Anna Freud (1968, pp. 506–507) put it, "Object constancy means . . . to retain an attachment even when the person is unsatisfying."

object permanence (Piaget)—an achievement of the 18- to 20-month-old child whereby he can believe in the continued existence of inanimate, transiently observed physical objects.

omnipotence/worthlessness—internal polarity experienced by the narcissist involving, on the one hand, intense feelings of power and personal effectiveness and, on the other, equally intense feelings of lack of value. These feelings are thought to persist in the narcissist as a result of lack of resolution of the polarity beginning in the rapprochement phase.

omnipotent responsibility—the feeling on the part of the young child that she has responsibility for others and for the fate of self and others. This belief by the child grows out of her own cognitive limitations—her egocentricity, her incomplete knowledge of true cause and effect, and her need to understand and have some control over her environment.

on the way to object constancy (22–30 months)—optimally, the child now has an idea of his mother as being mostly good, has a concept of self as separate from her and others, and has his own boundaries, self-confidence, and self-esteem. At this stage, he is beginning to be able to tolerate an image of himself and others as containing both good and bad elements.

optimal distance (Mahler et al., 1975)—the physical and psychological space between child and caregiver that best allows the child to develop those faculties that he needs in order to grow and to individuate. During the symbiotic stage, there will be little distance, as the infant molds into the mother's body; during the differentiation subphase, he begins to push away from his mother's chest to better explore her. The practicing infant begins to venture away from his mother in order to explore. During rapprochement, the toddler needs to be able to come and go even farther and to find the mother available on his return.

optimal frustration—challenges to the person's cognitive structure, belief system, and experience of self, other, and the world, which are in-phase and appropriately attuned to the individual's developmental level. The infant/child/person can gradually give up notions such as grandiosity, idealization, merger, etc., through such confrontations.

part-object—Rycroft (1973) views this as an object that is a part of a person, usually a penis or a breast. When the young infant views the mother this way, the mother is not recognized as a separate, whole person but, rather, as a need-satisfying object. This part, then, is all that is experienced, either in toto or in a certain state, when, for example, only the "good" or "bad" mother is recognized or only a certain function of the mother is acknowledged. These aspects are split off from other aspects, which may be experienced in other states.

practicing—the second subphase of separation-individuaition, lasting from about 9 to about 14 months of age. During this period, the infant is able to actively move away from his mother and return to her, first by crawling and later by walking. The infant is exploring the environment (animate and inanimate) and practicing locomotor skills.

rapprochement—the third subphase of separation-individuation, lasting from 15 to 24 months of age. The infant rediscovers his mother and returns to her after the forays of his practicing period. The toddler loves to share his experiences and possessions with his mother, who is now more clearly perceived as separate and outside. In optimal adjustment, the narcissistic inflation of the practicing subphase is slowly replaced by a growing realization of separateness and, with it, vulnerability.

rapprochement crisis—a period during the rapprochement subphase occurring in all children, but with greater intensity in some, during which the realization of separateness is acute and disturbing. The toddler's belief in his omnipotence is severely threatened, and the environment is coerced as he tries to restore both the union with his mother and his prior feeling of omnipotence. "Ambitendency, which develops into ambivalence, is often intense; the toddler wants to be united with and, at the same time, separate from mother. Temper tantrums, whining, sad moods, and intense separation reactions are at their height" (Mahler, Pine, & Bergman, 1975, p. 292).

real object—the other is seen by the developing child in a fashion that approximates that of an adult, i.e., he sees the object (person) as a whole and as separate from himself, a developmental achievement that follows seeing the other as a selfobject and a part-object, and the experience with transitional objects.

recognition memory—the ability of the human organism to recognize a stimulus by calling on the memory of having experienced it before. Recent child research dates this ability from birth, or even before; as Stern (1985) expresses it, "for some events, recognition memory appears to operate across the birth gap."

rejecting object (Fairbairn, 1958)—the repressed part of the original "bad" object, which is split off from the "exciting object." The rejecting object aggresses against the libidinal self and its original self-expressions exactly as did the original bad object. The rejecting object maintains connection or bonding with the "internal saboteur" or antilibidinal self through this antilibidinal aggressive stance. In this book, the rejecting object has been labeled the antilibidinal object.

role-relationship models (Horowitz, 1987)—the individual's expectations of self and others, which co-vary with one's states of mind. When one is depressed, for example, one might expect oneself to be weak and ineffectual and the other to be critical and powerful. In elated states, one might see oneself as brilliant and entertaining and others as captivated. These models of self and other may be conscious, partially conscious, or unconscious.

selfobject (Kohut, 1984)—similar to Stern's (1985) concept of self-regulating other, but defined by Kohut as an *internal representation* of that other used by the individual to maintain self-cohesion and identity. In practice, Kohut often uses this label to denote real external objects, but the key to the concept is their function in maintaining and defining the self—hence selfobject.

self-regulating other (Stern, 1985)—Stern sees this concept as similar to Kohut's selfobject, referring to an "ongoing functional relationship with (another) that (is) necessary to provide the regulating structures that maintain and/or enhance self-cohesion." Technically, Kohut's selfobject is an internal representation, but its function is self-maintenance and definition.

self-soothing—the infant's and, later, the child's self-comforting activities, derived partially from the child's internalization of nurturing from others.

separation anxiety—the infant/child's fear of being separated either physically, psychically, or both, from an object important to him. For Fairbairn, it is the infant's first anxiety.

separation guilt (Weiss & Sampson, 1986)—guilt felt by the child due to her belief that for her to separate from the parent (or other important figure) would be damaging to the parent and, thus, to the child's relationship with the parent.

separation-individuation (Mahler et al., 1975)—refers to the overall developmental process, which includes differentiation, practicing, rapprochement, and separation-individuation proper. During separation-individuation itself, the child gains a real identity of his own, can differentiate between self and object representations, and can maintain his ties with objects independent of the state of his needs (object constancy).

signal anxiety (Rycroft, 1973)—for Freud, the ego's response to internal danger. A form of apprehensiveness that alerts one to potentially upsetting and/or threatening stimuli and *signals* the need for an adaptive response.

stimulus barrier (Rycroft, 1973)—that part of the psychic apparatus that protects the person from excessive stimulation: It is directed against both internal and external stimuli. Stern (1985) has argued that this term is no longer necessary, as the infant very clearly begins this kind of regulation for himself.

stranger anxiety—one of an infant's possible responses to a stranger beginning at about eight months. According to Mahler et al. (1975), the infant in this state can display fear responses, avoid and/or shun the stranger, and may, in severe instances, cry or show significant distress. However, for Mahler, this reaction is not the norm, but rather, one that is more likely where "basic trust is less than optimal."

stranger reactions (Mahler et al., 1975)—"a variety of reactions to people other than mother, particularly pronounced during the differentiation subphase, when a special relationship to mother has been well established. Stranger reactions include curiosity and interest as well as wariness and mild or even severe anxiety. They subside at the beginning of the practicing period, but reappear at various times throughout the separation-individuation process" (p. 293).

survivor guilt (Modell, 1965, 1971; Weiss & Sampson, 1986)—guilt experienced by the individual as a result of the belief that for him to survive (or to thrive) is to deprive another with whom he is identified. The irrational belief is that survival is purchased at another's expense.

symbiosis—the symbiotic phase, which occurs as the one- to five-month-old infant and his mother or primary caregiver interact, is a stage of sociobiological interdependence between the two. Since this occurs before the infant has developed concepts of objects, Mahler believed the infant behaves and functions as though he and his mother were an omnipotent dual unity within one common boundary.

transitional object (Winnicott, 1953)—a blanket or other soft and/or cuddly object favored by the infant of about six months to a year. For Winnicott, it is the first object that exists for the infant neither totally internally or externally, but partakes of both; the infant can also use it as a stand-in for the mother. The transition is thus from infantile narcissism to object-love and from dependency to self-reliance.

transmuting internalization—this is seen by Kohut (1984) as a response to optimal frustration in which the person incorporates merged aspects of the "virtual selfobject" into his "virtual proto-self," thereby transforming the self and resulting in added psychic structure and organization with boundaries and a sense of identity.

twinship—Kohut describes this as the "damaged intermediate area of talents and skills seeking a selfobject that will make itself available for the reassuring experience of essential alikeness"; the other is experienced not as fused with the self but as like the self in essential ways—as being psychologically the same.

Therapeutic Objectives for Each Character Structure

SCHIZOID CHARACTER

Affective Objectives

1. Increase sensory contact with the environment—the sense of touch, hearing, visual, olfactory, and taste contact with the world—and develop an appreciation and awareness of the human touch of others.
2. Increase the sense of stability or *grounding*—the sense that one's feet are planted firmly on the ground, the sense that one can stand one's ground.
3. Increase the feeling sense within the body—the feeling of all movement, breathing, the sensation of tension versus relaxation, the specific bodily sensations associated with hunger, pain, joy, laughter, etc.
4. Reduce the chronic tension or spasticity in all affected areas of the body and the associated physical pain.
5. Open the feeling of rage and direct it at the appropriate target. Integrate the rage within the self until it becomes a source of power and assertiveness; in the simple poetry of the bioenergetic therapists, "Claim it, aim it, and tame it."
6. Open the access to terror in the person and assist in the recovery of its initial causes. Integrate the terror within the self until it becomes a source of the ability to feel fear, awe, and vulnerability.

7. Access the grief associated with the loss of love and the loss of self. Integrate that grief as a part of the reality of the person—a reality of tragedy and irony. Eliminate the denial of what was, so one can experience what is.
8. Develop the physical relationship between the person and the physical world (e.g., food, nature, home, familiar objects, etc.).
9. Open the feelings of love and the experience of joy grounded in reality.

Behavioral-Social Objectives

1. Initially establish or strengthen attachment and eventually resolve the symbiosis.
2. Strengthen the conscious and deliberate use of defenses such as social withdrawal.
3. Increase small group and community involvement.
4. Decrease perfectionism and specialness in performance and thereby affect procrastination and performance anxiety.
5. Help the client to discover current outlets for the denied aggressive impulses (i.e., the "game" patterns in social relationships, passive-aggressive or withdrawal patterns, aggressive fantasies, and so on).
6. Teach or arrange for the teaching of social skills (e.g., personal effectiveness, assertiveness, eye contact, display of affect in social situations, etc.).
7. Increase appropriate aggressive and assertive behavior in the person's social world.

Cognitive Objectives

Attitudes and beliefs

1. Identify, interpret, develop insight into, and change the ego ideal or false self (e.g., "I am all-accepting, understanding, and special. I am my ideas and accomplishments.").
2. Identify, interpret, develop insight into, and change the "script decision" (e.g., "Something is wrong with me. I don't belong. The world is frightening. Others can't be trusted.").
3. Strengthen identification of the self with the body and its natural life processes.
4. Strengthen the identification of the self with the person's history and

its resulting vulnerability. Eliminate the denial of what happened and its effects.

5. Strengthen identification of the self with natural aggression, assertiveness, and power.

Cognitive abilities

1. Identify, strengthen, and bring under voluntary control existing ego defenses.
2. Teach ego defenses not yet learned.
3. Reinforce, repair, or teach strategies for dealing with harsh or anxiety-provoking environments.
4. Promote or teach self-soothing and self-nurturing.
5. Establish the ambivalent experience of the self, others, and the world and increase the tolerance for ambivalence. Discriminate and integrate self- and object-representations with particular attention to the negative parental introject.
6. Assess and repair where appropriate: Assimilation, accommodation, discrimination, integration, and generalization.

ORAL CHARACTER

Affective Objectives

1. Open the feelings of need and longing, and assist the client in identifying with these feelings.
2. Work through the experienced sadness to the pain and deep despair at abandonment or chronic frustration.
3. Work through the rage at abandonment.
4. Work through the fear engendered by the release of all other feelings: the fear of rejection, abandonment, and continued frustration.
5. Develop a greater sense of grounding, strength, and clear energy flow in the feet, ankles, knees, and legs.
6. Strengthen the entire body and its overall musculature.
7. Strengthen assertive and aggressive expression.
8. Open the chest, the breathing, and the energy flow through the neck and throat.
9. Release the spasticity in the lower back and abdomen, shoulder girdle, base of the neck, and jaw.
10. Open the real love feelings, particularly for the central attachment figure, and develop the expression of this loving feeling.

Cognitive Objectives

Attitudes and beliefs

1. Identify, interpret, develop insight into, and change the ego ideal or false self ("I am sweet, soft, and entirely giving. I am needed.").
2. Identify, interpret, develop insight into, and change the script decisions ("I don't need. I have to do it alone. If I need, I will be despised and abandoned.").
3. Challenge, interpret, or explain the defenses (denial, projection, introjection, reversal, identification, turning against the self, and displacement) to effect their flexibility.
4. Assist in the recognition of the pattern of compensation and collapse. Assist the person in identifying and cutting off that repetitive pattern through the acceptance of responsibility for it.
5. Strengthen the identification of the self with one's needs, affirming the right to need and to have those needs met.
6. Strengthen the identification of the self with the history of abandonment or unmet need and the resulting vulnerability. Affirm the individual's right to the natural feelings engendered by the abandonment—rage, despair, and fear.
7. Strengthen the identification of the self with the natural aggression and assertion.

Cognitive abilities

1. Promote or teach self-soothing and self-nurturing.
2. Establish an ambivalent experience of the self and others and discrimination between the self and others.
3. Assess and repair construct formation: assimilation, accommodation, discrimination, integration, and generalization.
4. Strengthen the voluntary use of existing defenses to the extent that these are productive and useful.
5. Teach ego defenses not yet learned.
6. Reinforce, repair, or teach strategies for dealing with harsh or anxiety-provoking environments.

Behavioral-Social Objectives

1. Strengthen or teach self-care and self-soothing strategies.
2. Strengthen reaching out and asking for help directly in social relationships.
3. Strengthen aggressive, assertive, and instrumental behaviors.

4. Increase reality relatedness to the demands of adult functioning; strengthen the constancy of commitment to work, relationships, individual projects, etc. Develop stick-to-itiveness.
5. Strengthen mutuality, adult-adult contact, and individuated (as opposed to dependent or co-dependent) arrangements in love relationships.
6. Increase tolerance for being alone.
7. Discourage overwork, excessive drug use, exaggerated responsibility and nurturing, and other hypomanic, self-destructive behaviors in the compensatory phase of the cycle.

SYMBIOTIC CHARACTER

Affective Objectives

1. Increase self-expression of feelings.
2. Decrease guilt for all self-expression.
3. Decrease sense of obligation to others.
4. Decrease fear of hurting others or succeeding at others' expense.
5. Decrease harmful affects, which are the result of identifications with family or with family-imposed role.
6. Access aggression and calm the anxiety at its expression.
7. Access and correctly aim hostility, particularly at restraining and intrusive others.
8. Encourage pride and enjoyment in self-expression, power, adventure, accomplishment, success, indulgence, etc.
9. Assist in modulation of "optimal distance" through allowance and acceptance of impulses for closeness and distance.
10. Reduce fear of abandonment.
11. Reduce fear of engulfment.
12. Access and work through grief at the loss of the real self, the compensatory self relinquished in therapy, and destructive relationships relinquished during therapy.
13. Work through the grief for the losses sustained by parents or family.
14. Enhance the sense of self.

Cognitive Objectives

1. Access pathogenic beliefs underlying separation and survivor guilt.
2. Develop insight into patterns that serve to preserve a fused relationship with parent(s).

3. Develop insight into patterns based on excessive or pathogenic identification with parent(s).
4. Develop insight into the nature of one's real self (i.e., tastes, skills, aptitudes, etc.).
5. Develop memory for and understanding of the family and the history that produced the symbiotic self.
6. Assist with the realistic perception of the social environment (e.g., spouse, parents, coworkers, etc.).
7. Assist with the realistic assessment of social responsibility and obligation.
8. Decrease splitting and increase ambivalence in perception of self and others.
9. Increase awareness of compromise patterns such as passive aggression and "game" interactions, which express while denying aggression, hostility, success, etc.
10. Confront manipulative behavior, which seeks to maintain merger and externalize responsibility.

Behavioral-Social Objectives

1. Support behavior that expresses individuation from significant others.
2. Identify and support behavior that represents true self-defining expression and thereby furthers the experience of a real self.
3. Directly instruct or support social behaviors that smoothly modulate closeness and distance.
4. Assist in the behaviors for the mobilization, expression, and modulation of aggression and hostility in the client's "real" world.
5. Assist the client in using the past and present social environment for useful identifications and internalizations.

NARCISSISTIC CHARACTER

Cognitive Objectives

1. Access self-statements of worthlessness, distrust, self-criticism, inertia, depression, loneliness, etc.
2. Access the self-statements of reliance on achievement, grandiosity, pride, entitlement, manipulation, and the rationalization of such qualities.
3. Access the defensive functions of the false and symptomatic selves.

4. Assist the client in developing a historical and dynamic understanding of himself with regard to his feelings of emptiness, void, fragmentation of the self, his archaic demands of others and life itself, and his feelings of rage and deep hurt.
5. Assist the client in establishing an understanding of the process of discovery and development of the real self through the expression of his innate capacities, ambitions, and ideals.
6. Assist the client toward an integrated and ambivalent experience of the self and others.
7. Support a realistic assessment of the client's abilities, resources, and achievements.
8. Support a realistic assessment of the client's limitations, weaknesses, and vulnerabilities.
9. Assist the client in an integration and acceptance of all the above qualities of self.

Affective Objectives

1. Access the injuries caused by empathic failures in response to the needs for merger, twinship, and mirroring.
2. Access the injuries of disappointment at the failures of idealized others.
3. Access the fear of reinjury — the suspicion, distrust, and paranoia.
4. Access the narcissistic rage in response to injury and disappointment.
5. Access the continuing need for merger, idealization, twinship, and mirroring and assist in the differentiation and maturation of these needs.
6. Access all affective elements of the grandiose compensatory self — grandiosity, entitlement, pride, etc.
7. Access the feelings of emptiness, void, fragmentation, and discontinuity of the real self.
8. Nurture, support, and effect internalization of empathy and love for others.
9. Establish trust in the real self and trust for others.
10. Transform the grandiose false self into the "normal narcissism" of true self-love.
11. Transform the injury to vulnerability and the accepted limitations of the self, others, and life itself.

Behavioral-Social Objectives

1. Support or teach those ego-organizational abilities that will counteract fragmentation of the self in response to the therapeutic process.

2. Support realistic achievement and assertiveness in the client's life.
3. Support the client's social resources and assist him in using them as fully as possible.
4. Directly instruct the client in social behaviors that communicate empathy, regard, and understanding of others. Teach him to "let in" the warmth and human caring that others can provide.
5. Assist the client in the development of a self-discovering and self-sustaining support system, which incorporates others for merger, mirroring, twinship, and idealization. The goal of such a system is to provide internalization of resources resulting in greater autonomy in the context of greater support.

MASOCHISTIC CHARACTER

Cognitive Objectives

1. Reconstruct personal history leading to masochistic script decisions and pathogenic beliefs.
2. Elicit pathogenic beliefs in relation to all areas of functioning and interpret them in relation to history and their current dynamic function.
3. Interpret self defeating behavior to show its functions of (1) preserving original object ties, (2) paradoxically preserving integrity and entitled self respect, (3) rebellion or resistance, and (4) retaliation and the expression of hostility.
4. Establish responsibility for the self.
5. Label, interpret, and diminish problem flooding and negative success reactions.
6. Enhance internalization of good self-object models.

Affective Objectives

1. Elicit, disinhibit, and encourage the direct experience of spite, resentment, and rage.
2. Elicit, disinhibit, and encourage the direct experience of pleasure.
3. Reduce guilt associated with rage and pleasure.
4. Increase trust, hope, and the willingness to risk.
5. Reduce and modulate anxiety associated with the experience of rage, pleasure, trust, hope, and risk.
6. Work through the grief associated with prior losses, the loss of self,

and the loss of time, as well as grief at the loss of object ties and the loss of personal identity associated with change.

7. Assist the client in relinquishing revenge for injuries of the past.

Behavioral-Social Objectives

1. Establish new behaviors, which can serve the many functions previously served by self-defeat (i.e., maintain intimacy, express resistance or hostility, establish self-respect, etc.).
2. Establish behaviors that express trust, hope, and confidence in others and self.
3. Instruct, if necessary, in the well-modulated social expression of unfamiliar affects or states — anger, assertion, pleasure, love, etc.
4. Label, interpret, and diminish subservience, delay, self-victimization, self-defeating provocation, complaining, etc.

HYSTERICAL CHARACTER

Cognitive Objectives

1. Describe, confront, and interpret cognitive defenses of distraction, blocking, and premature closure, which prevent thinking and feeling through core issues.
2. Describe and interpret the dissociation between thoughts, feelings, and behavior.
3. Model and support staying with an issue to completion and resolution.
4. Encourage, explore, and interpret transference reactions in and out of the therapy setting.
5. Describe, confront, and interpret the denial of personal responsibility and power, passivity, insubstantiality, etc.
6. Describe and interpret polarities in self-concept such as naive child/evil seductress, good girl/bad woman, irresponsible/guilty, depressed/gay and superficial, helpless to men/castrating of men, etc.
7. Assist in developing an accurate, ambivalent, and shame-free self-concept.
8. Describe and interpret simplistic and oscillating concepts of men, women, and relationships and assist the development of more mature and realistic models.
9. Describe and interpret "affect defenses" or "hysterical states" in which emotional overwhelm can be both a natural consequence of over-

whelming conflicted feelings as well as a defense against the working through of such conflicts and the associated feelings.

10. Interpret depression as an essentially positive movement away from the usual hysterical defenses toward working, feeling, and thinking through core issues. But, interpret depression as defense when it serves to shut down all such processes.

Affective Objectives

1. Extinguish by non-response, description, confrontation, or interpretation the defensive use of affect.
2. Enhance the patient's ability to tolerate, explore, express, and contain genuine feelings.
3. Work through, using the aforementioned abilities, the feelings associated with the hysteric's "personal problems" (i.e., sexual, competitive, aggressive, guilty, and shameful feelings).
4. Work through the feelings associated with the experience of being exploited, corrupted, betrayed, and left unprotected.
5. Work through the polarized feelings directed at others and the self, e.g., (1) longing for and dependency on men versus hatred and envy of men and the power she has given them, (2) longing for mother love versus rage at mother for abandonment and collusion in the exploitation, (3) gratification versus guilt in obtaining father's attention, etc.
6. Assist the person in experiencing the sadness and grief associated with her family drama and her personal story of exploitation and abandonment.

Behavioral-Social Objectives

1. Provide a therapeutic setting in which transference is safe and welcomed—i.e., a respectful, warm but bounded relational style, which permits a solid therapeutic alliance.
2. By "working through the transferences" in and outside of therapy, develop the ability to relate to others in a genuine way.
3. Model and encourage genuine relating, ambivalent experience, and self-acceptance of human feelings—especially sexual, aggressive, competitive, and loving feelings.
4. Model, encourage, and teach directly assertive behaviors while extinguishing manipulative, coquettish, or indirect maneuvers.
5. Directly attend to addictive behavior to provide the support needed to stop it.

OBSESSIVE-COMPULSIVE PERSONALITY

Cognitive Objectives

1. Label, interpret, and diminish defensive cognitive maneuvers such as shifting of attention to the periphery, to the abstract, and to rapidly oscillating conflict or indecision.
2. Reconstruct personal history leading to anxiety, tolerance of imperfection, need for control, indecision, drivenness, rigidity, etc.
3. Elicit the personal script decisions or pathogenic beliefs.
4. Challenge the beliefs demanding perfection, freedom from anxiety, need for order and control, etc.
5. Educate concerning the difficulties inherent in controlling natural human responses through will.
6. Reduce "authoritarian" orientation in social relations and "rules" for being.
7. Label, interpret, and diminish the projection onto others of unreasonably high standards of performance.

Affective Objectives

1. Explore, interpret, and reduce anxiety through understanding, coping, relaxation, and other methods.
2. Enhance ability to tolerate anxiety.
3. Decrease shame and guilt and excessive obligation as motivating factors.
4. Develop full and ambivalent feelings towards parents and other figures of authority.
5. Increase client's ability to experience pleasure, love, and hate.
6. Develop ability to access and stand for client's own preferences and predilections.

Behavioral-Social Objectives

1. Attenuate the overly orderly, rigid, controlling, and frugal behavior.
2. Enhance ability to commit and to behave appropriately when anxious.
3. Reduce tension in the body.
4. Enhance expressive abilities particularly involving pleasure, expression of social warmth, love, and anger.

Content Research on Hysterical Personality

A LITERATURE SEARCH FOR THE thirty-year period, 1962–1991, was conducted on treatment and case study reports of hysterical personality. The search included *Psychological Abstracts* for that period, one computer-based journal search of the University of California, San Francisco, one computer-based journal search of the University of California, Berkeley, and a computer-based book search of the holdings of the University of California, San Francisco. The search also included the reference sections of the articles and books so obtained.

All treatment case reports were examined for the relationship between this diagnosis in women and the presence of behavior on the part of their fathers that could be characterized as seductive as defined by Herman (1981, see p. 000). The case reports were also examined for documentation of behavior on the part of the mothers or mother figures that could be characterized as cold-hostile, absent-neglectful, or competitive-rivalrous. Cases of childhood hysterical personality and hysterical conversion were not considered. Only three brief case reports from a single book were eliminated due to insufficient attention to the parent-child relationship.

Thirty-five case reports were obtained from the references listed at the end of this Appendix. After each of the references a code for the number of cases (e.g., C:2) and the number of those cases confirming the seductive father hypothesis and the cold, neglectful, or rivalrous mother hypothesis is given (e.g., F:2, M:1, M:?). Results show 26 of the 34 cases with sufficient father information (76%) support the hypothesis for fathers, while 17 of the 28 cases with sufficient information on the mother (61%) support the

313

hypothesis for mothers. Fourteen of these cases come from a book on the treatment of hysterical personality by Mueller and Aniskiewitz, and it is only in these cases where there was sometimes insufficient information to make a judgment regarding father (N:1) or mother (N:7). In these cases, the page numbers for each case determination are given. Separate analysis of these cases indicate that the observed ratios for the father hypothesis are virtually identical to the other cases from separate sources but the ratios for the mother hypothesis are considerably higher in the Mueller and Anskiewitz sample (86% versus 52% for the other 21 cases).

Allen, D. (1991). Basic treatment issues. In M. Horowitz (Ed.), *Hysterical personality style and the histrionic personality disorder*. New York: Aronson. C:1 F:1 M:0; C:1 F:0 M:1.

Chodoff, P. (1978). Psychotherapy of the hysterical personality. *Journal of American Academy of Psychoanalysis*, 6(4), 497–510. C:1 F:1 M:1.

Easser, B., & Lesser, S. (1965). Hysterical personality: A re-evaluation. *Psychological Quarterly*, 34, 390–412. C:6 F:6 M:0.

Guioa, A. (1966). Daughter of a Don Juan. *The Psychiatric Quarterly*, 40(1), 71–79. C:3 F3 M3.

Horowitz, M., Marmor, C., Krupnick, J., Wilner, N., Kaltreider, N., & Wallerstein, R. (1984). *Personality styles and brief psychotherapy* (pp. 68–109). New York: Basic Books. C:2 F:1 M:0; F:0 M:1.

Horowitz, M. (1991). Psychic structure and the process of change. In M. Horowitz (Ed.), *Hysterical personality style and the histrionic personality disorder*. New York: Aronson. C:1 F:1 M:1.

Jaffe, D. S. (1971). The role of ego modification and the task of structural change in the analysis of a case of hysteria. *International Journal of Psycho-Analysis*, 52, 375–393. C:1 F:1 M:1.

Mueller, W., & Aniskiewicz, A. (1986). *Psychotherapeutic intervention in hysterical disorders*. New York: Aronson. C:1 F:1 M:? pp. 25–26; C:1 F:1 M:? p. 27; C:1 F:? M:1 p. 32; C:1 F:1 M:1 pp. 32–33; C:1 F:0 M:? pp. 34–35; C:1 F:1 M:1 pp. 53–55; C:1 F:0 M:? pp. 109–110; C:1 F:1 M:0 pp. 123–124; C:1 F:0 M:? p. 131; C:1 F:1 M:? pp. 147–148; C:1 F:1 M:1 p. 247; C:1 F:1 M:1 pp. 164–165; C:1 F:1 M:1 pp. 168–169; C:1 F:1 M:1 pp. 190–192.

Prosen, H. (1967). Sexuality in females with "hysteria." *American Journal of Psychiatry*, 124(5), 687–692. C:2 F1 M:2.

Reder, P. (1978). A case of brief psychotherapy. *British Journal of Medical Psychology*, 51, 147–154. C:1 F:1 M:0.

Schmidt, D., & Messner, E. (1977). The female hysterical personality disorder. *The Journal of Family Practice*, 4(3), 573–577. C:1 F:0 M:0.

Zetzel, E. (1970). The so-called good hysteric. *International Journal of Psychoanalysis*, 49, 256–260. C:1 F:1 M:1.

REFERENCES

Adams, P. (1973). *Obsessive children: A sociopsychiatric study.* New York: Brunner/Mazel.

Adler, G. (1985). *Borderline psychopathology and its treatment.* New York: Jason Aronson.

Adler, G., & Buie, D. (1979). Aloneness and borderline psychopathology: The possible relevance of child development issues. *American Journal of Psycho-Analysis, 60*(83), 83–94.

Adorno, T., Frankel-Brunswick, E., & Sanford, R. (1950). *The authoritarian personality.* New York: Harper & Row.

Ainsworth, M. D. (1979). Attachment as related to mother-infant interaction. In J. B. Rosenblatt, R. A. Hinde, C. Beer, & M. Bushel (Eds.), *Advances in the study of behavior* (pp. 1–51). New York: Academic Press.

Allen, D. (1991). Basic treatment issues. In M. Horowitz (Ed.), *Hysterical personality style and the histrionic personality disorder.* New York: Aronson.

American Psychiatric Association. (1994). *Diagnostic and statistical manual of mental disorders* (4th ed.). Washington, DC: Author.

Ashmead, D., & Perlmutter, M. (1980). Infant memory in everyday life. In M. Perlmutter (Ed.), *Children's memory: New directions for child development.* San Francisco: Jossey Bass.

Baer, L., & Jenike, M. A. (1990). Personality disorders in obsessive-compulsive disorder. In M. A. Jenike, L. Baer, & W. E. Minichiello (Eds.), *Obsessive-compulsive disorders: Theory and management.* Chicago: Year Book Medical.

Beech, H., & Vaughan, M. (1978). *Behavioral treatment of obsessional states.* New York: Wiley.

Beloff, H. (1957). The structure and origin of the anal character. *Genetic psychology monographs, 55*, 141–172.

Bengtsson, H., & Johnson, L. (1987). Cognitions related to empathy in 5- to 11-year-old children. *Child Development, 58*, 1001–1012.

Berne, E. (1964). *Games people play.* New York: Grove Press.

Bertenthal, B. I., & Fischer, K. W. (1978). Development of self-recognition in the infant. *Developmental Psychology, 14*, 44–50.

Blacker, K., & Tupin, J. (1991). Hysteria and hysterical structures: Developmental and social theories. In M. J. Horowitz (Ed.), *Hysterical personality*. New York: Aronson.

Blanck, G., & Blanck, R. (1974). *Ego psychology: Theory and practice.* New York: Columbia University Press.

Blanck, G., & Blanck, R. (1979). *Ego psychology II: Psychoanalytic developmental psychology.* New York: Columbia University Press.

Blinder, M. (1966). The hysterical personality. *Psychiatry 29*, 227–236.

Bowlby, J. (1960). Grief and mourning in infancy and early childhood. *Psychoanalytic Study of the Child, 15*, 9–52.

Bowlby, J. (1969). *Attachment and loss. Vol. I: Attachment.* New York: Basic Books.

Bowlby, J. (1973). *Attachment and loss. Vol. II: Separation: Anxiety and anger.* New York: Basic Books.

Bretherton, I., & Beeghly, M. (1982). Talking about internal states: The acquisition of an explicit theory of mind. *Developmental Psychology, 18*, 906–921.

Briere, J. (1992, June 6). Theory and treatment of severe sexual abuse trauma. Workshop presentation, San Francisco, California.

Breuer, J., & Freud, S. (1893–1895). Studies in hysteria. In J. Strachey (Ed. & Trans.), *The standard edition of the complete psychological works of Sigmund Freud* (vol. 2). New York: W. W. Norton.

Briere, J. (1989). *Therapy for adults molested as children: Beyond survival.* New York: Springer.

Briere, J., & Runtz, M. (1991). The long-term effects of sexual abuse: A review and synthesis. In J. Briere (Ed.), *Treating victims of child sexual abuse.* San Francisco: Jossey Bass.

Brooks-Gunn, J., & Lewis, M. (1984). Early self-recognition. *Developmental Review, 4*, 215–239.

Browning, D., & Boatman, B. (1977). Incest: Children at risk. *American Journal of Psychiatry, 134*, 69–72.

Burgner, M., & Edgecumbe, R. (1972). Some problems in the conceptualization of early object relations. Part II: The concept of object constancy. *Psychoanalytic Study of the Child, 27*, 315–333.

Chodoff, P. (1978, June 12). *The hysterical personality.* Paper presented at the Joint Session of the American Psychiatric Association and the American Academy of Psychoanalysis, Atlanta, GA. Recorded by Audio-Digest Foundation, 7, 11.

Chodoff, P., & Lyons, H. (1958). Hysteria, the hysterical personality and hysterical conversion. *American Journal of Psychiatry, 114*, 734–740.

Clifford, C., Murray, R., & Fulker, D. (1984). Genetic and environmental influences on obsessional traits and symptoms. *Psychological Medicine, 14*, 791–800.

Daehler, M., & Greco, C. (1985). Memory in very young children. In M. Pressley & C. Brainerd (Eds.), *Cognitive learning and memory in children* (pp. 49–79). New York: Springer.

Davanloo, H. (Ed.). (1980). *Short-term dynamic psychotherapy.* New York: Jason Aronson.

DeCasper, A., & Fifer, W. (1980). Of human bonding: Newborns prefer their mother's voices. *Science, 208*, 1174–1176.

Easser, B., & Lesser, S. (1965). Hysterical personality: A re-evaluation. *Psychoanalytic Quarterly, 34*, 390–405.

Easterbrook, M., & Lamb, M. (1979). The relationship between quality of infant-mother attachment and infant competence in initial encounters with peers. *Child Development, 50,* 380–387.

Emde, R., & Sorce, J. (1983). The rewards of infancy: Emotional availability and maternal referencing. In J. Call, E. Gallenson, & R. Tyson (Eds.), *Frontiers of infant psychiatry* (vol. 2). New York: Basic Books.

Engel, L., & Ferguson, T. (1990). *Hidden guilt: How to stop punishing yourself and enjoy the happiness you deserve.* New York: Pocket Books.

Fairbairn, W. (1954). Observations on the nature of hysterical states. *British Journal of Medical Psychology, 27,* 105–125.

Fairbairn, W. (1958). On the nature and aims of psychoanalytical treatment. *International Journal of Psychoanalysis, 39,* 374–385.

Fairbairn, W. (1974). *Psychoanalytic studies of the personality.* New York: Routledge, Chapman & Hall. (Original work published 1952)

Field, T., Woodson, R., Greenberg, R., & Cohen, C. (1982). Discrimination and imitation of facial expression by neonates. *Science, 218,* 179–181.

Fiester, F. J. (1991). Self-defeating personality disorder: A review of data and recommendations for DSM-IV. *Journal of Personality Disorders, 5*(2), 150–166.

Finkelhor, D. (1979). *Sexually victimized children.* New York: Free Press.

Finkelhor, D., & Baron, L. (1986). High risk children. In D. Finkelhor & Associates (Eds.), *A sourcebook of child sexual abuse* (pp. 60–88). Newbury Park, CA: Sage.

Finney, J. (1963). Maternal influences on anal or compulsive character in children. *Journal of Genetic Psychology, 103,* 351–367.

Fischer, K. (1980). A theory of cognitive development: The control and construction of hierarchies of skills. *Psychological Review, 87,* 477–531.

Fischer, R., & Juni, S. (1982). The anal personality: Self-disclosure, negativism, self-esteem, and superego security. *Journal of Personality Assessment, 46,* 50–58.

Fisher, S., & Greenberg, R. (1977). *The scientific credibility of Freud's theories and therapy.* New York: Basic Books.

Foa, E., Steketee, G., & Ozarow, B. (1985). Behavior therapy with obsessive-compulsives: From theory to treatment. In M. Mavissakalian, S. Turner, & L. Michelson (Eds.), *Obsessive-compulsive disorder: Psychological and pharmacological treatment.* New York: Plenum.

Frances, A. J. (1986). *Diagnosis and treatment of DSM-III personality disorders* (4 audiotapes). New York: B.M.A. Audio, division of Guilford Publications.

Freeman-Longo, R. E. (1987). Child sexual abuse. Workshop presentation at Drake University, Des Moines, Iowa. Cited in Allen, C. M. (1990). Women as perpetrators of child sexual abuse: Recognition barriers. In A. Horton, B. L. Johnson, L. M. Roundy, & D. Williams (Eds.), *The incest perpetrator: A family member no one wants to treat.* Newbury Park, CA: Sage.

Freud, A. (1968). [Remarks in] panel discussion. *International Journal of Psycho-Analysis, 49,* 506–507.

Freud, S. (1896). The aetiology of hysteria. In J. Strachey (Ed. & Trans.), *The standard edition of the complete works of Sigmund Freud* (vol. 3, pp. 189–221). New York: W. W. Norton.

Freud, S. (1915). Instincts and their vicissitudes. In J. Strachey (Ed. & Trans.), *The standard edition of the complete psychological works of Sigmund Freud* (vol. 14). New York: W. W. Norton.

Freud, S. (1923). The ego and the id. In J. Strachey (Ed. & Trans.), *The standard edition of the complete psychological works of Sigmund Freud* (vol. 19, pp. 1–66). New York: W. W. Norton.

Freud, S. (1924). The economic problem of masochism. In J. Strachey (Ed. & Trans.), *The standard edition of the complete works of Sigmund Freud* (vol. 14, pp. 157–170). New York: W. W. Norton.

Friedman, M. (1985). Survivor guilt in the pathogenesis of anorexia nervosa. *Psychiatry, 48,* 715–720.

Gedo, J. E., & Goldberg, A. (1973). *Models of the mind: A psychoanalytic theory.* Chicago, IL: University of Chicago Press.

Geppert, U., & Kuster, U. (1983). The emergence of "wanting to do it oneself": A precursor of achievement motivation. *International Journal of Behavior Development, 6,* 355–369.

Golden, M., Montare, A., & Bridger, W. (1977). Verbal control of delay behavior in two-year-old boys as a function of social class. *Child Development, 48,* 1101–1111.

Golomb, E. (1992). *Trapped in the mirror: Adult children of narcissists in their struggle for self.* New York: William Morrow Co.

Gopnik, A., & Meltzoff, A. (1984). Semantic and cognitive development in 5- to 21-month-old children. *Journal of Child Language, 2,* 495–513.

Gopnik, A., & Meltzoff, A. (1987). The development of categorization in the second year and its relationship to other cognitive and linguistic developments. *Child Development, 58,* 1523–1531.

Greenberg, J., & Mitchell, S. (1983). *Object relations in psychoanalytic theory.* Cambridge, MA: Harvard University Press.

Greene, N. (1977). A view of family pathology involving child molest—from a juvenile probation perspective. *Juvenile Justice, 13,* 29–34.

Gross, H. (1981). Depressive and sadomasochistic personalities. In J. Lion (Ed.), *Personality disorders: Diagnosis and management* (2nd ed.). Baltimore, MD: Williams & Wilkins.

Guioa, A. (1966). Daughter of a Don Juan. *The Psychiatric Quarterly, 40*(1), 71–79.

Gunderson, J. G., Ronningstam, E., & Smith, L. E. (1991). Narcissistic personality disorder: A review of data on DSM III-R, a description of same. *Journal of Personality Disorders, 5*(2), 167–177.

Gunther, M. (1961). Infant behavior at the breast. In B. M. Foss (Ed.), *Determinants of infant behavior* (vol. 2). London: Methuen.

Guntrip, H. (1968). *Schizoid phenomena, object relations and the self.* London: Hogarth Press.

Guntrip, H. (1971). *Psychoanalytic theory, therapy and the self.* New York: Basic Books.

Gustafson, J. (1986). *The complex secret of brief psychotherapy.* New York: W. W. Norton.

Gustafson, J. (1992). *Self-delight in a harsh world.* New York: W. W. Norton.

Harlow, H., & Harlow, M. (1966). Learning to love. *American Scientist, 54,* 244–272.

Haugaard, J., & Reppucci, N. (1988). *The sexual abuse of children: A comprehensive guide to current knowledge and intervention strategies.* San Francisco: Jossey-Bass.

Haviland, J., & Lelwica, M. (1987). The induced affect response: 10-week-old infants' response to 3 emotional expressions. *Developmental Psychology, 23,* 97–104.

Hayes, P. (1972). Determination of the obsessional personality. *American Journal of Psychiatry, 129*(2), 217–219.

Heatherington, E., & Brackville, Y. (1963). Etiology and covariation of obstinancy, orderliness and parsimony in young children. *Child Development, 34,* 919–943.

Herman, J. (1981). *Father-daughter incest.* Cambridge, MA: Harvard University Press.

Hetzer, H. (1931). *Kind und schaffen* [Child and creation]. Jena, Germany: Gustav Fischer.

Holland, H. (1974). Displacement activity as a form of abnormal behavior in animals. In H. R. Beech (Ed.), *Obsessional hate.* London: Metheun.

Horner, A. (1979). *Object relations and the developing ego in therapy.* New York: Jason Aronson.

Horner, A. (1990). *The primacy of structure: Psychotherapy of underlying character pathology.* New York: Jason Aronson.

Horowitz, M. (1986). *Stress response syndromes* (2nd ed.). Northvale, NJ: Jason Aronson.

Horowitz, M. (1987). *States of mind: Configurational analysis of individual personality* (2nd ed.). New York: Plenum.

Horowitz, M. (1989). *Introduction to psychodynamics: A new synthesis.* New York: Basic Books.

Horowitz, M. (1991). Core characteristics of hysterical personality. In M. Horowitz (Ed.), *Hysterical personality.* New York: Jason Aronson.

Horowitz, M., Marmor, C., Krupnick, J., Wilner, N., Kaltreider, N., & Wallerstein, R. (1984). *Personality styles and brief psychotherapy.* New York: Basic Books.

Jaffe, D. S. (1971). The role of ego modification and the task of structural change in the analysis of a case of hysteria. *International Journal of Psycho-Analysis, 52,* 375–393.

Jehu, D. (1988). *Beyond sexual abuse: Therapy with children who were childhood victims.* New York: Wiley.

Jenike, M. (1990). Illness related to obsessive-compulsive disorder. In M. Jenike, L. Bau, & W. Minichiello (Eds.), *Obsessive-compulsive disorder: Theory & management.* St. Louis, MO: Yearbook Medical Publishers.

Johnson, S. (1985). *Characterological transformation: The hard work miracle.* New York: W. W. Norton.

Johnson, S. (1987). *Humanizing the narcissistic style.* New York: W. W. Norton.

Johnson, S. (1991). *The symbiotic character.* New York: W. W. Norton.

Judd, L., & Mandell, A. (1968). Chromosome studies in early infantile autism. *Archives of General Psychiatry, 18,* 450–456.

Justice, B., & Justice, R. (1979). *The broken taboo.* New York: Mormon Science Press.

Kagan, J. (1981). *The second year: The emergence of self-awareness.* Cambridge, MA: Harvard University Press.

Kegan, R. (1982). *The evolving self: Problem and process in human development.* Cambridge, MA: Harvard University Press.

Kendrick, M. (1988). *Anatomy of a nightmare: The failure of society in dealing with child sexual abuse.* Toronto: MacMillan.

Kernberg, O. (1967). Borderline personality organization. *Journal of the American Psychoanalytic Association, 15,* 641–685.

Kernberg, O. (1984). *Severe personality disorders.* New Haven, CT: Yale University Press.

Kernberg, O. (1988). Hysterical and histrionic personality disorders. In R. Michels et al. (Eds.), *Psychiatry*. Philadelphia: Lippincott.

Kline, P. (1981). *Fact and fantasy in Freudian theory* (2nd ed.). London: Methuen.

Kohut, H. (1971). *The analysis of the self: A systematic approach to the psychoanalytic treatment of narcissistic personality disorders*. (The Psychoanalytic Study of the Child Monograph No. 4). New York: International Universities Press.

Kohut, H. (1977). *The restoration of the self*. New York: International Universities Press.

Kohut, H. (1978). In P. Ornstein (Ed.), *The search for the self*. New York: International Universities Press.

Kohut, H. (1984). *How does analysis cure?* Chicago, IL: University of Chicago Press.

Kopp, C. (1982). Antecedents of self-regulation: A developmental perspective. *Developmental Psychology, 18*, 199–214.

Kuczynski, L., Zahn-Waxler, C., & Radke-Yarrow, M. (1987). Development and content of imitation in second and third years of life: A socialization perspective. *Developmental Psychology, 23*, 363–369.

Langs, R. (1973). *The techniques of psychoanalytic psychotherapy* (vol. I). New York: Jason Aronson.

Lazare, A. (1971). The hysterical character in psychoanalytic theory—evolution and confusion. *Archives of General Psychiatry, 25*, 131–137.

Levy, A., & Bleeker, E. (1975). *Development of character structure*. Paper presented at the annual convention of the California State Psychological Association, Fresno, CA.

Lewcowicz, D., & Turkewitz, G. (1980). Cross-modal equivalence in early infancy: Audio-visual intensity matching. *Developmental Psychology, 16*, 597–607.

Lichtenberg, J. (1983). *Psychoanalysis and infant research*. Hillsdale, NJ: Analytic Press.

Lieberman, A. (1977). Preschoolers competence with a peer: Relations with attachment and peer experience. *Child Development, 48*, 1277–1287.

Liebowitz, M., & Hollander, E. (1991). Obsessive-compulsive disorder: Psychobiological integration. In J. Zohor, T. Insel, & S. Rasmussen (Eds.), *The psychobiology of obsessive-compulsive disorder*. New York: Springer.

Lorenz, C. (1966). *On aggression*. New York: Bantam Books.

Lowen, A. (1958). *The language of the body*. New York: Collier.

Lowen, A. (1967). *The betrayal of the body*. New York: Collier.

Lowen, A. (1971). *The language of the body*. New York: Macmillan. (Original work published 1958)

Lowen, A. (1983). *Narcissism: Denial of the true self*. New York: Macmillan.

MacKain, K., Stern, D., Goldfield, A., & Mueller, B. (1985). *The identification of correspondence between an infant's internal affective state and the facial display of that affect by an other*. Unpublished manuscript.

Magaro, P., & Smith, P. (1981). The personality of clinical types: An empirically derived taxonomy. *Journal of Clinical Psychology, 37*, 796–809.

Mahler, M. (1968). *On human symbiosis and the vicissitudes of individuation*. New York: International Universities Press.

Mahler, M., Pine, R., & Bergman, A. (1975). *The psychological birth of the human infant*. New York: Basic Books.

Main, M., & Weston, D. (1981). The quality of the toddler's relationships to mother and father: Related to conflict behavior and readiness to establish new relationships. *Child Development, 52*, 932–940.

Maisch, N. (1973). *Incest*. London: Andre Deutsch.

Mandler, J. M. (1983). Representation. In G. H. Flavell & E. M. Markman (Eds.), P. H. Mussen (Series Ed.), *Handbook of child psychology: Vol. 3. Cognitive development* (pp. 420–494). New York: Wiley.

Manfield, P. (1992). *Split self/split object: Understanding and treating borderline narcissistic and schizoid disorders*. Northvale, NJ: Jason Aronson.

Marks, I. (1981). Review of behavioral psychotherapy I: Obsessive-compulsive disorders. *American Journal of Psychiatry, 138*, 584–592.

Marmor, J. (1953). Orality in the hysterical personality. *Journal of the American Psychoanalytic Association, 1*, 656–675.

Masson, J. (1984). *The assault on truth: Freud's suppression of the seduction theory*. New York: Farrar, Straus & Giroux.

Masterson, J. (1976). *Psychotherapy of the borderline adult*. New York: Brunner/Mazel.

Masterson, J. (1981). *The narcissistic and borderline disorders*. New York: Brunner/Mazel.

Masterson, J. (1985). *The real self: A developmental, self, and object relations approach*. New York: Brunner/Mazel.

Matas, L., Arend, R., & Sroufe, L. (1978). Continuity of adaptation in the second year: The relationship between quality of attachment and later competence. *Child Development, 49*, 547–556.

Meissner, W. W. (1986). *Psychotherapy and the paranoid process*. Northvale, NJ: Jason Aronson.

Meissner, W. (1988). *Treatment of patients in the borderline spectrum*. New York: Jason Aronson.

Miller, A. (1981). *The drama of the gifted child*. New York: Basic Books.

Miller, A. (1983). *For your own good: Hidden cruelty in child-rearing and the roots of violence*. New York: Farrar, Straus & Giroux.

Miller, A. (1984). *Thou shalt not be aware: Society's betrayal of the child*. New York: Meridian.

Millon, T. (1981). *Disorders of personality: DSM-III: Axis II*. New York: Wiley.

Mitchell, S. (1988). *Relational concepts in psychoanalysis*. Cambridge, MA: Harvard University Press.

Modell, A. (1965). On having the right to a life: An aspect of the superego's development. *International Journal of Psycho-Analysis, 46*, 323–331.

Modell, A. (1971). The origin of certain forms of pre-oedipal grief and the implications for a psychoanalytic theory of affect. *International Journal of Psycho-Analysis, 52*, 337–346.

Montgomery, M., Clayton, P., & Friedhoff, A. (1982). Psychiatric illness in Tourette syndrome patients and first degree relatives. In A. Friedhoff & R. Chase (Eds.), *Gilles de la Tourette Syndrome* (pp. 335–339). New York: Rouen.

Mueller, W., & Aniskiewicz, A. (1986). *Psychotherapeutic intervention in hysterical disorders*. Northvale, NJ: Jason Aronson.

Murphy, L., & Moriarty, A. (1976). *Vulnerability, coping and growth*. New Haven, CT: Yale University Press.

Niederland, W. (1961). The problem of the survivor. *Journal of Hillsdale Hospital, 10*, 233–247.

O'Connell, B., & Gerard, A. (1985). Scripts and scraps: The development of sequential understanding. *Child Development, 56*, 671–681.

O'Connor, N., & Franks, C. (1960). Childhood upbringing and other environmental factors. In N. J. Eysenck (Ed.), *Handbook of abnormal psychology*. London: Pitman.

Peters, S., Wyatt, G., & Finkelhor, D. (1986). Prevalence. In D. Finkelhor & Associates (Eds.), *A sourcebook on child sexual abuse.* Newbury Park, CA: Sage.

Pfohl, B. (1991). Histrionic personality disorder: A review of available data and recommendations for DSM IV. *Journal of Personality Disorders, 5*(2), 150–166.

Piaget, J. (1936). *The origin of intelligence in children.* New York: International Universities Press.

Pollack, J. (1979). Obsessive-compulsive personality: A review. *Psychological Bulletin, 86,* 225–241.

Pollack, J. (1981). Hysterical personality: An appraisal in light of empirical research. *Genetic Psychology Monographs, 104,* 71–105.

Pollack, J. (1987). Obsessive-compulsive personality: Theoretical and clinical perspectives and recent research findings. *Journal of Personality Disorders, 1,* 249–262.

Prosen, H. (1967). Sexuality in females with "hysteria." *American Journal of Psychiatry, 124*(5), 687–692.

Putnam, F. W. (1989). *Diagnosis and treatment of multiple personality disorder.* New York: Guilford.

Rangell, L. (1959). The nature of conversion. *Journal of the American Psychoanalytic Association, 17,* 632–662.

Reder, P. (1978). A case of brief psychotherapy. *British Journal of Medical Psychology, 51,* 147–154.

Reich, W. (1961). *Character analysis* (3rd ed.—enlarged). New York: Farrar, Straus & Giroux. (First English edition published in 1945)

Reik, T. (1941). *Masochism in modern man.* New York: Farrar, Straus.

Rice, A. (1985). *Beauty's release.* New York: Penguin.

Rush, P. (1980). *The best kept secret: Sexual abuse of children.* Englewood Cliffs, NJ: Prentice Hall.

Russell, D. (1986). *The secret trauma: Incest in the lives of girls and women.* New York: Basic Books.

Russell, D., & Finkelhor, D. (1984). The gender gap among perpetrators of child sexual abuse. In D. Russell (Ed.), *Sexual exploitation: Rape, child sexual abuse and workplace harassment.* Beverly Hills, CA: Sage.

Rycroft, C. (1973). *A critical dictionary of psychoanalysis.* New York: Basic Books.

Sagi, A., & Hoffman, M. (1976). Empathic distress in newborns. *Developmental Psychology, 12,* 175–176.

Salzman, L. (1980). *Treatment of the obsessive personality.* New York: Jason Aronson.

Salzman, L. (1985). Comments on the psychological treatment of obsessive-compulsive patients. In M. Mavissakalian, S. Turner, & L. Michelson (Eds.), *Obsessive-compulsive disorder: Psychological and pharmacological treatment* (pp. 155–165). New York: Plenum.

Salzman, L., & Thaler, F. (1981). Obsessive-compulsive disorder: A review of the literature. *American Journal of Psychiatry, 138,* 286–296.

Schmidt, D., & Messner, E. (1977). The female hysterical personality disorder. *The Journal of Family Practice, 4*(3), 573–577.

Shapiro, D. (1965). *Neurotic styles.* New York: Basic Books.

Shapiro, D. (1989). *Psychotherapy of neurotic character.* New York: Basic Books.

Sherrod, L. (1981). Issues in cognitive-preceptual development: The special case of social stimuli. In M. Lamb & L. Sherrod (Eds.), *Infant social cognition.* Hillsdale, NJ: Erlbaum.

Sifneos, P. (1979). *Short term dynamic psychotherapy.* New York: Plenum.

Sifneos, P. (1985). Short term dynamic psychotherapy for patients suffering from an obsessive-compulsive disorder. In M. Mavissakalian, S. Turner, & L. Michelson (Eds.), *Obsessive compulsive disorder: Psychological and pharmacological treatment* (pp. 131–154). New York: Plenum.

Silverman, L., & Weinberger, J. (1985). Mommy and I are one: Implications for psychotherapy. *American Psychologist, 40,* 1296–1308.

Simner, M. (1971). The newborn's response to the cry of another infant. *Developmental Psychology, 5,* 136–150.

Slade, P. (1974). Psychometric studies of obsessional illness and obsessional personality. In H. Bush (Ed.), *Obsessional states.* London: Methuen.

Slavney, P., & McHugh, P. (1974). The hysterical personality: A controlled study. *Archives of General Psychiatry, 30,* 325–329.

Solomon, R., & Wynne, L. (1954). Traumatic avoidance learning: The principles of anxiety conservation and partial irreversibility. *Psychology Review, 61,* 353–385.

Sperling, M. (1973). Conversion hysteria and conversion symptoms: A revision of classification and concepts. *Journal of the American Psychoanalytic Association, 21,* 745–772.

Spitz, S. (1982). *Infant recognition of invariant categories of faces: Person identity and facial expression.* Unpublished doctoral dissertation. Cornell University.

Stern, D. (1977). *The first relationship: Infant and mother.* Cambridge, MA: Harvard University Press.

Stern, D. (1985). *The interpersonal world of the infant: A view from psychoanalysis and developmental psychology* (pp. 118–119). New York: Jossey Bass.

Thorman, G. (1983). *Incestuous families.* Springfield, IL: Charles Thomas.

Tinbergen, N. (1953). *Social behavior in animals.* London: Chapman & Hall.

Tisak, M., & Turiel, E. (1988). Variation in seriousness of transgressions and children's moral and conventional concepts. *Developmental Psychology, 24*(3), 352–357.

Torgersen, S. (1980). The oral, obsessive and hysterical personality syndromes. *Archives of General Psychiatry, 37,* 1272–1277.

Tronick, E., & Adamson, L. (1980). *Babies as people.* New York: Collier.

Tronick, E., Als, H., Adamson, L., Wise, S., & Brazelton, T. (1978). The infant's response to entrapment between contradictory messages in face-to-face interaction. *Journal of Child Psychiatry, 17,* 1–13.

Tronick, E., Ricks, M., & Conn, J. (1982). Maternal and infant affective exchange: Patterns of adaptation. In T. Field & A. Fogel (Eds.), *Emotions and early interactions.* Hillsdale, NJ: Erlbaum.

Tupin, J. (1981). Histrionic personality. In J. Liew (Ed.), *Personality disorders: Diagnosis and management* (2nd ed.). Baltimore, MD: Williams & Wilkins.

Turner, J., Beidel, D., & Nathan, R. (1985). Biological factors in obsessive-compulsive disorder. *Psychological Bulletin, 97,* 430–450.

Vaughan, B., Kopp, C., & Krakow, J. (1984). The emergence and consolidation of self-control from eighteen to thirty months of age: Normative trends and individual differences. *Child Development, 55,* 990–1004.

Waters, E. (1978). The reliability and stability of individual differences in infant-mother attachment. *Child Development, 49,* 483–494.

Waters, E., Wippman, J., & Sroufe, L. (1979). Attachment, positive affect and competence in the peer group: Two studies of construct validation. *Child Development, 51,* 208–216.

Watzlawick, P., Weakland, J., & Fisch, R. (1974). *Change: Principles of problem formation and problem resolution.* New York: W. W. Norton.

Weinberg, S. (1976). *Incest behavior.* Secaucus, NJ: Citadel Press.

Weiss, J., & Sampson, H. (1986). *The psychoanalytic process: Theory, clinical observation, and empirical research*. New York: Guilford.

Wellman, H., & Estes, D. (1986). Early understanding of mental entities: A reexamination of childhood realism. *Child Development, 57*, 910–923.

Wenar, C. (1982). On negativism. *Human Development, 25*, 1–23.

Winnicott, D. (1953). Transitional objects and transitional phenomena. *The International Journal of Psychoanalysis, 34*, 89–97.

Winnicott, D. W. (1958). *Collected papers*. London: Tavistock.

Winnicott, D. W. (1965). *Maturational processes and the facilitating environment*. New York: International Universities Press.

Winnicott, D. (1971). *Playing and reality* (pp. 144–145). New York: Basic Books.

Wittels, F. (1930). The hysterical character. *Medical Review of Reviews, 36*, 186.

Yuill, N., & Perner, J. (1988). Intentionality and knowledge in children's judgments of actor's response and recipient's emotional reaction. *Developmental Psychology, 24*, 358–365.

Zetzel, E. (1968). The so-called good hysteric. *International Journal of Psychoanalysis, 49*, 256–260.

INDEX